Prais

"David Bain has brought together a stellar line-up of experienced SEO professionals from around the world, covering a wide range of important topics for websites of all different sizes. If you are looking to improve your SEO, you should definitely check out 'SEO in 2022'."

MARCUS TANDLER
Chief Evangelist, Ryte

"It is hard to come across a resource these days that has input from so many brilliant and knowledgeable people in the SEO community. This is a must-read for anyone who is looking to take their SEO knowledge to the next level."

JOY HAWKINS
Owner, Sterling Sky Inc

"This book is what every SEO needs to start 2022 in the right direction. I would consider it a survival, and championing, kit for website owners and those working for someone with a website. It contains all you need to know, not just for your SEO strategy in 2022 but for the long run. The advice in here is timeless and should be read by everyone."

AIALA ICAZA GONZALEZ
SEO Director, Reflect Digital

"There are multiple layers to successful SEO. Certain key elements remain the same through the years, but you can only remain highly successful if you continue to layer the newest SEO tactics on top of your existing strategy. Reading 'SEO in 2022' is a wonderful way to stay on top of the current thinking from many of the world's leading SEO minds."

ELI SCHWARTZ
Author, Product-Led SEO

"With so many changes afoot, it's incredible to have such a comprehensive look at the SEO landscape. From planning to user behaviour, semantics and more, 'SEO in 2022' has some excellent actionable insights from some of the industry's top minds."

CRYSTAL CARTER
Senior Digital Strategist, Optix Solutions

"If you combine the SEO Experiences of the contributors, it totals over 3 centuries' worth of advice! 'SEO in 2022' features today's best SEO minds and covers everything from a Holistic Understanding of SEO to Semantic and Technical SEO requirements in the modern era."

KORAY TUĞBERK GÜBÜR
Founder, Holistic SEO & Digital

"Want to know where to focus your SEO efforts in 2022? Yes? Then, this book is for you! SEO is a vast topic, but in just a few hours of reading time, 66 world-leading experts break through the fluff, avoid the chaff, and identify the areas that will make all the difference in 2022 and beyond."

JASON BARNARD
Founder, Kalicube

"'SEO in 2022' is a book that should be read by every marketing professional - up-and-coming or established. It's jam-packed with advice from top talent in SEO, including insights and best practices on what it takes to have good organic performance in 2022, including bits on internal linking, building brand and topic authority, content strategy, prioritization, and so much more! Each piece of advice comes with an in-depth review of the complexities and opportunities, as well as talks about processes and tools, so getting started could not be easier. Implementing the tips in the book will undoubtedly help you really skyrocket the performance of the sites you're working with and become a superstar in the niche."

LAZARINA STOY

Tech SEO Analyst, Skale

"One of the most comprehensive collections of expert opinions available in one place. It's insane that this is free! There's not a stone unturned in this 'SEO in 2022' series."

LUKE CARTHY

eCommerce Growth Consultant, LukeCarthy.com

The hard thing about SEO is, that it can be approached from many different angles. There is no one-fits-all solution. Wouldn't it be great to have the knowledge acquired over decades of running smart SEO campaigns across different sites and industries? 'SEO in 2022' is an incredibly insightful collection of ideas and techniques covering various areas of SEO. Full of actionable expert advice so you can learn from what's been tried and tested. A true knowledge powerhouse of people leading the industry that have all come together to share their best advice for SEO in 2022. Massive congrats and thank you to Majestic and David Bain for pulling this together - an essential SEO guide for starting the new year with a bang!"

KERSTIN REICHERT

SEO and Content Lead, SeedLegals

"David has put together an extensive library of best practices in SEO. Learning from the list of different experts that collaborated with David in this book was very insightful. This is really the one-stop go to resource for learning how to implement SEO to grow traffic and revenue of any business. I highly recommend checking it out."

AMEL MEHENAOUI

Head of SEO, Puffy

"SEO in 2022 is a must-read book for anyone who is looking to make the most value out of their SEO strategy in the coming year. It covers all needle-moving elements of an effective SEO strategy, from building strong foundations and prioritization, to user behaviour, content creation, links, analytics and so much more - all from the point of view of experienced SEOs with a proven track record in some of the biggest companies in the world. I highly recommend it."

ORIT MUTZNIK

Director of SEO, DataCamp

SEO in 2022

66 of the world's leading SEOs share their number 1, actionable tip for 2022

DAVID BAIN

TO THE SEO AND DIGITAL MARKETING
COMMUNITY –
THANK YOU FOR YOUR CONTINUED SUPPORT

CONTENTS

FOREWORD

In my role as Operations Director at Majestic I have oversight of the many relationships we maintain with our customer base and the wider SEO community. It has been a delight for us to collaborate with David and the amazing contributors to 'SEO in 2022'.

I've been involved in the web since the mid 90's. Like so many things in life, I first discovered the web while at university. Back then, the web was new. Because of its novelty, there wasn't much in the way of a guide, leaving the intrepid to discover this brave new world in their own time.

In those days, home internet access was often based on a 56k baud modem. This noisy "dial up" hardware required your computer to make a telephone call to a remote machine before you could get online. These modems were capable of downloading less than one percent of a megabyte per second and resulted in an online experience almost unrecognisable to what we see today.

A great deal has changed since I started out. The web has become very, very big. So large that words describing its magnitude start to seem a little irrelevant. Suffice to say that, in the West, the internet permeates so much of our everyday life that many may struggle to imagine life without it. Whichever way you look at the web, the one constant seems to be change.

The online world is highly competitive. Digital is a highly dynamic environment where short-term success has been no guarantee of long-term gain. We live in a world of disruption. Even the language of business has changed. "First Mover Disadvantage" may have overtaken "First Mover Advantage" as the ruling philosophy for online business. Consider GeoCities, Altavista, Friends Reunited, Friendster, Ask Jeeves...

These are interesting, exciting times. How many of today's household names in the digital world will be as popular in another 20 years' time? Who, or what, will replace them?

This dynamic landscape presents significant challenges and opportunities for entrepreneurs and digital marketers. Novelty may have been the leading challenge for those attempting to master the web of the 1990's. Have the 2020's seen this challenge overtaken by the demand of navigating a blizzard of often contradictory information and advice?

If we accept that Change is a constant, then a result of that may be that we find ourselves asking the same question again and again. How do we best confront the task of marketing an online business in these tumultuous times?

One might suggest that as the web has grown, so too has the complexity associated with it. I don't have the answers. I doubt any one person has. Is it fair to say that best practice has migrated from the "one man brand" of the 90's to a more collaborative model where best practice is held within the collective knowledge of those working in our industry?

This notion may have contributed to the excitement I felt when David first approached us to see if we could help facilitate the creation of a guide based on the principle of a collaborative approach to knowledge sharing.

This project began earlier this year in discussions between David and the team here at Majestic. We wanted to do something bold and relevant. The idea for 'SEO in 2022' was the result of these discussions. We wanted to capture the contemporary thinking of our community, for our community. We deliberately focused on '2022' to drive a sharing of insight into key areas of interest to digital marketers over the next 12 months.

This collaborative approach to excellence is at the heart of our philosophy here at Majestic. If you've used Majestic, you may have noticed that it's a bit different to the backlink checkers you may find built into an integrated

SEO toolset.

We don't try to solve every problem in SEO. Instead, we focus on one area – Link Intelligence. We recognise not all links or domains are made equal. We've built a platform on which one can explore how sites establish visibility and discover new approaches to enhancing opportunity online.

We believe Majestic empowers its customers to dig deeper into backlinks than other simple backlink checkers facilitate. We aim to provide a platform that offers a very different perspective on link-related matters than a dedicated SEO link checker can afford to give. Our belief in the diversity of use of our product is reflected in our customer base. Majestic provides Link Intelligence data and insight to a rich community of users - Domain Name traders, Academics, Affiliate researchers, Digital PR specialists, and, of course, Search Engine Optimisers. There are others. I can remember receiving praise from an early crypto investor around ten years ago who used Majestic as a research tool to discover new mining opportunities.

Majestic is, at its heart, a platform which aims to work with other specialised platforms to support insight. The vision Majestic fits into is one where a rich ecosystem of tools are used by expert Digital Marketers. This ecosystem then supports the creation of a value proposition by in-house teams, agencies and consultants who can pick and choose the technology that works for them. We recognise that our platform is just one of many which are skilfully deployed by experts in the battle to enhance their clients' online visibility and seek new opportunities online.

I believe this guide reflects the values we hold dear at Majestic. David has curated a guide jam-packed with insight. The guide is free to access, spanning a podcast series, YouTube video, and, for those like me who are still infatuated with print, this book.

I hope the singularity of purpose and focus on actionable insight for 2022 results in an experience as stimulating to consume as I've found it exciting to be involved in.

As I've seen the project come together, I'm delighted to say it has exceeded the high expectations I had at the outset. SEO in 2022 has been an inspiration to me. While Majestic has been involved in video and podcast before, this is the first print book which I am aware that the company has sponsored. We hope our involvement is a positive contribution to the sharing of knowledge this project represents. On a personal level, being involved in the production of this guide has been an amazing learning journey. I'd like to finish this Foreword by recognising those who have helped this project come to life.

The project's contributors are experienced, recognised thought-leaders in their field. A huge thanks is owed to the 66 contributors who have made this guide what it is. The panel don't just know their stuff – they live it and breathe it on a daily basis. We are delighted to be able to facilitate the sharing of their generously contributed wisdom and experience.

The author and project lead on this project is David Bain, founder of Casting Cred, a podcast agency for B2B brands. David produces a number of shows and podcasts, including "Old Guard, New Blood", a live 45-minute show which looks at hot topics in SEO and digital marketing. "Old Guard, New Blood" is hosted by Dixon Jones and sponsored by Majestic.

David is an experienced and skilled interviewer. You only need to watch one of his podcasts or livestreams to recognise the deftness of touch he brings to his work. As a published author, podcast presenter and producer, David embodies the multimedia ethos of this project, facilitating a conversation on 'SEO in 2022' over video, audio and the written word. If you enjoy this book, please take time to discover, and share more ways of accessing this content at seoin2022.com.

It would be remiss of me to write a Foreword without acknowledging the contribution of many of my colleagues, some of whom will not thank me for naming them.

I hope you enjoy reading this book as much as we have enjoyed facilitating it.

Steve Pitchford
Operations Director
Majestic.com

OPENING THOUGHTS

SEO's a funny old game. Techniques change rapidly if you're always trying to 'beat the system', but on the other hand - if you're in it for the long-term - there are many core-guiding principles that tend to stay the same. The key is to differentiate between what's core, what needs to be added, and what needs to be removed from your SEO strategy in 2022.

I've been actively involved in SEO for the past 18 years and, as I'm sure you're aware, SEO is night and day from what it used to be.

Back when I got started, Google was still just getting established and links were King, Queen, and Emperor. Any type of link was good, and you were happy to exchange links with anyone. The more links you exchanged, the higher your rankings rose.

It got a bid daft - many SEOs ended up creating general internet link directories on their own websites as a way of maximising the number of links that they could exchange.

The advice has changed through the years

If I had created a series like 'SEO in 2022' in 2003, the advice would have focused on user-hostile tactics - such as keyword stuffing, link swapping, and PageRank sculpting.

I'm happy to say that those days are gone but it's interesting that, as we approach 2022, links are still a critical signal to inform search engines about the authority and relevance of your site.

However, there is so much more to SEO than link building nowadays. A series like this is eye-opening, in terms of the breadth and depth of SEO tactics in operation today.

What is your number 1 SEO tip for 2022?

You would have thought that if I asked 66 SEOs the same question (What is your number 1 SEO tip for 2022?) then I would receive lots of similar answers. Not at all. The industry is now so rich and varied that most contributors came up with an entirely different answer. Even where the topics were similar, the perspectives were very different. The advice ranges from doubling-down on evergreen strategies to finding new and better ways to identify opportunities, how the SERP is changing, next generation tech, and so much more.

I felt that these tips naturally broke down in to 12 different chapters, and that those chapters fell into 4 main sections – EVALUATE, PLAN, DELIVER, and CANI.

SECTION 1: EVALUATE

The first section, EVALUATE, contains the first 3 chapters – 'Modern SEO', 'Strong Foundations', and 'Prioritise'. These tips are focusing on the ongoing, key elements of SEO that you can't ignore, year after year. Included are tips on focusing in the areas where you are likely to have the biggest impact, how to build a technically sound website in 2022, and how to determine your ongoing strategy - partly based upon thorough competitor analysis.

SECTION 2: PLAN

After the evaluation phase, Section 2 looks at how to PLAN your SEO activities for 2022, under the chapters: 'Site Structure', 'Keyword Research' and 'User Behaviour'. Here we include tips on how to use Schema to educate Google about the uniqueness and specificity of your content, why mapping keywords to personas and user journeys is essential, and how search engines are moving towards gaining a better understanding of user intent.

SECTION 3: DELIVER

Next up is the DELIVER section, including the chapters 'Content Creation', 'Links' and 'Keep an Eye on the SERP'. Shared in this section is the fact that your job as an SEO is to help searchers get the answer that they're looking for. Also included are tips around how to build high-quality, original content assets, and why the SERP isn't just the place that sends you traffic – it can also be a wonderful source of competitive intelligence.

SECTION 4: CANI

Finishing us up is section 4: CANI - CONSTANT and NEVER-ENDING IMPROVEMENT. An SEO's work is never done – and if you ever think it is, that's probably a sign that your competitors are about to surpass you. In this section of 'SEO in 2022', we look at topics such as why you need to be using Google Search Console on a daily basis, how machine learning could improve an SEO's life, and why training the next generation of SEOs is so important.

There's a lot to explore – some of it will already be top-of-mind. Other elements will be waiting for you to discover.

Join in the conversation

We'd love for you to join in the discussion. Why not share what resonates with you as you make your way through 'SEO in 2022'? @Majestic on Twitter using hashtag #SEOin2022 is probably the best way to connect socially and share your thoughts.

N.B. 'SEO in 2022' was produced as a free video and podcast series as well as a book, so check out the links to the video and audio episodes at SEOin2022.com if you haven't done so already.

Thanks so much for taking the time to read 'SEO in 2022'. We hope that it's as helpful and enjoyable for you to consume as it was for us to create!

David Bain
Author, '*SEO in 2022*'
Founder, *CastingCred.com*

SECTION 1:

EVALUATE

1 MODERN SEO

Get your basics covered first - with Izabela Wisniewska from Creatos Media

Before becoming side-tracked by shiny, exciting, new things - let's get started by ensuring that the basics are covered first.

Izabela Wisniewska says: "Cover your basics before attempting anything fancy. I've seen so many companies and brands try to do new, great things whilst they don't have their basics covered. They don't have their own page content or their technical aspects covered, like getting rid of old code or updating something that's not being used anymore. Then, when they try to implement the 'fancy' new stuff, it doesn't work. They might start to question why they are not ranking, or why their pages are dropping, when they upload a new blog post. You need to prioritise your growth and your technical updates, and you need to make sure that your tech is up-to-date first of all.

I understand there's probably no CMS that can handle all SEO recommendations, but you need to make sure you are doing what you can. I do a lot of SEO updates, and I still see unused JavaScript, or unused CSS, in pretty much every single update I do. You should be getting rid of this before you push the website live. Similarly, if you don't have H1s, or your titles are not optimised, you need to start there. These are the basics - this is SEO 101 - and for some reason, people have stopped doing them. We have to walk before we can start running.

I think this is what people are beginning to struggle with because they want to do everything new. Make sure you have your basics covered and educate your staff, not only your SEO colleagues, because everyone in your team should know how these things work. In this way, you will avoid simple mistakes and you won't have to go back and redo your pages."

You talk about H1s and titles, are there any other key on-page elements that are part of the basics and need to be right at the beginning?

"Besides H1s and titles, you need to look at content on the page. This is often the missing key. Brands tend to have headlines and titles, and maybe even alt tags, but usually they are missing content. You don't want to push a page without anything on it, or with only pictures, unless it's vital for the brand."

What's the minimum amount of content for each page? 200 words?

"It depends on what kind of business you are running and what kind of page you are talking about. In a category page, 200 words is probably going to be enough - you need to think about what people are expecting and what they want to see. If you write an article, for example, or a research piece, then obviously you want more words. How many words also depends on the industry and the subject matter. Make sure it makes sense and looks natural - try to show what people are expecting to see. It has to be appropriate for the page type, but you need some content on every page."

What's your standard structure for H1s and titles? Do you have a go-to length or format?

"For titles, you want to keep to under 60 characters. Some crawlers tend to identify H1s as too long, so if you use a blog title, or an article title, make sure it makes sense. If it doesn't make sense, make it shorter. You want it to display properly in Google. However, you don't want it too short either. You have to remember that the title is what people see in Google's search results. We want the title and the meta description to actually describe what they're getting into.

These things influence click-through rate because this is the first thing that people will read on your website. If 30 characters make sense, then 30 characters is fine. It is about what makes sense - if you think of the user first, then Google will probably be happy. If you try to think of the search engine first, and forget about the user, then they won't be."

What sort of unused JavaScript and CSS do you think needs to be addressed?

"It might be anything. One common example is tracking codes for software that's not used anymore. I find them through crawls and the technical things I do. You need to start with your crawl and make sure, because you might have already gotten rid of your unused JavaScript, but you might have something else."

What's your favourite software for doing crawls at the moment?

"My favourite is Sitebulb - I'm in love with that tool. You really get value for what you pay for, and visually it is amazing. I like Screaming Frog as well, because they tend to give a different view on the website. It depends on what type of client you have or how you work. If you are a more visual person then Sitebulb is great.

Also, it is good for people just starting out in the industry, and in technical, because they've got an amazing library. If you're not sure what type of error you're dealing with, you can just click through the library from the crawler and there's a huge list of articles and resources you can reference. Even if you've been in SEO for ages, this is an industry that is always changing. You might not have worked with that particular type of client before or seen that particular type of error.

If you're looking for a web-based crawler, then my go-to is DeepCrawl. It is slightly more expensive, but you can get it going on the web, forget about it, and come back to it later."

Is there a general rule in terms of the size of a site, and if it's over a certain number of pages, you'd go for DeepCrawl instead?

"I haven't had a problem with the size, but if a website was on Shopify, I've had to move from SiteBulb to DeepCrawl because Shopify is blocking crawlers. Also, if the settings are not set properly then it can take ages on a computer-based program, but Sitebulb has mostly dealt with this now. Perhaps if the site was huge, and you needed to have your machine turned on for days, you may encounter issues, like internet connection outages. In this situation, I would go for something web-based, like DeepCrawl, just in case."

What should you teach your PR people about SEO, and how do you efficiently educate team members?

"Obviously you can't make everybody a specialist in SEO, but you have to understand that it is all part of digital marketing - it has to work together. You may have different channels, but these channels all have the same goal. With PR, for example, you want the content on your page to rank and you want it to be optimised but you also want it to work from a PR perspective so journalists are interested, and it will be promoted elsewhere. If the PR and content teams don't know the SEO basics, and don't consult with SEOs, the content won't add up and you end up with things that Google hates, like keyword confusion.

In a digital marketing agency, for example, all of the staff should at least have a basic understanding of SEO. I'm not saying they need the ability to do it, but they need to know what they are working towards, and how they are going to achieve it. Everybody needs to understand, for example, that you need quality, optimised content to rank in SEO so you can't pack the content with keywords.

This is also true the other way around. SEOs need at least a basic overview of what kind of content the PR team needs. That way, you don't end up going back and forth between the two teams to achieve the right content. It is similar with development teams. If they are educated on the technical side of how good SEO works, they would understand why it is needed, and implement it in the first place."

Are the basics of SEO likely to change moving forward?

"Everything can change. We had title and meta description updates, but the core of what we need will remain. We will always need keywords somewhere, and we will need quality content. Since I started working in

SEO in 2014, I've been hearing they're not going to look at links, or they're going to find something else to focus on - but they haven't. The quality metrics are changing. They want more quality, but they still want good links and good websites talking about you. The core basics are not likely to go away. They might be changing, but they will not disappear."

What's one ineffective activity that an SEO can stop doing to focus on the basics?

"Some people believe that pushing out as much content as possible is the way to go. We have shouted about quality content, and how Google likes fresh content, but that takes time. If you have time to create quality content every month, go ahead and do it. But it is a cost in terms of time and ideas. You are better off doing one great piece of quality content every quarter, rather than trying to push 500 words every week just to put out some content. Everybody used to do it, but it no longer matches the quality that users and search engines are looking for.

We have to remember that great pieces of content need research and more people involved. A great piece will have graphics, and maybe videos, and not just come from a copywriter writing 500 words. It's better to take more time so you can publish something great."

You can find Izabela Wisniewska over at CreatosMedia.co.uk.

Don't forget the basics - but also make sure you monitor Javascript - with Freelance SEO Consultant Natalie Arney

Natalie shares a message similar to Izabela's, however, she's also keen to convey the importance of JavaScript monitoring.

Natalie Arney says: "Don't forget the basics. A lot of people focus on what's trendy and what everyone's talking about, but SEOs should make sure that best practice, and everything that's quick and easy, is also remembered."

What would you prioritise as the key basics for 2022?

"Site structure, information architecture, and hierarchy. They're seen as more advanced in the content side of things and are often only thought about early on when creating and structuring a website. SEOs need to consider these things throughout the process, rather than just at the start of something.

You also have to think about things like meta content, which can affect click-through rate. We've seen the changes that Google has made in the last year, such as displaying page titles in SERPs. Obviously, you need to make sure that you are trying to get users to the site as much as possible. At the end of the day, we're here to get traffic, that converts and qualifies, to a website."

What are you looking at in terms of site structure?

"For site structure you're looking at the coding of the site, but particularly where it's linked to information architecture. You need to be doing things like creating content hubs, but also making sure that the content is properly and adequately internally linked to as well. For an eCommerce site, make sure that your navigation is well-structured, it appeals to the user, and they are using it properly. Don't just create for creation's sake."

How is information architecture different to site structure?

"Site structure is more about the technical side and the structure of the site. It's things like internal links. For information architecture, you're not just looking at the physical structure of a site, you're also looking at how the information is organised. That may be content hubs, blogs, domains, subdomains, etc. There are many different areas involved in that."

Does hierarchy refer to the number of links from the homepage?

"It does, but there are lots of different types. Alongside information architecture and site structure, looking at the hierarchy of the content on your site is very important. Often, you'll find that you have really informative, helpful pieces of content sitting thousands of layers down on a random blog. Things like that need to be analysed and prioritised, because you don't want useful content sitting further down in a site structure. You want users to be able to find that informative and informational content. By prioritising your hierarchy, that content will rank better."

Is there a maximum number of levels deep that pages can be in a hierarchy?

"I don't think so. It all depends on the site itself; how it's already structured and how you want it to be laid out. If you are migrating, or making changes to your site, make sure that your user journey is supported as much as possible. You need to consider that. You will obviously have different types of users visiting sites at different times, so it's not going to be perfect. Make sure that the journey to that piece of information, or content, is as accessible as possible."

What JavaScript is it important to monitor?

"Tracking scripts, and sites created completely in JavaScript are both relevant. The use of JavaScript is increasing every single year. People are moving to different types of platforms that either use a lot of it or are fully built on JavaScript. People often aren't aware of how that might impact SEO. A lot of SEOs are still on a big learning curve with JavaScript. We know that the market is changing, and you need to make sure that you're keeping on top of that, and understanding what issues may arise. You also need to know who to go and speak to with regards to getting those issues fixed.

You might have a client that wants to re-platform to a site that's fully JavaScript. In that case, you will need to know a bit about JavaScript SEO and how that's going to affect you, and any issues that you need to be aware of initially. It might be that you're getting a new client and pieces of JavaScript in their site are affecting how their content is being crawled, indexed, and ranked. There are lots of reasons why you should look at and monitor JavaScript. Using tools is one step, but there is also education to be done around it. You want to understand why it's used by developers and why clients want to use it, as well as the impact and restrictions it has on you as an SEO."

Could search engines have difficulty crawling JavaScript sites in the same way that they had trouble with flash-based sites in the past?

"It depends. Search engines should know and understand JavaScript as it does take up a large proportion of the web itself. They should be able to crawl that content. They're slowly getting there, but I don't think it's fast enough. As SEOs, and as developers, we need to be aware of the restrictions, and what we need to take into consideration around JavaScript. It does impact many different things - from server-side rendering to whether search engines can crawl internal links or see links in navigation. There are lots of different issues. If you don't have clients or developers on your side with those difficulties, then it presents you with a whole other layer of problems."

Should crawlers like Deepcrawl and Screaming Frog be able to give you the same information about a JavaScript site as a regular HTML site?

"I think so, yes. Certain crawlers, including Sitebulb and Deepcrawl, provide response vs rendered co-coverage, which is really helpful. Before a lot of crawlers were able to do that, you had to rely on Chrome plugins - and a lot of SEOs still do. Having crawling tools give us things like response vs render also enables you to present that information to an internal team, a developer, or whoever you're trying to get buy-in from. You can actually show them the issues that you're having."

What tools do you recommend for monitoring JavaScript?

"Personally, I use a number of different tools. Sitebulb is a great tool and Screaming Frog is very useful - it doesn't give you response vs render yet but that should be implemented soon. ContentKing is great at highlighting any issues and changes. If a developer has implemented a fix regarding JavaScript, it will tell you whether that's been completed without having to constantly run crawls."

How often should a site be crawled for JavaScript monitoring?

"It will depend on the team, what developers are doing, and what's being implemented at that time. We all have different workloads and devs will have different views. A lot of SEOs run crawls on a weekly or monthly basis, but it shouldn't be up to you to crawl a site every day. Having something that will alert you to those issues will really help."

What are the most common, and most important, issues to be aware of?

"Canonicals is a big issue. Years ago, I had an issue where a whole site was canonicalized to one folder. If we had a monitoring tool that alerted us to that at the time, we would have been able to jump on it a lot quicker. Issues like that can arise.

It does depend on what's going on internally, what's going on in the developer's queue, and what's going on in the sphere. The type of platform will affect the issues as well because they can change things themselves, especially if they're not custom-built or use a lot of plugins that need to be updated, like Shopify and WordPress."

What's one thing that SEOs should stop doing to focus more time on securing the basics and monitoring JavaScript?

"Stop creating content without strategy. If you're creating content for content's sake, you should spend that time doing something else. A piece of news that is not optimised or SEO-lead is not going to get traffic to your site. You could be spending that time elsewhere. The main priority for SEOs is traffic acquisition and user acquisition. You're not going to acquire customers through a piece of news that's not going to be distributed, and is not going to be ranking."

You can find Natalie Arney over at NatalieArney.com.

Stop being a magpie and focus on what actually moves the needle - with Laura Hogan from Sweet Digital.

Laura feels that it's all-too-easy to spend your time on areas of SEO that don't have the highest levels of impact.

Laura Hogan says: "Stop being a magpie and actually focus on what's important, and what's going to make a difference. We're definitely very guilty of liking shiny new things and forgetting about our basics."

What are the shiny new things that SEOs are spending too much time on?

"Anytime Google tweets something or makes a change, we freak out - instead of taking stock, waiting and actually seeing the impact of that on our data. We've always been prone to do it and it can lead to rash decisions.

It makes much more sense to, first and foremost, look at your basics - the foundations of SEO such as technical optimization, content, and links. Quite often these things get overlooked. Remember when FAQ schema came out, and we all took advantage of it and had 10 FAQs on every page? Did this actually have as big of an impact as having clean technical health and really strong content? Possibly not. We just got distracted and blinded by something new, rather than focusing on what we know actually works."

What does work at the moment? What are the absolutes that SEOs have to be doing in 2022?

"Having a clean bill of technical health is always going to be important. Always consider the context of things that come through when you are looking at any audits. This will help you understand whether it is actually important to fix or not. There are some things from an accessibility point of view that may not move the needle from an SEO perspective, but you want to have strong website accessibility. For instance, alt tags – they're not going to make a huge impact, but if you are in certain spaces it's important to have that accessibility angle.

We know that content is always strong, especially with the meta changes and Google pulling information from different places now - where we specifically tell them to. We also know that you can drive strong traffic from good pieces of content - and they can convert really nicely.

There's always a debate around links but there's enough evidence, from over the years and recently, to show that links can help you move those positions - particularly when you're on the first page. Everybody's got good technical and good optimization, so having those really strong links can be the difference.

It's things that we've always known, but the nuances of how we do them have changed over the years, and what we need to consider when doing them has changed slightly. It's always been those core foundations, and they will stay the same - particularly in 2022."

What are the key elements from a technical perspective that are going to deliver that great user experience in 2022?

"Definitely addressing site speed where you can and the elements of Core Web Vitals and usability. It's not easy, and it may not even be possible for everybody to have really high scores. This is where the consideration of your customer base has to come in. If you're an e-commerce store, you actually want your images to be as high quality and beautiful as possible. You may even want 360° views of them - but you know Google wants things to be really fast. It's about maintaining a balance. Do you want to use lower quality images, or less video, that might not actually convert?

The speed side of things, and Core Web Vitals, are really important. However, you also have to consider what the company needs, and what's going to help the company to convert more as well. 404s and crawl errors have always been important – you don't want people to be falling onto error pages or clicking on links throughout the site and getting stopped on their journey. The likelihood of these users carrying on is slim.

We're seeing canonicals, and HREFs particularly, making a big impact. On the hreflang side, we've been making sure that they're implemented correctly for international clients. Particularly for clients on WordPress sites, we've seen the plugins they're using for recipes and similar elements aren't doing the hreflang tagging correctly on the international version. These things are still quite important for international ranking, so it's a case of making everything as easy as possible for Google to crawl an index.

Google is very clever, as we all know, but we sometimes forget that it's a piece of software. It's a spider, it's a machine - it doesn't understand context. We just need to make life as easy as possible for Google to find what we want it to find."

It's amazing that around 40% of websites have WordPress as the backend. How often should you do an audit on the WordPress plugins to make sure everything's performing as intended?

21

"We do it every month, or every six weeks. I've found that WordPress has been updating more this year than in previous years, so we seem to have had more versions come through. Particularly if we have very plugin-heavy new clients, one of the first things we do is audit the plugins and make sure they're using things that make sense to use.

Again, the 'magpie syndrome' can come in here. For example, you might find a plugin that's going to redirect users as soon as you turn off a discontinued product. Now, there are possibly better options for the discontinued product page. You could take people to the most relevant product that still exists rather than throwing them to the homepage. We find quite a few tools that don't need to be on sites, but people are using them because they think it's going to help with something, or it's an SEO factor. However, they're just adding bloat to the site in the long run."

So, it's not about trying to achieve 100% in the technical scores - it's about you against your competition in your specific industry?

"100%. That's where our obsession with tools, scores and numbers works against us. We don't always think about the context of the client. Sometimes, we're too focused on getting 100% on our tech score, or Core Web Vitals, and it's not always possible - especially if you need high-quality images and videos. You have to get past looking for high scores because that's not what will drive revenue all the time for clients. Instead, focus on what's driving your clients' revenue and make sure you're improving in these areas."

What changes have you seen in terms of the content that works now versus a few years ago?

"Definitely long-form seems to be working really well. I know that's been around for a while, but there was a phase where SEOs were focussed on producing lots of content in terms of frequency, such as three blogs a week, rather than its depth. Now, I'm seeing a lot more content that's very in-depth. Using the table of contents element, and breaking content down into strong sub-headings, seems to be performing well and having really strong ranking longevity and breadth.

Instead of having five pieces of content driving bits of traffic, you have one that's working extremely hard and driving in the same amount of traffic as those five. It's much easier to get one piece of content to work as a conversion trigger. You can build your downloads into it, capture email addresses, and build products into that content to drive revenue if it's eCommerce. Spending more time on a smaller number of content pieces is going to be key to next year."

How has link building, and the type of links that an SEO should be looking to acquire, changed?

"It's become harder - that's for sure. Clearly, relevancy is key, and gone are the days where you could just include links about puppies! I think digital PR is brilliant for getting a large volume of links in a short space of time.

However, I think it's moving towards trying to target a smaller number of links that are super relevant to you. Rather than going for all the national press and lifestyle magazines that may have relevance, but talk about completely different things, you need to be more industry-focused and targeted. Instead of trying to create something to appeal en masse, create content specifically for one publication. That's where I see things moving in 2022."

Should a site still be looking to acquire new links on a monthly basis, or should it be an annual project?

"I think a mix of both is always good. There's always some consistent link building to be done through channels such as HARO, where you can give your expertise in return for a link credit. Keeping an eye on this is always really useful and can drive some good opportunities.

The bigger campaigns have a lot of value from a brand perspective, so I think it's good to keep running those - but think of them as having a different objective than just building links. Consider them from a branding, and maybe social virality, perspective as well.

Then, use your wholly focused, specific campaigns that you're running to one or two publications, with the consideration of improving the performance of a specific page. That way you can monitor the performance of the page based on this activity."

What are one or two things that an SEO should stop doing in 2022?

"Stop panicking and jumping to conclusions. We all need to take a step back and get back into the data. Things always change on Google – look how different things are now compared to pre-Penguin. We need to stop being so reactive to any change. Take stock of a change and make an informed decision from a place of strategic evaluation.

Just because something has worked for one person doesn't mean it's going to work for you. You've got to think about your clients and what works for them - not what everybody else is doing."

You can find Laura Hogan over at SweetDigital.co.uk.

Go Big, Go Bold, Go Against SEO - with Alina Ghost from Debenhams.

Alina wishes to emphasise that if you play it too safe in 2022, the competition might just gobble you up!

Alina Ghost says: "I am going to be controversial and say that you should do something different - completely different.

I've been in the industry for many years and it's always the same stuff. It's always about knowing the basics and doing the three core pillars: coding, links and content.

However, what makes you stand out is doing things that nobody else is doing. The reason we even know what actually works these days is because people try out everything, and not just what we are told to do. Think outside of the box and try something new."

What's an example of a different campaign? What have you done or seen, that wasn't a traditional SEO campaign but resulted in incredible SEO success?

"Firstly, you need to be thinking about brand, which we know is increasingly important these days. Consider creating those huge campaigns that will get eyes and traffic onto your website. It's about getting people to think about you in a specific way - you have to show that on the site and across the web as well. Your E-A-T has to be good. I'm not saying disregard the ranking factors, I'm suggesting you go about it a different way to get to that point. If you are building your brand, think about how you are doing it.

You have to think differently and come up with new ideas. For example, you could use emotion to help people remember you and revisit. This is something that Google looks at as well. They assess the brand and how people actually think about - not only across the web, but also on social media."

What if your boss says, 'I just want to rank for red woollen socks for Christmas'?

"I've had that in the past where people were fixated on one keyword. It's a matter of telling them to look at the bigger picture. It's not just about specific keywords, it's about knowing the categories you're ranking for and clustering what you stand for. Going back to the brand, you need to make sure that the content you're producing is giving back to the users, providing them with more information, and making you an authority."

How do you measure success if you're creating articles for entertainment, rather than targeting specific keyword phrases?

"Use as many tools as you can to actually understand what is happening. Every tool has its own great functionality that it can showcase. You obviously need to track visibility, and sessions and clicks are your number one consideration. However, understanding the keywords within that is also important. Are they branded or non-branded?

Additionally, be aware that as SEOs, we touch on many different things. I say, 'Go big and go bold' because it's not just about the SEO metrics. It's also about looking at your conversion rate, or your Average Order Value. Is there a way that you can increase these values? Discover what people think when they come onto your site, what they are currently feeling, and how they actually want to purchase."

You talked about the expanding role of SEO. How does an SEO influence and work with other departments? Do you have any managerial tips?

"There are plenty of different things an SEO can be doing, including training. Showing the numbers to managers always works. If you can show someone how much they might be losing, which is something you can forecast, it's a really strong message.

SEOs are not just about one area, and the traditional activities, anymore. Now, you can be writing code one day, and creating PR campaigns the next. We've got such a breadth of things we need to be looking at. Because it's growing, it's about trying something different to see whether that's working or not. Make sure you are constantly testing - especially when it comes to the CRO factor. Meanwhile, UX is equally important as we need to make sure that developments are actually workable for our users as well."

What are your thoughts on the importance of doing more testing? What are the typical metrics or areas of a page that needs to be tested, and where are the quickest wins?

"The low-hanging fruit would probably be something that you already rank for. Are you able to improve their click-through rates, add some stuff and even use PPC or affiliate data? For example, you can use any ads you create, do A/B tests on different snippets or content, and take the one that saw the highest click-through rate - and the most conversions as well."

To decide what to split test, and how to improve your SEO, what is the best way to take data from your pay-per-click campaigns to map against your organic success? Do you match things together by syncing your data from Google Ads to Google Data Studio?

"The quickest and easiest thing is not to waste your money on brand. If you are showing up for brand, and people are actually looking for you, don't waste that money on PPC.

You can use the content that you're writing for the PPC ads, pull the data out, and discover what is working. This doesn't have to be for that particular category - you could potentially use it in a different category. If it is working for one area, perhaps it's working for something else as well. Having said that, sometimes it's category-specific. For example, if you're trying to push something seasonal, such as clothing, then it might be completely different to something you do with, say, makeup."

One progressive area of content marketing where SEOs should probably have more involvement is digital PR. How can those campaigns help SEOs to achieve results?

"I used to work for AMARA, a luxury interiors brand. I knew about them because I did interior blogging, and they had an annual event around the Interior Blog Awards. They would get lots of bloggers, interior designers with websites, and experts from the main brands. They brought all of them together and had different categories, such as Best Colour Award.

This all resulted in amazing feedback. Not only was it great PR for the brand but also, they managed to get loads of natural links because people were naturally talking about them. It was driving people to the site. That traffic was great because people were being told to go to the website and vote for each of the nominees. It was also a great, organic way to build that community. That event worked for them in a number of ways.

That example shows the importance of planning. SEOs need to be thinking about how they can take advantage of the countdown to an event, to drive as much awareness and links as possible towards their brand."

Are SEOs (and digital marketers, in general) too reactive, and are they not planning enough for opportunities like these? Is there anything that digital marketers can do to be more strategic?

"Definitely. Another thing to mention about that example is that, on the night the awards took place, there were journalists interested in coming as well. Not only was the blog linking back to us, but also the press.

Planning ahead is so important and so strategic. Sticking with this campaign, as an example, we began talking about it months in advance of starting the process every year. We discussed what we're going to do this year, what kind of categories we are going to get, and what isn't getting much traction. This is because the trends are always changing.

Thinking ahead, and being strategic, is always important. Use the data you have in front of you. It's going back to the basics, like doing your keyword research and looking at Google Trends. Is there anything new you can jump on, to offer more information or actually create this campaign around? There are a number of ways you can be strategic, both in the short and long term, when it comes to trends. Sometimes, people want something right here, right now. Other times, if you are thinking about the bigger picture, it's about planning and making sure you go back to see what data you've got, and how you can it mix together.

The reason I'm saying, 'Go big and go bold', is because everybody knows that's what we're doing for digital PR. We are going and looking at the data, but what can you bring to the table that's different? What kind of data can you bring that other agencies can't get? Think outside the box, be strategic, and actually try a bit harder."

What's one thing SEOs should stop doing to spend more time thinking about how to go big and go bold?

"This will be controversial. If you went to the recent BrightonSEO, you might have seen Tom Capper speak, and he said that Core Web Vitals is a bluff. It resonated with me because he's saying to take it with a pinch of salt. Yes, everybody is working towards those Core Web Vitals, but if you actually breakdown what the metrics ask you, you might make your UX worse. Your website might look awful as you try to improve. Is it actually a ranking factor, or is it more of a tiebreaker? This is a conversation that you need to have with the wider business. Consider whether you are wasting your time trying to improve things when you actually don't need to do everything. You can save your resources to do other things that will make more of an impact. We're trying to chip away at things, but ultimately, we want to make the best and biggest impact as quickly as possible."

Alina Ghost is SEO Manager for debenhams.com.

Modern SEO is similar to Heisenberg's uncertainty principle in quantum mechanics - with Sante J Achille

Sante warns that no matter how well you think you can plan your SEO success, you're never going to fully understand the algorithms.

Sante J Achille says: "Be very wary about relying too much on your rankings and performance, as far as reporting is concerned.

I have been thinking about the Heisenberg principle recently, which was one of the first things I learned when studying chemistry many years ago. It was on one of the first pages of a very thick Inorganic Chemistry book. It laid the foundation for modern chemistry and the understanding for how matter is built. Heisenberg's Uncertainty Principle disrupted the old theory on the structure of atoms - that electrons were rotating around the nucleus, etc. It basically stated that it's not possible to exactly predict the state, position, or momentum of particles. I see a strong similarity between that and what is happening now, and will continue to happen, in SEO."

How does this affect the way you think about SEO?

"Right now, there is an extensive use of tools that give you predictions. They produce reports on your performance, in terms of your position and ranking. I am reluctant to rely on that kind of information and I try to stick as much as possible to whatever Search Console comes back with. It's not the entirety of the information, because it's only a portion of what is going on, but it is a significant order of magnitude of what is happening. It will tell you where your site is, who it's being presented to, in what form and with which kind of queries your pages are surfacing on the search engine results pages.

That will give you an idea of who is looking for your pages, or even better, what the intent is of people that are looking for pages like yours. You can then identify how close you are to that kind of need, and how close you are to solving someone's problem. However, it is always an unpredictable situation. Flying blind is the right way of looking at it when you're doing this kind of thing. You are trying to understand where you are, what you have to offer, and what are the needs of the people that are looking for you.

It used to be easier to see where you were on the SERPs. You could see yourself across different browsers in different locations, which is literally impossible at the moment. Now, you can hop on a proxy, change locations, change browser, be logged in or not logged in, and you'll see completely different sets of results. It's too simple to say that you have a certain position or ranking. You have to rely more and more on performance results and business transaction contexts to guide you."

What does this mean for SEO forecasting? How can you predict the financial outcome of your activities, and communicate the value of the process?

"It can be challenging. Sophisticated SEO goes beyond most people. Look at things like natural language programming and you are just scratching the surface of what rankings actually entail - the mathematics behind them, and how words become numbers. It changes the way you look at the entire activity. When words are no longer words, and they become numbers, they're in a different space, and a different league. It's a matrix of zeros and ones, sparse matrices, principal components, and eigenvalues. That needs to remain under the carpet - you cannot talk to the majority of people with this language. It is a challenge; most people don't understand it and it can be intimidating.

The other problem is that it's totally unpredictable. The time lag means that it can take a while for results to actually surface. I've recently had a bad experience with a client that freaked out because they thought I was taking advantage of them. They thought I was talking nonsense and that I wasn't going to deliver, because it took a couple of months for the first results to come through. The problem is crossing that desert and waiting for the results to come along. Once the results are there, they realise how quality SEO can change the course of events for an enterprise.

Explaining the process is something that has to be carefully processed, depending on the person that is sitting in front of you. That can be more challenging than doing the technical SEO itself."

You've stated that ranking and performance are stochastic variables, what does that mean?

"To say that they are stochastic variables is to say that they are equivalent to random elements. It means that it's a process that is not, by any means, under our control, and there is no recognisable pattern that we can follow to identify a strategy and fulfil an objective. There is a slight difference between this meaning and the purely mathematical terminology of 'stochastic'.

I am not a mathematician; I am an engineer - I studied engineering. I worked for the aerospace industry for about eight years before I changed path. My approach to modelling and mathematics has always been a very practical and less theoretical one. I've always been a fan of mathematics and modelling, but in using the tools for a purpose and not for the sake of studying the tools themselves."

If it's now almost impossible to measure cause and effect, and predict outcomes, should SEOs simply try to deliver on user experience, oversee great content that's relevant to users, and hope that the machine will recognise your value?

"I tend not to believe the fairy tale: that delivering great value for the user through a wonderful experience will magically float you to the top of the search results pages. You can try to follow a philanthropic approach, with a mission to make people feel wonderful, but SEO doesn't work like that. There can be a lot of science behind the way you approach SEO. Orders of magnitude are what typically 'guarantee' that you will fulfil the objective of providing quality traffic at a steady rate, both on-site and off-site.

Off-site, your backlinks are important: developing a strategy, writing the right content to attract good backlinks, and using tools like Majestic to analyse your performance and that of your competitors. Try to find the right opportunity for developing rewarding editorial backlinks. That is one strategy that is, and will remain to be, very beneficial. Backlinks might lose their force as a ranking factor, but the fact that you have good links from good websites will always bring quality traffic.

On-site, the way you actually build a page can have a big impact. One thing to focus on is paying attention to your use of images and having enough of the right images with the right name. People don't like to use images very much, or don't use them in the best way, because it's time consuming. You need to write a piece and include the right image with a caption, a title, an alt tag that describes the right thing, have the name of the image be the right name, and then combine the right elements of intent.

SEO is becoming less about specific keywords and more about the topics around which people search. You need to be there with your content and be able to pinpoint a certain query that people put into the search engines. Try to determine the right keywords for those topics and how they can be combined in different ways. The keywords are not the focus - the focus is the topics that are then illustrated, described, and enforced throughout the copy with those keywords."

What's something that has become less relevant now, that SEOs can spend less time focussing on?

"If you want to succeed, you need to be less attached to minor details. SEOs spend too much time chasing ghosts that don't exist. As the Germans say, people look at the tree, but they miss the forest. They're very focused on trying to pinpoint small details but miss the big picture. For example, before writing an article, just go onto Google and analyse the top 15 relevant pages, (excluding the 800-pound gorillas that are there because of their brand or because they're Wikipedia). Look at those pages and try to understand what they have done, and what kind of problem they're trying to solve. Then try to combine these concepts in a meaningful and optimised way. Think less about the minor details and look at the bigger picture.

Also, dive into your own Search Console. SEOs overlook a lot of what is in Search Console, you can do wonderful things with the information there. Look at combining it with the API that Google allows you to use. With a pivot table, you can combine your URL and all the search terms that Google has associated with that URL. That is what you should be looking at, not fussing about whether you have two images or three, or if they are at the top or the bottom of the page."

You can find Sante J Achille over at Achille.name.

2 STRONG FOUNDATIONS

Compete on technical quality, and stop re-building things - with Jono Alderson from Yoast

Jono feels that the best use of your time is to ensure that your site's technical infrastructure is significantly better than that of your competitors.

Jono Alderson says: "Stop looking at technical debt as something that we have to fix, and technical SEO as a way to prevent errors, and start looking at it as something we can compete on. If we make our technical infrastructure, and our platform, twice as good as our competitors we get paid dividends in rankings, performance, conversions, and much more. We need to look at technical SEO as a positive thing, not a negative thing."

What does competing on technical quality mean, in practice?

"Instead of saying, 'How do we take our inaccessible website from a 4 out of 10, to a 6 out of 10?', you say 'What would perfect look like?'. You can't just tick some boxes and get by, slightly ahead of the competition. You need to consider how much money you could make if you were twice as fast as the next fastest player in the market.

Don't just fix the basics; achieve excellence and embrace the new standards. You want to get to a position where you never have to worry about 404s, or 301s, and wasting time fixing things that break all the time. When you get to that place then you've got more budget, time, and resources to be doing the things that matter - like brand building and content strategy - rather than fighting fires."

Why do you want to be twice as good as your competitor, instead of just number one in the search results?

"With speed and quality, there are many benefits, other than just SEO ranking boosts. A few milliseconds can be the difference between somebody spending or looking away. The perception that users have of brands as they browse influences how likely they are to return, or to recommend. If you are looking at how little you can get away with, you're never going to start surprising and delighting customers.

Simply ranking first puts you at risk of one of your competitors going above and beyond. Then you lose customers, you lose hearts and minds, and your addressable market size diminishes. You need to win the consumer, not do as little as you can get away with. SEO is becoming even more of a 'winner takes all' game. The old joke was that the best place to hide a body was on page two of Google. But the world has changed - now it's on the second result. You need to be the best result. If you're getting away with being okay, it only takes a tiny shift in the marketplace for you to be gone."

Is it an SEO's job to stay on top of the changes in things like CSS and JavaScript?

"Yes, and no. Core Web Vitals has given us a watershed moment. The entire technology stack has become something SEOs need to have an opinion on. However, even as a technical SEO nerd, I find myself struggling to keep up with some of it. It moves so fast. In conversations about things like Chrome experimental features, I can get lost in the level of technical jargon and terminology. There is no way that, as an industry, SEO can be expected to know it all.

I started working on a conference presentation recently, where I decided to describe all the moving parts for building a perfect website. I thought that it was just a case of knowing the ingredients and standards. I started a slideshow on How to Build an Image Tag: 'img src=picture.jpg' is fine, but it needs an alt attribute, and you need a source attribute for different screen sizes, and it changes if the image is landscape, or a document.

I got to 70 slides on how to put an image on a web page and I was still learning things. If putting a cat on an HTML web page takes an hour to teach at a basic level, with the modern standards, then there's no way we can do it all. We need to be involved, but this is not something that SEOs can own completely."

Where are some educational resources online, that you would recommend?

"There are two places and they're both from Google. One is web.dev, which is Google's general web dev portal. It's a little sprawling and busy, but it's worth digging through. There are a lot of blog posts and articles - some are truly phenomenal, but others are incomprehensibly technical. It's really good for 'ad hoc' learning.

For something more structured, I would recommend Google's PageSpeed Insights documentation - not the PageSpeed Insights tool, but the web fundamentals documentation around it. It covers everything from what a server is, to how to minify your CSS. The problem is that it's still far too much to consume. At some point, you have to rely on frameworks, platforms and CMSs. You can't do all of this manually and keep on top of it. My 70 slides on images has turned into 75, because five new things have happened since I wrote it last month."

Should every site be using AMP to make their site fast?

"I'm a huge proponent of AMP. I should disclose that I'm on the AMP Advisory Committee, which means I have opinions on what it is and where it goes. I'm involved because I think that it is a good solution to this kind of challenge. It's not enough to chase perfection and build a perfect site. You also need to maintain it as standards, policies, personnel, and expectations change. AMP is a very good framework for solving that kind of thing.

With it, you offload all maintenance and knowledge requirements to the developers who work on it, which tends to involve a large amount of Google developers. I run my website on the 'AMP for WordPress' plugin, the main developers of which work for Google. I can wake up in the

35

morning and see that my site scores 98 on Core Web Vitals, and in the source code there's a bit that I don't recognise. That's because a Google employee has spent the evening working on my website, or rather all the websites running the software, so that I rank better in Google. They're operating at a technical level which far exceeds my ability as a developer - they are right on the cutting edge of what's possible. Every day my site gets better, not worse. I'm not fighting technical debt, I'm ahead of the curve.

Imagine the impact of not using this resource. A brand will start to build a gap against their competitors who are working from scratch, reinventing the wheel, and not competing on technical perfection. AMP is not perfect for all sites; it has its limitations. It is a platform and an approach. For many sites, however, it can be a catalyst for not only fixing but transforming how you approach tech."

Are there benefits for using AMP on different content on your site, like product pages?

"Initially, it wasn't great for that, but a lot of the constraints have changed. There's been a lot of changes to how AMP is governed and operated, and how it functions technically. It is still not trivial to build a product page in AMP, but there's no reason it can't be done. It covers all elements, like checkout, interstitials, modals, and payments like Stripe and PayPal. It's not the easiest thing in the world to build complex pages at the moment, but it's definitely achievable.

People tend to struggle with AMP when they're still building in 'paired mode'. They have both the AMP version and the original version of the page they're maintaining. The right way to do it is to build just the one.

The next evolution is Bento AMP, which is AMP as standalone components. If you want a carousel, a product image, or a pricing unit, then you just load in the bits you need. That will be transformative, and that'll be when it really starts to shape the web."

What's a quick summary of Progressive Web Apps and how can SEOs use it?

"A lot of people have only just started to encounter it, because they've seen bad scores for it in a Lighthouse test and Core Web Vitals. We have a paradigm at the moment, which doesn't help Google, in that we have web pages and websites, and we have apps. They are two entirely separate ecosystems that work in two different ways. That makes things like crawling, indexing, and monetization quite difficult for Google.

The dream is that you could have a website that behaves like an app – it could live on your phone, have an icon, and could access APIs on a phone, like making a phone call. PWAs are that bridge, and they can be surprisingly easy to set up. If you're on WordPress there's a plugin, again maintained by the same team of Google employees who continually update it. You can practically plug-and-play, whack an icon in, and suddenly your website can behave as if it's an app. You have the best of both worlds.

It also acts as a framework to allow a website to act as an API. If I want to be able to integrate into or out of any other system, say Salesforce or Zapier, it's easy for all of my bits of content to be pushed and pulled in different directions. I see the combination of AMP and PWAs as a pairing, and it's a smart move for any content sites wanting to take advantage of that."

Will PWAs work alongside apps on an Android or iOS device, or are they in competition?

"I think they will work together, though this is a contentious issue. A few years ago, Cindy Krum first mentioned PWAs at a conference and she said it would kill the app ecosystem. She was laughed out of the room because Apple had firmly stated that they would not support PWAs, but then they changed tack. Now, Google openly crawls and indexes the content of apps and PWAs in much the same way. Cindy has a lot of insight into how the back end of Google Play is changing to disambiguate those things.

In the longer term, those distinctions will go away. We will see PWAs in the app store, and apps in search results, and the difference will be academic."

What's one thing that SEOs should stop doing to focus more time on the technical success of their website?

"The simple answer is link building. I know that links still 'work' for some purposes, however, as an industry we spend far too much time building, buying, or otherwise acquiring links. It's easy to commoditise and it's a convenient deliverable. If you're an agency, judged on what you've achieved this month, it's easy to do externally. That doesn't mean it's the right way to be spending our time, or the best way to be spending our time.

Some of that time, budget, and resource should be spent having challenging conversations. Are we on the right platform? Is it beneficial to spend 10 hours a month fixing 404s? Is it sensible to adopt the new JavaScript framework, when our current website is experiencing errors? In the industry, there's a huge amount of focus in the wrong places. We need to ensure our websites are healthy before we worry about getting some promotion and some PR coverage. It's not 'shiny' but it's a good investment."

You can find Jono Alderson over at Yoast.com.

Rubbish in, Rubbish out - with Fili Wiese from the Search Brothers

Fili would like to emphasise that, even though your natural instinct might be to blame Google's algorithms for your site's ranking declines, the problem actually lies much closer to home.

Fili Wiese says: "You want to make sure you control what goes into the algorithms of search engines. As webmasters, we are responsible for what goes into the algorithms. We need to make sure that our website is crawlable, indexable, and that search engines understand our content. Now, a lot of the algorithms are like a black box, and we don't have control over how those algorithms are programmed or executed, and what comes out of the search results.

However, as webmasters, we do have control over what goes into those algorithms, so we want to make sure we send the right things into them. If we want to change the output, we need to change the input, and if we're sending in rubbish, we're going to get rubbish out. To improve our rankings, we need to focus on what we send into those algorithms."

What are examples of rubbish that SEOs typically send into the

algorithms?

"Common examples include problems with trust signals, like canonicalization that is done wrong, or sitemaps that are basically sending the wrong signal by having non-indexable patterns in them. Also, content pages with barely any content that is indexable. You're asking Google to index a particular page, but it doesn't have a unique sales proposition or value, so it shouldn't actually rank in the first place.

If you have too many of these, you're basically sending a lot of rubbish into the algorithms. You need to be very careful about what signals you're sending. Can Google actually trust your server codes? Can Google trust the content that you're sending?"

Will this give Google a degree of confidence in what you do, and impact its willingness to rank you for contextual terms?

"Yes. You've heard all the terms being tossed around, such as 'content quality', 'expertise, authoritativeness and trustworthiness', and 'Domain Authority'. It's true that a lot of these signals matter. It's a way of evaluating the quality of your content and seeing if you stand out enough. Do you have enough authority so the user would indicate to Google that this is a very good website? The overall trend of the signals you're sending into algorithms determines your level of trust and authority, and whether you should rank for certain terms or not."

What are specific aspects of sitemaps that SEOs are getting wrong at the moment?

"It's not just SEOs - it's primarily webmasters. What webmasters often get wrong is they only generate one sitemap. They have a dynamic website, but they don't generate a new sitemap when they add new content. You end up with content that is indexable and discoverable in your website, but you don't have it in your sitemap.

Another common mistake is having non-indexable patterns in the sitemap, such as redirects, 404s, or deleted content. Another example is people trying to rank in news because there are different rules for news sitemaps."

How important are Sitemaps in the grand scheme of things? If you

have a brilliant website for users and content, but you've got a terrible sitemap, is this likely to impact your ranking significantly?

"I'm going to narrow the field to XML sitemaps because HTML sitemaps is a completely different topic. When it comes to XML sitemaps, it doesn't impact your ranking significantly if everything else is brilliant. The idea of a sitemap is to provide a list of all the indexable URLs that you would like to have indexed and be considered as an SEO landing page - something that can be used in the search results to provide value for actual users. However, it's not just a list alone that gets you crawled. Google also wants to see if there is any internal linking or canonicalization to it. There are multiple different signals that Google uses to prioritise which URLs it crawls, and the sitemap is just one of them."

What would you describe as poor content nowadays?

"You need to provide content that users are actually interested in and solves their problems. If you're not solving that problem, it's content mostly for SEO purposes. We see this a lot in eCommerce - there's hidden text that's not there for users, it's just there for search engines. This is not a good approach for users. The content isn't attractive to users and it's not carrying much weight either. Poor quality content doesn't necessarily mean lack of content, although that could be one of the reasons as well."

What constitutes important user signals that search engines pick up on?

"Keep in mind that when a user starts to search on an engine like Google, they are Google's user - they're not your user. They're not anywhere near being your user at this point. Google wants to satisfy the need of their users - not your users. The user will type in a query, see a bunch of search results and click on the first one. If the page loads very slowly, the content is very poor, or they run into errors, the user is likely to go back.

Also, you need to manage users' expectations. You need to make sure your meta tags and page titles are optimised and demonstrate the benefit of clicking on this search result versus the other nine. This search result is going to give them the answer, and what they expect when they click on it. What is the unique sales proposition? If they click on it, and you don't deliver on these things, the user will go back.

Any situation where the user goes back to Google indicates that this search result did not satisfy them - and there can be plenty of reasons why. Basically, the user has just communicated that your search result isn't great. The key is that it's all about trends. I know there's a lot of people who are focused on specific numbers – but they change all the time and are based on a snapshot of what Google has crawled at that given moment. The web is continuously changing by removing, editing, and adding new content on a daily basis, on a whole bunch of URLs.

Stop focusing on specific numbers and focus on the overall trends. What are you sending as a trend into the algorithms? This is also very important from an off-page perspective. Not necessarily for PageRank purposes, but for discovery purposes - to prioritise which URL Google should crawl next."

How do you explain algorithms to non-technical marketers?

"It's pretty simple - we're talking about formulas. If you change the number in the sum, then you're going to get a different output. A very basic way to explain algorithms is using the analogy of a navigation system in your car. If you're going to a certain destination and the navigation system is telling you where to go, but you're not paying attention, you will miss your turning. This means it takes longer to get there.

This is what happens with algorithms. They are basically calculating in the backend to see where you should be placed. They do continuous testing, and they're trying to figure out the best result for their users. Once a user converts on our website, then they become our user."

What's one thing an SEO needs to stop doing to spend more time focusing on the quality of the signals they're providing to search engines?

"I'm going to give you two things. Firstly, you need to make sure that you check what you're sending in. You need to do some audits of your website. You can do it yourself, or you can go to third parties - but you do need to check what goes in. There are many tools out there in the industry for you to discover. Don't just check what you are sending in from an on-page perspective - also, check from an off-page perspective,

Secondly, you need to stop buying links for the sake of PageRank. That doesn't work, and it's not beneficial in most cases. If you're spending a certain amount of money every month to get 20 links pointing to your website – you're throwing your money in the garbage bin. Instead, you should be spending that budget on getting converting traffic. If you build links, make sure you build links that convert traffic on your website."

You can find Fili over at SEO.services.

Don't leave accessibility out of your SEO Strategy - with Billie Hyde from The SEO Works

Billie urges you to consider how accessible your site is, and how much revenue you could be missing out on by not making your site truly accessible in 2022.

Billie Hyde says: "Focus much more on accessibility. Recently, Google has really been pushing page experience, with Core Web Vitals and site speed. It's heading down a route of making the user experience better, and that includes accessibility. Google says, in its mission statement, that it wants the Internet to be accessible by everyone, for everyone. That means that as well as having fast sites, to be available for people that have slower connections, we need to start thinking about a wider range of users. We want to think about users that are neurodiverse, visually impaired, have limited mobility, etc., - the people that struggle with using devices.

This is going to be a massive thing over the coming years. Google recently shared documents on how they like content that contains more inclusive language. Gone are the days where we just think about SEO as creating content and ranking pages for neurotypical people, now we want the internet to be for everyone."

Does making your website more inclusive have a measurable, positive impact on your SEO?

"That's a difficult question to answer. Around 20% of all the people on the planet have some sort of disability. That's 20% of the world's population which could potentially be excluded from your site. In 2020, there was an average of around 60 billion sales made online and 3% of those were made by people using screen readers. It's hard to have a measurable way of tracking that because Google Analytics doesn't allow us to see whether a screen reader has been used. However, 3% of 60 billion is a lot of people - it's a large amount of potential revenue.

It's also common decency to make sites accessible. If it's something you choose to target, you are much more likely to see an increase in traffic, and in users with disabilities. Some studies have shown that neurodiverse users are much more likely to become returning customers compared to neurotypical users, if a website caters to their needs."

If you're doing the right thing for the user, then will search engines catch up with that and reward you for doing so, if they're not already?

"Absolutely. Every SEO knows that Google is planning the MUM update, and we don't really know much about it because everything's been held really close to the chest. What really stood out to me was that they said you might be able to take a photo of your hiking boots and ask: 'Can I use these to hike Mount Fuji?'. There's got to be a tag of some kind that they will use to be able to do that. I am convinced that it's alt text, which is always the last thing SEOs do on their optimization plans. If you push that to be done sooner then, even if you're not actively thinking about accessibility, you're becoming more accessible, as well as helping yourself be ready for whenever Google decides to drop the MUM bomb."

How does an SEO get started with this if they haven't done much work providing better accessibility in the past?

"As with anything in SEO, the first steps that you need to take are in self-learning. Jump on LearningSeo.io and see what documentation is on there. There are some fantastic people to follow on Twitter as well, like Lucy Pickering and Diane Kulseth, that are constantly dropping knowledge bombs around accessibility.

There's a lot of DIY to learn even further. What really got me into accessibility was the tool Sitebulb, that added an accessibility option for their crawls. I'd recommend that. It uses the axe DevTools framework, and it provides you with a lot of information on not just issues on the site, but also why these issues are important to people with various disabilities - and how you can resolve them. There's so much reading that you can do, but my practical advice is to start applying things. Also, question why things have been done a certain way, and if it's actually helpful for all the users that might need the site."

What's driving this awareness and change? Is it government legislation or more general awareness?

"It's a bit of everything really. In America, there have been some big cases on accessibility in terms of excluding certain users from your sites. That's where legislation has been more involved, and there's been a lot of publicity around that. As the internet has grown, and social media is connecting individuals all around the world, more people are being given a voice. We're more aware and connected to people and their pain points. We should listen to the people that are using our site, and if they are struggling to use it, we need to change things. That affects everyone, from marketers to SEOs to developers and user experience teams. We need to come together on this and make the internet a better place."

How do you listen to the people that are using your site?

"One of the things that originally helped me listen to the users was working on a site for a client who are a big charity for people with autism. I saw that the pages created specifically for people with more severe levels of autism had a high bounce rate, and the users weren't connecting with the content. You can look at bounce rate, you can do heat maps, and there are various triggers you can look at in Tag Manager to see how a user relates to the site, but the best way to understand how someone uses a site is to ask the users.

We were lucky with that client, to be connected to their users and be able to ask how they feel about a page - how they feel using it, whether it makes sense and whether it's what they want. From asking those kinds of questions, we were able to take on their advice. Some of it was really small things, like changing the text colour. The text colour wasn't being picked up as an accessibility issue by the various tools we were using. It was grey on a white background, so it stood out quite nicely, but our specific target audience was struggling with that. Simply changing the text colour had great results.

Especially for people that are working with specific niches, like people with learning difficulties or severe disabilities, you really need to listen to your users. You can also check things yourself. It's easy to change the way you use a computer for a little while. Instead of using your mouse, go on your website and try to tab through it, like a user with limited mobility would have to. Things like that will help you with understanding their experience."

How often should changes be made? Is this something that can only be affected by website redesign?

"These changes don't need to be made too regularly. You could do them once and then review in a year, or 18 months. However, it also doesn't need to be a big website overhaul. You don't need to completely restructure the site - making small changes can provide a massive benefit. For something like text colour, it could be a tiny change in the CMS that will result in a change across the site. It depends on how involved you want to get on this. It's hard to say exactly what the results will be. You could be increasing your audience by 20%, but you can't guarantee it."

What's one thing that SEOs should stop doing to spend more time considering the accessibility of their site?

"This might be controversial because some people love a meta description. Personally, I find them boring to write and they're not always used. I'd recommend that you still write meta descriptions but automate them, so you don't have to spend as much time on it. In a spreadsheet, with a bunch of 'If' statements, create a few sentiments around the site and what you're trying to say. Doing something like that will allow you to pull it together more quickly, and you could save yourself hours of work. Then you could just focus on something else while it's still getting done, like ensuring that your site is accessible for all of your users."

You can find Billie over at BillieGeena.co.uk.

Start optimizing for accessibility - with Amel Mehenaoui from Puffy

Amel shares a similar mindset to Billie, advising that Google's algorithms are evolving to consider site accessibility as part of the mix.

Amel Mehenaoui says: "All SEO professionals need to start thinking about accessibility in 2022. It's really important to think about making the web accessible for everybody because we've seen that Google did a lot of algorithm updates about UX in 2021. Page experience, ranking factors, and Core Web Vitals are all actually related to the user experience. By not focusing on accessibility, you're actually overlooking certain users and not helping them use the web how they want to.

You need to start thinking about optimising for accessibility and making the design part of the user experience for everyone. Looking at how the Google algorithm is evolving; accessibility could become ranking signals and factors at some point in the near future."

What aspects of accessibility do you envisage becoming part of the algorithms in the future?

"Sometimes web designers only design elements on the page, and they don't think about how the contrast, or the colours they pick, affects uses. This means it can be very difficult for users with disabilities to see the design or read the text.

It's about designing in a way that makes the usability of the site easy, and in the future, Google will be able to pick up on these things. In fact, if we audit a website for Core Web Vitals, we can already see that Google is picking up some metrics for accessibility - although they are not scoring them yet. Therefore, it's clear that Google knows how to find elements that are not optimised for accessibility."

What metrics are they picking up at the moment?

"The one that comes back a lot is the contrast between the text and the colour elements - so that could be an easy thing to start with for SEOs.

This is one of the beauties of SEO - we're not just doing content and technical optimisation; we're actually moving to user experience and also design. We can work much more closely with the UX teams.

When you think about it, there's one element of the current algorithm that came up with the page experience matrix, which looks at the spacing between the design elements. This is pure UX - but now it's affecting SEO."

What online resources can an SEO use to learn how their website's accessibility can be improved?

"The easiest one to use is Google PageSpeed Insights. If you audit your website, the last metrics are related to accessibility - although there is no score for them as they are currently greyed out. This is really interesting because if it's there, and Google is actually able to see them, it means at some point they may be able to add them to the algorithm itself.

You can also access these results through the DevTools. Just go to any website, click on Inspect, and you will have access to what we call the DevTools. From here, you can run the Lighthouse audit report."

What are the different ways that SEOs can articulate the value of what they're trying to do, to help other teams fully embrace the value of SEO?

"All SEOs have this struggle of showing the value of SEO to all these different teams. When it comes to accessibility, and the latest algorithm update, working closely with the UX and design teams is very important. It's our job to look at PageSpeed Insights, understand what it's telling us and learn more about UX. We need to keep evolving in our profession and understand why Google is asking us to care about UX. We need to work with other teams to optimise UX, but also educate them on algorithm changes - not only for the users but also for Google. Let's face it, if you are not ranking on page one and not getting traffic, this will affect sales.

If you share the recommendations from Google to improve the UX, the design elements on the page, and accessibility, then you can work together as a team to make improvements for your users. At the same time, Google will reward you with ranking improvements.

SEO has changed so much over the last five years, so internal education is more important than ever. For example, we knew that the user experience matrix would, at some date, become a ranking factor. Our job is to understand the main goal of the algorithm. Once we share this knowledge with the rest of the business, it's going to help us improve not only the ranking for the site but also the user experience - which is the goal of it all."

Should an SEO sit down and work with a UX team on a quarterly basis when they're looking to implement larger projects, or does this need to be done more regularly?

"The success of a website depends on SEOs working in a cross-functional way and collaborating with all teams on a regular basis. Obviously, each company is different, but most have to do ongoing releases, and you need to be part of those universal releases and the QA of the entire process.

It's your role to help other teams understand that anything that is added or removed to the website can affect SEO. That's why you need to always have an SEO at the table during the brainstorming and scoping. After implementation, you have to QA from an SEO perspective to make sure that nothing is affecting the site, such as speeds, user experience and rankings.

If the other teams have considered SEO throughout an implementation project, it's a win-win for everybody - the users, the bots, and the website. And it's the SEO's responsibility to get them thinking about these questions."

How do you measure accessibility improvements on your site?

"There are lots of tools out there that can record actual users' experience of browsing on your website. You can find users with accessibility challenges and run a test with them, or record their experience of using your site. You can watch on videos afterwards how they navigated the website and how they found the text, contrast of images with the text, and the colour contrasts."

How do you find users with accessibility challenges?

"There are companies out there who provide this service for you, such as UserTesting.com. You just tell them your criteria - for example, 100 individuals from the US that have these specific accessibility challenges. They might already have these users in their system, or they will work with you to build this segment.

They have everything set up, so you don't have to do a lot. They just need to know the tasks you want the users to do. They'll record the customer journey and the user's verbal description of the experience."

What's one thing SEOs need to be doing less of, so they can spend more time thinking about accessibility over the coming year?

"Obviously, all the things we do in SEO are important. But I think we need to start thinking about accessibility more, and optimising for it, before anything becomes a signal and then a ranking factor. One thing I would recommend doing more strategically is backlink building. We all know that everybody's doing them - but let's do them in a more strategic way that uses less resource. This will give you more time to work with the design team to think of the website's user experience and how it can be improved."

Amel Mehenaoui is head of SEO for Puffy.com.

Make the search engine embarrassed that your site isn't ranking for your target terms - with Barry Schwartz from Rusty Brick.

Barry has an unusual perspective on how you should think about your relationship with Google, and its SERP results.

Barry Schwartz says: "The number one goal for any SEO or site owner is to make a website, and have a Google (or other search engine) algorithm representative notice it should be ranking for the relevant keywords but is embarrassed that it isn't."

What would make a Google engineer embarrassed that your site isn't ranking number one for relevant terms? Is it typical on-site SEO,

content or relevance?

"It's not even thinking about SEO. You can build a website any way you want and create something you think your users would find really valuable. Search engines are going to want to rank it, even if it's a flash website that couldn't be indexed. I don't think you should really think about the fundamentals. When you build your website, you are building your business, and you should be thinking about what you're marketing, selling, and putting on your domain name that is useful for the user. You want them to read it, and for your site to be more useful than your competitors."

It's thinking of the way Apple releases their products. They put them in really nice boxes because it represents something that is very valuable to the company and the brand. You want to make sure to package your website, and your content, in a way that represents the highest level of quality possible."

In the future, will keywords and the standard optimisation of things like titles or headings be less important, and will it all be about thinking about the user?

"If you look at the progression that Google has been making with MUM, RankBrain, BERT, and all these different types of algorithms, AI and machine learning they've been deploying - it's about trying to find content that isn't optimised. They're looking for content that SEOs haven't had their hands on, trying to convince Google this is the best type of content, because Google wants to truly find what the best type of content is.

Not every website published every day is thinking about SEO. They just want to produce the best type of information for the users. This is why Google, and other search engines, are building the technology to find this type of content, even if it isn't optimised."

Does that mean you still do competitor analysis and benchmarking?

"You should definitely look at your competitors. However, I don't think you should get bogged down in what they are doing in an obsessed way. When I build products, I think about the user, and I don't want my thinking to be affected by what my competitors are doing. You need to think outside the box, think differently and come up with a new solution to help your customers. I've built many software applications and apps over the years, but I never try to replicate what the competition is doing in any way. Yes, I monitor them, but it's more about finding a new approach to what they're doing."

How do you define who the user is, and how do you build your site for them?

"Usually, the best businesses, and the best products that come out, are solving a need for the founder of the company. They need something and hate the way existing tools solve the problem. They build something that is great for them, knowing that other people will want it. That's how the best products are built - building a solution that fills a gap. They already think from the perspective of the user, so they don't need to do much market research.

You just have to have a passion to meet a need. Square was a company built based on this principle: I need a credit card machine that I can carry around with me and plug into my phone. It's simple concepts that solve big problems."

Are you advising SEO to stay one step ahead of Google in terms of what they're using to rank today?

"You won't lose if you're just thinking about where Google wants to be in the future. If you think that Google wants this type of content to rank, you will probably be one step ahead of the game, no matter what you do."

Do you think that the same will be true for the other search engines out there?

"That's the goal for any search engine - to rank the most relevant search results because they are the most helpful for the user. Google and all other search engines want to send you to the best type of search results, and the best website for that query. This will mean the user will come back to that search engine in the future when they have another query to make."

How do you measure the value of doing this if you're not looking at more traditional SEO metrics?

"You can still look at those metrics. It takes a while to build this up if you're doing something new and out of the box. But it will all lead to traffic on your website, engagement on your pages, and hopefully, your revenue goals. Maybe it's a form being completed or a download of a white paper. All these things are still accessible and trackable via Google Analytics, or any analytics tool.

All these SEO metrics are still relevant, but I think the best sites don't necessarily worry about measuring them. I don't think they care. They're just passionate about building something that they think is very valuable to the users in a way that people haven't been thinking about before. That's the way to approach it - but it's easier said than done."

For the last 15 years, we've seen blog posts saying SEO was dead. Are we actually heading towards this now?

No, I don't think SEO is dead. You still need to do the basics at some level. You can't launch a WordPress website and use the title tag: 'homepage'. Well actually you can, because Google recently made some changes to how they handled title tags and titles in the search results because they see a lot of people are not implementing titles in the 'proper' way. Google's now going to try to use other methods, maybe the header of the page or anchor text, to come up with a new title for your result.

But the point is, you don't want to give Google mixed signals. You don't want to have anchor text saying your website's about blue widgets, while the title tag says it's about red widgets. That just doesn't help."

How do you implement this advice in a larger organisation that has several hundred people within a marketing team? Do you formally have to sit down with all the different elements and decide on an approach together?

"If you're a founder, you have the vision and the idea, but you want to hire the best UX person that maybe thinks outside the box to bring your vision to life. You want to hire the best programmers that have a unique way of using a new technology. And of course, you want to hire an SEO that's able to implement this in a way that's search engine friendly. You want to hire people that are able to deliver stuff and produce your vision. You need a whole team behind you to make that possible. Deciding on an approach together is definitely the right route to take."

If your clients are used to focusing on traditional SEO metrics, how does an SEO agency articulate the value of doing this?

"Traditional SEO metrics are short-term and available after three to six months of SEO. This new approach is much longer term. It could take a year or so to see results – which is hard. It's hard to say we should be doing Y, when all the competitors are doing X – and doing well. The answer is, eventually Y is going to be the thing that actually gets you more traffic. It's a bigger risk, and it might not work. But those who take risks usually get the biggest reward.

Larger businesses can actually handle this. They have budgets and resources to take the bigger risks. But smaller businesses have so much more flexibility to make these things happen. It's basically about understanding who you're working with and making that pitch for them directly."

How do you articulate this approach to your marketing team?

"Marketers would probably eat this up! Most of them aren't worried about title tags, technical SEO, or boring stuff they might not care about. Ask them what you could build that is unique and out of the box without worrying about SEO. What do they think your users are going to love? Maybe it's a creative widget, maybe it's a mobile app, or maybe it's a cool marketing campaign. It's a good thing to go to marketers and ask them to forget about SEO and instead tell you what they think is great for your users."

What can SEOs stop doing to spend more time thinking out of the box to create incredible and unique content?

"That's the hard part. You have your SEO daily tasks, and you do your SEO audits and reporting every day, week, or month. Getting bogged down in the routine takes out the creativity in your experience. And without creativity, and thinking about things at a higher level, you're not going to produce the stuff that Google is looking to rank in the future. That's an issue.

Focusing too much on Domain Authority or looking at different link metrics is looking backwards. Google can make one change tomorrow, and links could suddenly become unimportant. A lot of these things we're doing are focused on the minutiae, and they're preventing you from thinking on a higher level. Step back and think strategically about what you can produce. Stop wasting your time on the smaller SEO metrics."

Will there still be room for more conservative and technical SEOs in the future?

"100%. There are massive sites that do this really well, like Amazon. On the other hand, you might have somebody building crazy, amazing stuff that users love, but you have six different domains with the exact same solution, and there's duplicate content all over the place. That's confusing the search engines. A lot of this SEO stuff is just common sense. It's about making sure you're consistent and have everything in one domain, in one brand. Sometimes you can lose that focus if you don't hire the right SEO – who knows what they are doing."

If you are doing a one-off incredible creative project, is it best to do it on your core domain name?

"Keep everything on your brand, on your domain name. Your domain name is your brand. You could make a subdomain if you think that's applicable for this specific type of thing, but I wouldn't publish it on Facebook - I wouldn't publish it on somebody else's thing. You could share it there, but I wouldn't make it live in those areas. You want to control it for the rest of your life."

You can find Barry Schwartz over at rustybrick.com.

3 PRIORITISE

Convince your stakeholders to make SEO a priority - with Kerstin Reichert from SeedLegals

Kerstin believes that many organisations aren't treating SEO seriously enough – and that SEOs need to be doing a better job of articulating its value.

Kerstin Reichert says: "Convince your stakeholders to make SEO a priority. Time and time again, SEOs are unable to implement all the amazing things they could be doing because of this. You need to bring people on board before anything else. Make sure that all your wonderful ideas actually have a chance of coming to life."

Why don't stakeholders have SEO as a priority?

"I wish SEO was front and centre but it's not that simple, and there can be different reasons. Usually, it's because SEO is not sexy. It can take quite a long time and it's not as measurable as other channels, so the results can sometimes be a bit vague.

Stakeholders are often not able to forecast as well for SEO as they can for other channels. They are not able to know exactly what's going to happen when they invest more. Plus, it takes longer than other channels to implement. A lot of times, SEO is the ugly stepchild within marketing, and it can take a bit more effort to get people to buy in."

Are SEOs at fault for not articulating its value, or is it stakeholders that are not recognising it?

"I don't want to point fingers; I think it really depends on the type of company you're dealing with. The background of the senior stakeholders, or the marketing leaders, will have an effect. If you're lucky, everyone's already on board when you start, and that's fine. Usually, if you're working on your own projects then it's not an issue. At a smaller company, you might have the liberty to do things that demonstrate the success of SEO.

However, there are situations where SEO gets deprioritised in favour of other channels. It's not that other people in the business don't think SEO is important, it just falls behind because it is slower, and harder to measure. Business objectives, and targets to hit, are often easier and faster to achieve through paid channels.

SEOs can also be quite technical. We often don't use the right language to be convincing, especially when communicating with people that don't have a background in SEO. I would highly recommend that you adjust your language, adjust your communication, depending on who you're speaking to in the business. To you, KPIs are super important, it's what you look at every single day, but senior management probably don't consider individual rankings. They are focussed on business impact, and meeting targets."

How should SEOs communicate the impact of their work, and what kind of business impact are most stakeholders looking for?

"It depends on who you are speaking to; the key is to tailor your message to your audience. Senior management, in every company, have their targets. It could be to increase revenue, increase the customer base, or both. You should know what the business is trying to achieve. That usually gets broken down into overarching marketing targets. As an SEO, you should be able to say how you will be able to contribute to hitting those targets.

That's for senior management, but you also need to get other people on board with SEO. You need people from many different areas to get your campaigns implemented - developers, designers, product owners, and more. Again, you have to adjust your language and focus on what the individual is trying to achieve, and how your work contributes to that. Tailor your approach, depending on who you're speaking to.

In most cases, you will have to start very early to create awareness about SEO - what it is, how it works and what it can achieve. For example, you could run workshops across the business, that would be different depending on who you're running them for. That's a way to start the conversation and get a seat at the table, where important decisions get made."

Do you need to get SEO involved in the marketing strategy conversation, so the business understands how it can be implemented effectively?

"Definitely, especially at the planning stage. You have to be there to explain what's realistic, and what the expectations should be, because SEO does take longer. If the awareness isn't there, then you might not be able to deliver against expectations. It might look as if you're not performing, when in reality you were not involved in planning, so you didn't set the right expectations.

You need to be plan how you can contribute to the goals of the business. It's hard for someone else to do that for you. SEO is not as well understood as it could be, and it can be harder to relate to than other channels. Paid search can say that 'Investment X' is going to give 'Output Y'. SEO is not like that. There are so many areas to cover within those conversations - from tech, to content, to off-page. So many things influence performance in SEO that it can be difficult for people to understand.

SEOs should have the opportunity to input in planning, budgeting, and performance reviews as well."

Is it helpful to describe SEO as something that can funnel new traffic and awareness to the brand, or is that too simple?

"I'm not sure I would describe it that way, though it is one option. We always discuss with our data team that there are so many different touchpoints to SEO that it's like a football team playing together. Many different people are involved before one person at the end scores a goal. Within my setting, I think everyone's aware that different channels play together, and that they are needed at different stages.

Marketers should recognise that SEO has touchpoints throughout the user journey, not only at the top of the funnel, especially if you consider content marketing as well. You need to communicate that SEO is not only there at the beginning, with discovery. At midpoint, you've got potential customers asking questions, that you can provide a direct answer to. Further down the funnel, brand queries may almost be resulting in a sale. It provides the opportunity to optimise the brand online. SEO is present throughout, to increase the awareness and reach of the company's marketing."

How do you deal with a stakeholder that's fixated on vanity metrics, like ranking for a particular keyword phrase that doesn't really matter?

"It takes some convincing, but it starts with a bit of education. It's up to us as SEOs to take a step back from using keywords as a success metric and change the conversation. We should be talking about traffic, or lead generation, or conversion – things that are relevant to the business. We should be the ones to take the conversation in that direction, so that people don't measure us against the ranking of one particular keyword.

As an SEO, you need to take the responsibility to communicate more effectively within your business. You need to proactively train different departments and start speaking in a language that people understand. You should be creating awareness and providing education to get the people you work with on board."

What's one thing that you suggest SEOs should stop doing to focus more time on educating their business about SEO?

"Don't worry about how to counter Google's updates. Google wants to show the best results for any given search query. You should try to be user first - focus on the audience and creating the best user experience and worry about Google second. Don't get too hung up on every single update and trying to chase external factors. You will save yourself time. Don't ignore it completely, and do test things, but don't focus all your energy on the next Google update.

You are better off investing time in championing SEO within your business, getting people on board and making sure they understand and buy into it. Then you will have the freedom to do what you need to do for good performance. If you come back with results, you get more buy-in for SEO. It's a cycle that you need to start at some point, and you need to invest the time to make it happen."

You can find Kerstin Reichert over at SeedLegals.com.

Benchmark your search market to find the quick wins - with Lidia Infante from BigCommerce

Lidia feels that the key to SEO success lies in truly understanding who your competitors are and determining their strengths and weaknesses.

Lidia Infante says: "Look at what your competitors are doing, benchmark them, and find the quickest way to outrank them."

How do you define who your competitors are?

"You can identify your competitors from different areas of the business. Look at your competitors in sales, speak to customer service and marketing, and compile a list. Then, look at who your search competitors are. There are two ways to go about that. You can work from the bottom up: look at all your keywords, what sites are ranking on those keywords, and which competitors appear most often. Alternatively, you can work from the top down: take the list you've compiled from conversations within your business and go for a tool like SISTRIX, or Semrush, or Ahrefs. Make sure that those competitors are relevant. Find the ones that appear both on your compiled qualitative list, that comes from within the business, and also within the tool."

Are your competitors' businesses that do similar things, or ones that are ranking for the keyword phrases you're targeting?

"You're looking at the sweet spot between the two. Which competitors are more likely to show up in search and steal your customers? Those are the ones that you want to outrank."

When benchmarking, how do you analyse and keep track of where your competitors are ranking?

"There are two different approaches, again it's bottom-up or top-down. My favourite approach is the top-down approach. In that case, you start by looking at how many keywords they are ranking for and what their estimated traffic is. Out of that estimated traffic, look at what traffic is branded and non-branded, and what is editorial. Non-branded, non-editorial traffic would be product-focused, and editorial traffic is typical How To informational stuff that would lead to a blog."

How do you differentiate between editorial and transactional content?

"Look at the destination of that traffic; look at the landing page. If one competitor has an estimated traffic of 100 that's branded, 200 that's not branded, and 3000 that's editorial, you know that this competitor has a solid editorial strategy that you might want to look at. If you only look at traffic numbers, this competitor's brand might look bigger than it actually is. Don't just analyse the traffic on the bigger numbers, dive a little bit deeper into what kind of traffic you're looking at."

How do you decide if you have an opportunity to surpass a competitor's rankings?

"With this benchmarking, you're looking at the three main sides of SEO: authority, content, and tech. What you're trying to do here is determine whether you need to work on your brand and authority, your content, or your tech SEO. There are a few ways to choose the area that's most feasible to outrank your competitors in. Maybe you are weak in that area, maybe your competitors are weak, or maybe you are average and want to take it one step further. It's going to be a strategic decision that should inform a wider strategy. Once you've identified the aspect that's going to be your focus, benchmark further. Investigate in more depth what your competitors are doing in those areas, and how you're planning on surpassing them."

How do you determine if a website has high authority?

"Look at links and backlinks. I don't usually condone this metric, but Domain Authority is a good way of benchmarking how authority is flowing to that site. Domain Authority is a bit of a one-size-fits-all that doesn't fit every case, because it doesn't account for whether the content of the links is relevant to the page.

You also want to be looking at brand search volume and the amount of branded traffic in the links that you're seeing."

Is benchmarking the volume and relevance of content a manual task or can it be automated?

"It can absolutely be automated and there are different metrics that you can automate. An easy option is to put the list of competitors into the Batch Analysis tool on Ahrefs, and it will give you keywords, index pages, estimated traffic, etc. Then, go to each of the competitors and play with 'Include/Exclude' to get the estimated traffic and the number of keywords for branded traffic, non-branded traffic and editorial. If you want to get the exact number of URLs that these competitors are ranking for on the editorial side of things, you could use a formula and Import XML into Google Sheets to scrape it from the search results. That's usually not needed because it's faster to just copy-paste the numbers."

How do you measure and benchmark for tech?

"It's very difficult. I've been trialling different metrics and methods. I'm working on this with a wider team because I want to reach a universal conclusion, and a metric that we can use. Lately, I've been using Core Web Vitals for it, and Lighthouse scores, but I'm not particularly happy with those. It's a good starting point because it will tell you which of your competitors have been taking the tech side of things more seriously. However, it won't tell the entire picture of their technical health, especially if you're looking at eCommerce or massive sites.

There's much more to be talked about, like architecture and how they're overcoming specific challenges. I've been trialling adding health scores from auditing tools and doing some more manual work as well. It's complicated to measure."

How often should this benchmarking be done?

"I would do it on a monthly basis for clients that are looking to get results fast. Firstly, start with an overview of the entire search market for the client. Depending on how involved they are on search, you can do top-down or bottom-up. Once you've identified the area of growth, dive a little bit deeper into that specific area to create a goal and a benchmark. For example, if the average number of branded searches for a specific market is 1000 a month, and you know that you're at 500, maybe the goal is 1500. Then, you know you need to work with a PR agency to improve the brand.

You should be looking at this on a monthly basis to see how you're progressing towards the goal and towards the benchmark. You will need to modify that benchmark as your competitors move. If your benchmark is an average number, and the average changes, your goal needs to change. It needs to be updated. When you're planning your goal, you need to consider how you think the average is going to move and move your goal accordingly. If branded searches are decreasing, maybe you only need to get to 1000. If branded searches are increasing by 10% every month, you need to take that into account as well."

Is it difficult to measure the bottom line for these efforts?

"When it comes to measuring the real success of SEO, I always bring it back to revenue. Everything can be tracked to revenue, even if you have different models for doing that. If you are a SaaS company, you might look at leads, then which of those are qualified leads, then how many of those turn into customers, and then the lifetime value of those customers. You can track it back down to the value of a lead and get the estimated revenue growth from the growth of your SEO efforts. In the end, there's always a way to bring it back to revenue in the world of SEO. That's what matters to businesses."

What's one thing that SEOs should stop doing to spend more time benchmarking their competitors?

"Stop immediately panicking about rank drops and rank changes. Don't track them daily. Track them globally around the topic more than on specific keywords - unless there's something that's absolutely vital for you. Don't work reactively because you might be looking at a Google test of the SERPs, or something that your competitor has done, that doesn't necessarily fall in your hands. Take a deep breath and look at your rankings with a little bit more perspective. Look at them over time, whether the drop is consistent, how volatile the SERPs are in your industry, and what level of drop you are comfortable with."

You can find Lidia Infante over at Lidia-Infante.com.

SuperGAP analysis: Using your competitor's rankings to guide your SEO success - with Lukasz Zelezny from SEO.London

Lukasz reveals that he uses his competitors' rankings to identify and select his own target keyword phrases.

Lukasz Zelezny says: "My analysis is called SuperGAP because I use a super high number of competitors, often between 20 and 40 depending on how much memory my local machine has. I use Excel and data sources like Semrush, and export the rankings of the competitors to build a matrix of all the keywords the competitors are simultaneously ranking for, and my client is not. As competitors are players of the same industry, this gives me a perfect view of the areas where my client is not ranking and should be doing so."

How do you get started with this? Do you have to define a list of keyword phrases to begin with?

"When my clients are onboarding, I send them a form where they can add anyone they consider to be a competitor. If they struggle to provide many competitors, I use metrics to find the most similar websites to my client's site, such as the number of their ranking keywords that overlap with my clients'. The websites can't be ranking on too few or too many keywords. If there are only a few keywords, often the competitor will be not relevant, and it will not be a competitor. If it's too many, you are probably talking about Wikipedia or Amazon. Every eCommerce may say at some level that Amazon is a competitor - but this is not the type of website we're looking for.

You're looking for a website of similar size, traffic, and number of keywords that rank. Semrush provides a metric which measures the similarity of the keyword set. It provides all the keywords that competitor A is ranking for versus your client and all the keywords that competitor B is ranking for versus your client. This shows you what the similarity level is. The higher the similarity level, the better - as long as the other metrics also makes sense."

How do you ensure that you don't get keyword recommendations that are irrelevant for your client? Could this happen if your competitors have additional lines of business that your client doesn't operate in?

"The outcome of the SuperGAP is just a final suggestion that needs to be digested by an in-house team. You know that there are other areas which your client is not interested, so when the gap analysis is prepared, you can work through the list with the client and exclude all these areas until you hit your sweet spot.

SuperGap analysis is so powerful that I can do keyword research for a Russian website written in Cyrillic and provide relevant topics for a Chinese website. You don't need to know the language or the alphabet because you're using numbers.

Often, after I've presented the gap analysis to clients, there is a 'Wow' moment when they see the highest priority keywords. They can't believe they are not ranking for them and have to check on Google. This is that moment you know you've done a great job as a consultant, and provided very relevant research for your client."

So, you're delivering such accurate information and appropriate recommendations to your clients because you're selecting a high number of competitors. Have you determined that you need to find at least 20 competitors to achieve this level of precision?

"That's correct. Normally software only allows analysis of five competitors, but I use many more. I'm currently analysing 35 competitors of a client who provides golf equipment, and they are ranking most highly for keywords such as 'How much does a golf simulator cost?' That means my client needs to provide advice on this. Maybe they should start selling simulators, because it's definitely something that resonates highly with their potential customers.

You're getting super deep knowledge about the industry, and this is also very valuable information for eCommerce websites. It can show you which products need more marketing, or even which products they should consider selling. You can do gap analysis to understand why your competition is doing so well. If they are predominantly selling men's clothing, you can see they are now also doing women's clothing to inflate traffic. Do they want to follow this path? If yes, you know what products they need to upload. If not, you can dig deeper."

Are there certain types of business or website sizes that SuperGAP analysis is not appropriate for?

"The only exception to using this gap analysis would be highly B2B websites, such as the petroleum industry. This is not because the methodology is bad, it's more due to the behaviour of potential customers. It's very rare that someone decides that today they're going to dig a shaft and search to find out who can help them. The purchase process is much longer and very complicated.

Every small, medium and large company can grow – as can the industry leaders. There are always areas where you are not ranking. I use three metrics in my gap analysis. Firstly, 'match' - which is the number of competitors that simultaneously rank. Secondly, 'average' - which is the average ranking of competitors. Thirdly, 'prioritisation' - which is a special formula used to aggregate everything, including cost per click. Despite the fact we're talking about SEO here, this is important because a higher cost per click means the keyword has more commercial benefit.

When I've aggregating this, I sort by 'match' and then 'priority'. The keywords that are most visible across competitors are always on the top of the list. Of course, my clients might decide they don't want to go for specific keywords, and that's fine. This is the role of the consultant. This is the moment when you can marry the knowledge of external SEO expertise and in-house know-how about the company and the industry."

How often should an SEO be doing this? Is it only done at the start

of a client project, annually, or more often than that?

"I recommend doing this every three to six months. You don't want to have a situation where you're bombarding in-house people with new gap analysis every two weeks. The other determining factor is when they can actually execute the findings from the gap analysis. I do this analysis during the client audit, and they are getting the peak benefits for the next three to six months.

There is one key step in my analysis I haven't mentioned that makes things a lot easier. At the end, when I'm left with 100,000 keywords in my spreadsheet, I only choose the keywords which have at least three competitors ranking for them and 100 searches a month. The list is suddenly reduced to 5,000 records.

Previously at this stage, I had to manually group these keywords into what would constitute a landing page, blog post, or category for eCommerce. Now there is a software, SE Ranking, which has a tool called Grouper. The problem is this tool is pay-as-you-go, so every keyword costs a very small amount. If you're going with 5,000 keywords, it will be an additional cost to the audit - but it's worth it. You know that you are only loading keywords that are very prominent in delivering extra traffic to your client. Let the tool start grouping, and it looks at the Google search results to identify keywords that return the same URLs multiple times, which is a strong signal that multiple keywords should belong to the same page. You end up with a beautiful spreadsheet with grouped keywords' search volumes. Send this to the content writers, and they can deliver amazing content."

Is optimising existing pages one of the biggest initial wins after you've provided this information to your clients?

"Gap analysis is predominantly for writing new pages. 99% of the time, it's used to design and create new content to expand on the existing number of pages.

I have another pillar in my audit, which is Snapshot. Here, I take the keywords that are already ranking from the Search Console using an API. I can have about 400,000 keywords and then identify 5-10 keywords per URL that are ranking quite well but are not yet first. Then you optimise this in-house. It can be a very long process, especially if you have a lot of content, but it's very beneficial."

What's one thing an SEO needs to stop doing to spend more time on SuperGAP analysis?

"Firstly, in-house people need to remember that to scale up, they need to outsource. They can outsource all the menial tasks, and that will give them much more power.

The second problem I see is too much writing for writing's sake - and no one measures what value it brings. You may have articles that are not even generating traffic, let alone leads or conversions. Nobody's searching for terms like, 'Top 100 things you should see in Budapest this week' anymore. Instead, people are searching with a problem focus for phrases such as, 'Where should I go for a holiday during lockdown'. Now, you need to get to the point. People are using Google because they have a problem, and they want to find the solution. It's your job to give them that solution."

You can find Lukasz Zelezny over at SEO.London.

Tailor your SEO content strategy around your first party data - with Michael Bonfils from SEM International

Michael urges you to harness your first party data, to give you an unfair advantage in your content marketing campaigns.

Michael Bonfils says "Look at first party data as a way to enable better content strategy for your SEO plans."

What first party data do you think is most useful to SEOs?

"It's data that comes from the customers. That could be through email marketing, email capture, etc. Right now, there is a war on third party data, all the assumptive technologies are going away due to privacy regulations and more. For your own data from your customers - the people who have signed up for newsletters, for example - you have a choice. You can either give that data away to companies like Google or Facebook, or you can hold onto that data as preciously as you possibly can. It is highly valuable. Reach out to the marketing teams, or to customer support, and find out who these people are - their names, their email addresses, or any other data that you can get on them internally. That's all within the realm of first party data."

How can you start to use first party data?

"Obviously, there are a lot of things you do in regular paid marketing when it comes to first party data, like look-alike modelling. However, I want to focus on understanding your customer. You can do that through surveys, or polls, for example. One thing that we did, that was great for content strategies, was we surveyed all our first party data to find out where the customers fit within a psychographic profile. Psychographics refers to the study of consumers based upon their psychological and cognitive attributes such as beliefs, values, thoughts, hopes and goals.

We saw that a large fraction of our customers matched a specific intent psychographic profile, that engages with certain types of content, yet we'd been spending all our time on content that's not very engaging for them. We could learn from those customers and tailor the content to what they wanted. That's what this is all about: understanding your first party data and tailoring your content around that, for the benefit of your entire SEO content strategy."

How does an SEO form a strategy based on first party data?

"A focus group is a really good strategy, especially if that group is made up of your customers. One of the psychological models that we like to use is from a book called The People Code. It basically profiles everybody into four different 'colours', and each group has certain psychographic elements to it. For example, somebody who is in the 'yellow' profile is fun-loving and looks at life through rose-coloured glasses. These profiles can have significant attributions. For somebody in the 'white' profile, who is more engineering-focussed and research-heavy, they will take a lot of time to think before they make a decision. There are four of these profiles that every human has within them.

Using this model, taking the questions and surveying your first party data, you get some knowledge of what your clients look like. You can see if they are all within a certain profile, or if they are a mix and what that mix might be. You may find that the content you've been creating has been attracting one segment, but you're missing out on people from other profiles because your content doesn't suit them. Somebody from the 'yellow' profile wants content that is appealing to them in the here-and-now, they don't want to do research and stuff their brains with too much information. Somebody in the 'white' category, however, could want to absorb as much as possible. You can create a strategy with this, by using the same topic but developing your content to suit your audience. You can design the perfect amount of content to appeal to people in the 'white' profile - the engineers that are thinking of research. You can also decide that for people who don't want all that research, you just need to present the fun facts so they can move forward. It's about understanding what these individuals look like. When you focus on first party data, you get to know your audience instead of making general assumptions.

Marketing departments, SEOs, and content writers fall into these classifications themselves, which means that often they're not thinking outside their box. You could be a very research-centric engineer, but there's probably a lot of people in your audience who are not like that. You may have a hard time writing content for different profiles. Look at your own content staff, so that they understand these different quadrants within themselves and can reach all these different audiences. Then they can develop the same content but tailored to different mindsets."

Should SEOs be publishing different forms of content, and perhaps different pages, for different audiences? If so, does that make it difficult to build one authoritative piece of content to appeal to search engines?

"It may have an influence on trying to build one piece of content for a search engine. However, things are moving as search engines are getting smarter. They want to know your content, the user intent behind it, and how relevant you are to your users. The technologies are getting faster and are starting to better understand consumer behaviour. By developing content that's tailored to a consumer mindset, especially that of your customers, there's an opportunity to leverage.

You may want to design four different pieces of content, that are all based on the same core material, for the four different behaviours. Then you can determine which one of these has the authority. It could be a majority, so you would figure out how to craft the content to appeal to all four, and then test it with your focus groups. You could produce one piece of content but introduce elements, like specific case studies, that load within it based upon which audience you are targeting. That way the content could appeal to different audiences from the same page and URL, so that search engines can see it as one piece.

There are ways around this, but it's not perfect. It's still relatively new. On the paid side, we're always targeting specific people based on their psychological mindset. SEO is a whole different ballgame because you've got authority here."

How do you measure the success of this kind of strategy?

"You can look at all the regular metrics: engagement, click-through, traffic, and ranking for some pages compared to others. You can see who progresses through the site, completes a call-to-action from a certain piece of content, or spends longer on a certain page. There's nothing specific that really stands out except when you're testing using your own data. You can get a lot of information testing on your customers with the content that you've created, perhaps even using a focus group. They could win a prize or get a discount by giving their feedback. That's a great way to get an idea of what is successful."

Does this affect how keywords should be used?

"I am an advocate for keywords, I don't think they're going away. There are opportunities to take your keywords and place them within a customer journey segment, while understanding your audience. When we do this, we look at psychological profile per persona, so we end up with four psychological profiles for each persona. Then we analyse all the keywords per persona profile and start bucketing them into segments. That can be a segment for the awareness phase of the customer journey, all the way down the different levels of intent on the customer trail. Most of the time, it doesn't change too much. There are very few words that are specific to one psychological profile. However, you can do per persona keyword segmentation and build your content strategy around that."

How often should the content marketing strategy be looked at?

"It depends on the budget. Personally, I would be doing content strategy every month, at least quarterly. That content is key to everything that you do. It's about trying to leverage your content in every way possible, create fresh content and keep your customers engaged with your brand. That's really important. When you compare an SEO content strategy with the amount that's spent on paid, the returns differential is ridiculous. Content strategy and SEO should be as important as a campaign on YouTube or other places, if not more so."

What's one thing that SEOs should be doing less of to focus more on using first party data to form their content strategy?

"Cut out what everybody else is doing. SEOs spend a lot of time on very general, very basic, content marketing, like Article of the Week or deciding whether the number one keyword should change. Stop doing as much of the traditional stuff and start thinking out of the box.

Paid marketing is really good at focusing on target audience. They usually let Google run their smart campaigns, but they're really good at finding out who their customers are and developing strategies that are super targeted. SEOs have been the reverse of that. The 'old school' mentality was to be broad and get as much traffic as you can. Things are changing now. Look at what Google's doing with FLoC - getting rid of cookies and having their browser be the data centre of everything. That is going to impact search in the future, and we've got to be prepared. They are going to be looking at your customers, and they're going to relate your customers' intent and engagement with the content that you have. First party data is how you can be ready for the future."

You can find Michael over at SEMinternational.com.

Forecast your projected SEO success based upon business metrics - with Kevin Gibbons from Re:signal

Following on from Kerstin's tip at the beginning of this chapter, Kevin shares that to get greater decision-maker buy-in, SEOs need to start communicating using more conventional business metrics.

Kevin Gibbons says: "Make sure that you start everything with a forecast. SEOs often go wrong when they rush into problems and start off too tactical. They may try to improve areas of weakness on their website, or look to strengthen areas up, but without considering why. I like the framework of Simon Sinek - start with 'Why', and go from there to 'How', then to 'What'. I've been reiterating that for years. Rather than starting with 'How', and the tactical, look at 'Why' with forecasting.

From a business level, there's so much to get out of that. Rather than sprinting in the wrong direction, you're developing a strategy first. With that approach, you know that you're going in the right direction. Once you are, then it's time to accelerate.

It's about starting with a strategy first, then building that into a clear forecast you can use to set expectations with clients. You want to know what success looks like in the next 12 months, or even in the next 5-10 years. A longer-term vision of the business should be aligned to your SEO strategy."

How does an SEO decide on the metrics to incorporate within the forecast?

"Keep them as business-focussed as possible. There's not a one-size-fits-all -it comes from conversation with the client. You need to know what their business objectives are, and what they are looking to achieve. It may fall back to organic revenue, but you don't want to make assumptions. Too often, agencies go straight into 'pitching mode' without listening to what successful means within the business.

I have a mix of experience, with nearly 20 years in SEO and running a business for around 15 years. Business owners should treat SEO as an investment. When they're looking at the tactical parts of SEO, sometimes that can be viewed as a cost. They end up looking for deliverables like an audit, or keyword research, and looking at the rate. The client sees this an investment in SEO. That money could have been spent on paid search, or email marketing, or even the stock market for direct returns. It's not about SEO versus PPC, there's always been a place for both channels, but SEO needs to be creating something that is adding value.

The metrics should be about what the business is trying to achieve, and that's normally a return on their investment. It could be cost savings, or brand awareness, but SEOs need to identify what success look like from the client's perspective. Whether it's revenue, number of sales, or profit, you need to dig into it so that you can start working backwards.

I advocate having a hierarchy of KPIs and picking one target. Otherwise, you're chasing two rabbits. If organic revenue is that one target, then you can start to work back and figure out the type of traffic that you need, or the type of rankings to secure. More tactically, you could then even identify what type of links you need to get from different publishers, or which pages need to be optimised. When you have these lead and lag indicators, clients don't have to make an SEO 'leap of faith'. You can show progress all the way through, that keeps you heading towards the end goal without losing sight of why you're doing that in the first place."

Should SEOs be focussed on things that are likely to convert straightaway, and how long should it take to pay back on the investment in SEO?

"To a certain extent, that's the right way to approach it. If you're having a short-term impact, then you can get more investment and buy-in for what you're doing. Prioritise terms like page two rankings, that you can tip over the edge on to page one. Those are great for forecasts, because you're almost there, you're just not yet getting the traffic and revenue to match the hard work that's been put in. If you can get that easy win, you can build towards more competitive terms that might take a while.

The timeframe does depend on the market that you're in and the competition that you're against. Remember that you're fighting a moving target. Often, forecasting is done because businesses want to get to where their competitor is already. They want to know what it will take to close the gap. That assumes that the competitor will do nothing, which is often not the case - they're switched on and heavily invested in themselves. You need forecasts on where they will be in two years' time, to surpass what their success will look like in the future.

In terms of ROI, a marketing director will be looking to make a return within 6-12 months at a minimum and want to reap the rewards within a couple of years. This isn't paid search, where you can put money in and get traffic back quickly, it's a longer-term investment. However, at the end of those 12 months, if you've secured a lot more organic traffic, you have a much stronger base from which to start the next year. Your outlook does need to consider the long-term timeline as well. If you're always invested in short-term tactics, you have to keep investing to keep it going. It's a tap that can be turned off. You need realistic expectations, but you need to look at the return that you're getting from the cost."

What SEO tactics are likely to bring a ranking that's just off page one onto it?

"We've had some good wins purely with content and making the experience stronger. Think of E-A-T, particularly the authority of content. You need to make sure that you've got content that can be trusted. You can take keywords that are on the edge of page one, and tip them over the edge just by improving the content.

The UX will sometimes help as well. Certainly, there are things you can do to boost your click-through rate, like title tags and meta descriptions. Make sure that it's as targeted as possible for those terms. Give Google a signal that you deserve to be amongst the page one listings, if not higher.

The three pillars of SEO have always been the same: technical, on-site content, and link reputation. In an ideal world, you would be as strong as possible in all three. The quickest wins though, unless you have serious technical issues, are from investing in the content experience."

How do you challenge business owners that want you to focus on bad metrics, and what types of metrics are those, typically?

"I'm not a fan of link metrics because I think you're choosing the wrong target. I think link metrics can be a KPI, but it shouldn't be the main goal.

The main goal should be a business metric. Ideally, it should be revenue focused. Whether you've generated 40 links, 100 links or 300 links shouldn't be the main outcome. That doesn't do much from a brand, or business performance, perspective.

I would even question focussing on domain and link authority metrics. That's not Google, it's from a third-party tool that gives an indication of strength. If your whole strategy is built on wanting to change a score of 60/100 to 70/100, that can be changed by the way the tool provider calculates things. It's not a bad metric, but it's not the end goal - it's a way to help you secure that goal.

If you're judging the success and failure of SEO on KPIs it's hard to get true investment. If you're judging on ROI, it's much easier because you can show the business owner that there's been, say, a 5-6 times return for the spend, and how you did it. It goes back to those lead and lag indicators. Set the importance levels of what you're doing in the right way and understand what the true goal is."

What do you think SEOs should stop doing to focus more time on proper business metrics?

"There are two things. One is that not all clients are great clients. By which I mean, not all agencies are a good fit for every single client. If you are an agency or an SEO provider, you need to know what to say 'No' to. Sometimes you might want to focus on organic revenue, and they might want to focus on specific KPIs that you don't feel are the right target. Most failures come from a misalignment of goals from the very start. You need to be clear in stating what you want to be judged upon. Be prepared to walk away. It's hard because agencies want to win new business and take on new work. Things go wrong when they end up adapting to the way the client wants to work, and not playing to their strengths.

The second part of that is, once you are clear on your goals, to put all your effort into focusing on them. That sounds obvious, but too often when SEOs are trying to increase organic revenue, they get distracted by doing X, Y, and Z to improve blog awareness traffic. First, hit the target. Make the client happy. If there are ways to extend the strategy to generate more awareness long-term, then you can look at it later. Start with what's most important.

It's about prioritisation. You can do SEO all day long for, pretty much, any website on the internet. You're not going to run out of things to do. You need to prioritise what's most important, and where your efforts will have the most value."

You can find Kevin Gibbons over at ReSignal.com.

Prioritise your SEO business funding efforts based upon their level of efforts, over level of impact - with Keith Goode from Cox Automotive

Keith concludes Chapter 3 by sharing a formula that he utilises to prioritise his SEO business-funding efforts.

Keith Goode says: "Prioritise your efforts, and request business funding based on the LOE/LOI Matrix - the Level of Effort versus the Level of Impact, or 'Return on Investment'. This is the way to gain, or retain, legitimacy in the minds of corporate leadership. SEOs need to prove their value."

How many SEOs are doing this at the moment?

"A lot of SEOs tend to be running around in circles based on whatever news is coming out of Google. When there's an algorithm update, or a core update, coming, the Twittersphere descends into chaos as SEOs start worrying and gnashing their teeth. Instead, they should be focused on the basics: doing the right thing and avoiding Black Hat techniques. 90% of the time, if you are running an ethical SEO practice, you don't have to worry about an algorithm update."

Is this only for SEOs working in big business?

"It is for everyone who is dependent upon other people to get something done with their website, or anyone who has to request funding. It's for agencies as well.

A friend of mine, who works for one of the largest military banks in the United States, has just received a 50-page audit from a highly respected SEO agency. It was just a list of things that they saw as problematic with the site. The audit didn't tell them where to start, what to focus on, or what would have significant impact for their efforts. These clarifications weren't forthcoming from the agency. It was a blanket, 50-page list of problems. You end up with a Paradox of Choice. Like going to a restaurant with too many items on the menu; it becomes impossible to choose or you default to the most basic choice that may be the least impactful.

When you do an audit for a site, break it down for them and let them know what you recommend. Show them which efforts will have the greatest impact in the short-term and what will take a bit longer and have a long-term benefit. You need to explain the options that are available. As SEOs, we need to be able to discern what is valuable and what isn't valuable.

Kristina Azarenko recently posted a quote from John Mueller that said, 'Any SEO tool will spit out 10s or 100s of 'recommendations', most of those are going to be irrelevant to your site's visibility in search. Finding the items that make sense to work on takes experience'. This is where SEOs step in. Your customers, or your company, can get any of the bigger tools that will spit out recommendations daily. However, without an SEO to make sense of it for them, it's going to go to waste."

How does an SEO really calculate the level of impact, and then articulate that for a client to understand?

"It is largely through experience. A tool might tell you what to change to have a big impact, but experience is going to be wiser. Essentially, you have to use the LOE/LOI Matrix, and sit down with your writers and developers. Ask the people who are actually going to be working on these items how long it will take and what the effort will be. Agile methodology can help for a 'T-Shirt Sizing' type of request, where you simply want to know how large the request will be.

Once you've communicated with the relevant people, you can ask yourself if something like changing page titles or rewriting the content to answer the user's intent is going have a greater impact on ranking. Likely the latter, but that's going to take a bit more effort. A lot of it is on experience, but it's also a matter of collaboration.

If you're new, and you don't have the experience, then experiment. Start on a smaller site, see what changes you can make now, and measure the impact. Gain the experience that you don't have. Also, reach out to your fellow SEOs - I have never been in an industry more giving, and willing to share information."

Is the Level of Effort as simple as calculating the number of hours required?

"In the corporate world, everything comes back to money. If it's developer hours, those are hours they have to pay the developer. Those hours are your costs. When they pay that cost, they are hoping to get a 10X Return on Investment for that. If I'm not returning 10X ROI every year when I'm earning, from a salary perspective, then I feel like I'm not really adding value to the company. If I'm looking to meet that 10X criteria, then any of the resources or requests that I make need to meet that 10X criteria as well."

Where are some specific areas that you can implement this within SEO procedures?

"It really starts at the planning stages for everything. I break SEO down into the URA SEO framework - Usability, Relevance, and Authority. I break all my needs down into one of those three categories. Usability covers crawlability, your Core Web Vitals, and everything related to coding on the page. Relevance is your content – how relevant you are to the query and to the user needs. Then Authority covers everything from external links to social to PR. It even includes internal linking, because the goal there is to build the collective equity of the site.

Look at the tasks you feel are important and put them in the appropriate category, then use that to talk to the appropriate team. You're not going to talk about content with your developers or talk to your content team about coding issues. Then you can get estimates from the right people on what it would take to fix a problem and you can estimate, based on experience, what the ROI is going to be. This means that, when you hand in your budget requests, you've got all the numbers that you need. You can show what is important, what is costing money, and what it would take to fix."

How do you articulate the value of SEO to other marketers that aren't technical?

"It depends on their area of expertise. We have marketers who focus on programmatic, and others on paid media, or on social. It's a matter of demonstrating what SEO offers to their discipline. I'll give you an example. We noticed that our paid campaigns had terrible Quality Scores when I first started. A bad Quality Score, from a paid perspective, means an increase in the amount that it costs to pay for each click. With an increase to the Quality Score, you can decrease the amount of money you're having to pay per click. As an SEO team, we could help them optimise the pages, to be better suited to the queries that they were going after. We could get rid of the queries that had nothing to do with the content and we could save tonnes of money.

It's a matter of collaboration. You can show other marketers that if you make pages better from an organic perspective, you save money on those pages from a paid perspective. It's about working together and letting them know how you can benefit them."

What is one thing that you think SEOs should stop focussing on to spend more time considering the impact of their efforts?

"Stop chasing your tail. I'm specifically referring to being on constant algorithm watch: obsessing over Search Engine Roundtable and letting every hint of a potential shift in the algorithms throw you into a panic. Instead, focus on doing the right thing.

If you're going to pay attention to what's happening in the industry, be pragmatic. When there's an algorithm shift coming, you can put an annotation in Analytics, in case anything does happen to the rankings, or the traffic. If it does, you can then investigate which particular change is negatively affecting you, and where you might look to fix it. Use those updates as an annotation opportunity. Otherwise, focus on what really matters: the user."

You can find Keith Goode on at KeithGoode.com.

SECTION 2: PLAN

4 SITE STRUCTURE

Have an SEO-friendly taxonomy to maximise traffic to your product listing pages - with Luke Carthy from lukecarthy.com

Luke shares that many sites are missing out on the opportunity to drive significant volumes of traffic to their product listing pages.

Luke Carthy says: "I spend the vast majority of my time in eCommerce, and I find that taxonomy, or product categories, are often left to their own devices and don't really have an SEO centricity to them. There's a real benefit to spending the time building a taxonomy in a SEO-friendly structure. Not only because it's going to draw more traffic, but it's going to help customers find the products they're looking for - whether it's parent categories, subcategories, or something in the middle.

Make sure you're building a category structure that's based upon demand - what people are searching for and the questions they are focusing on. Let's use the healthcare space as an example. If you are building structure for shampoos and conditioners, normally you might have focused more attention on allowing people to shop by brand. However, what's equally important is making sure people can shop by condition, which is something that has real intent. Users will be searching for 'dandruff' or 'sensitive scalps'. Allowing customers to shop in a way they would be searching helps set the scene, and it makes it easier for them. Additionally, it gives you that competitive advantage in the SERPs when it comes to people spending their money."

When you're saying structure your taxonomy based upon demand, does that mean you can automatically generate product pages that are easier to discover based upon search volume that tends to go up because of factors like seasonality?

"Exactly. There's no reason why you can't do that, and seasonality is a great factor to focus on. Q4 will always be a peak for many retailers, so there might be particular gifts where it's worth investing into taxonomy to bring more traffic to those products in those categories.

Another good example is Valentine's Day. The usual way of structuring content is by Him or Her, or Husband or Wife - and there's nothing wrong with this. However, there might be additional opportunities due to new trends this year where the market is shifting because people are searching differently. It could be organised by gift type rather than For Him or For Her. It allows customers to shop and explore in different ways and could help you attract an audience that you may not have been able to get away with.

In the world of paid search, these are well accommodated for because we chase the commercial keywords and build specific landing pages for them. In SEO it happens as well, but what I typically see with clients is a taxonomy - as far as product catalogues are concerned - that's fairly set in stone. It was often created when the eCommerce site was built five years ago, and it sticks.

There's a real benefit for your customers, and your traffic, to building a taxonomy that allows people to shop in the same way they search. This gives you greater penetration and visibility of products, and equally can improve the rankings of those products as well if you're getting traffic to the right places on-site."

Many fashion websites start off with an option to shop for Him or Her, but when you're trying to rank for brand names, you don't necessarily want those landing pages to be associated with male or female shoppers. How do you best structure optimising landing

pages for these fashion brand names?

"Structuring for Him and for Her, or for Boys and Girls, is a good way to approach fashion and apparel in most cases. However, I understand the need to optimise outside of gender bias. In cases like this, you can build experiences, and it could be a different taxonomy branch altogether, which allows people to shop by brand, by design, or by season - and these can all exist in silos.

Allowing customers to shop in an alternative way is also more modern, as gender is now more fluid. The increasing number of non-binary people won't necessarily shop by gender - it's more about the clothes they like. There's definitely an appetite, and a real appreciation for your customer, to give them an alternative way to browse and buy than the stereotypical Men's, Women's and Children approach."

Obviously, you're optimising for users but also for search engines. Do XML sitemaps still play an important role in helping guide search engine bots to decide which page fits where?

"Yes, they're very important. When it comes to discoverability, they become more significant as your taxonomy structure, or eCommerce site, becomes bigger and more cluttered. If Domain Authority is thin, the efficiencies of crawling are going to be challenging. Remember, sitemaps have to be maintained - ideally, automated and generated in a way that is really beneficial. For example, if you create a new product, release a new range or promotion category, then ideally your sitemap gets updated every day or week. This allows search engines to get onto those new products and categories sooner rather than later. It's equally to remove products that get sunset."

Is it worthwhile using your own first party data to define the queries that are more likely to convert, and then prioritise those URLs over others that are less likely to convert straightaway?

"Site search is a huge opportunity to find queries that people are looking for. The downside is you really need to have a lot of numbers, traffic, and other search activity for site search to be properly useful. However, it's very powerful in allowing you to understand gaps in your taxonomy. If people can't find a category they're looking for, they might just go ahead and search for it, in which case, there's an opportunity there. Look in Search Console as well and see what queries you've got impressions for, but maybe not so many clicks. Leveraging the first party data you have is very beneficial.

Additionally, there's nothing wrong with having a look at your competitors' search for queries and ways you'd like to shop and see who's ranking there and whether it's a product or category page. Have a look at their taxonomy structure - it might reveal an opportunity you may have missed."

If an SEO is starting on an eCommerce Store, where are the quickest wins to focus on?

"The biggest way to get started is using the Keyword Magic Tool, which is available in Semrush. This allows you to start with a very broad keyword, such as 'shoes', and then get more specific as you get into the data. It allows you to understand all of the variations, questions, and additional keywords that contain the word 'shoes'. Normally, you'd find things like 'shoe size 12', 'brown shoes' or 'trainers'. Now, you can start to build a case for not just keywords, but also the popularity and seasonality of these keywords and what pillars of these keywords you can use to build your taxonomy.

'Shoes' would naturally be your departmental category, but how do you get to your second-tier and subcategories? Do you do it by gender, design, or colour? This tool allows you to answer those questions and start to define and build how your category structure should look from the top down. I would highly recommend that everyone does this exercise - whether you're starting out or reinvigorating your taxonomy."

How often should SEOs look to reinvigorate their taxonomy, or is it an ongoing job?

"You might just be inquisitive, have a look, and do a bit of research, and before you know it, you're proposing a whole new taxonomy structure a few weeks later. This comes with its own issues of redirects, mega menus, and all sorts of other stuff in there.

If you're looking at rebuilding your taxonomy completely, it's a big job. I'd suggest doing this annually. It really depends on the vertical you're in. Fast-moving consumer goods, cutting-edge fashion, and children's toys are completely different ball games to groceries - which is typically quite stable in terms of velocity of product categories.

I'd also recommend a quarterly soft review. That's just looking for any opportunities to extend and revise your taxonomy."

What arguments can an SEO use to encourage other people in the business to agree to their recommended taxonomy changes?

"There's a few of ways I like to build my case and get buy-in. Firstly, you need to prove or disprove the performance of category landing pages to products. That could be using the click-through rate from landing on a category page, or engaging with the capture page, and seeing how many visitors engage with the product, go somewhere else, or leave. This really helps to give you some data on the context.

Additionally, I'd always recommend looking at categories collectively across the entire site. Globally, identify how well your categories are performing organically versus something like paid. If you've got a strong gap between all of the traffic sources and organic, that would indicate there's an opportunity to improve the rankings, relevancy, and traffic through those categories.

Another approach is to see how users are browsing the site. Are they typically in tune with categories, using the mega menu a lot, or just getting frustrated and using alternative ways to find products? Taxonomy can be twofold. It can be a UX issue, which is separate to an SEO issue, although they're normally quite closely intertwined. If you have an under-optimised taxonomy structure, you can be pretty sure it's going to be quite challenging for customers to find what they want."

What's one thing that SEOs need to stop doing to focus more effort on taxonomy?

"I've always been a massive advocate of site search. However, with directories and some eCommerce sites, there has been a lot of focus on optimising site search for specific queries. That means allowing your site search to almost become a dynamic extension of your taxonomy. Nowadays, in almost all cases, this causes you dramatic problems. It causes canonicalization, makes the site huge and bloated, and is difficult for search engines to crawl. This absolutely needs to stop."

You can find Luke Carthy over at lukecarthy.com.

Mark up your website with every bit of Schema that you can - with Jonny Ross

Jonny feels that Schema is still very much overlooked, and that marking your site up with as much Schema as possible will greatly assist Google in understanding the context of your content.

Jonny Ross says: "It's clear from Google that marking up content is what they want. If you have a website with content on it, you need to mark it up so that Google understands it. You need to give Google the content on a plate - what it's for and what it's related to - so that Google can use it in its search."

Is schema essential for every type of website?

"There's not a single website that shouldn't have some schema on it. Even if you are a local business, you could mark up your contact page with your address, phone number, Facebook account, etc. This is true all the way up to if you're an airline. There is airline schema, sports organisation schema and government organisation schema. If you look at local businesses, there is schema for animal shelters, childcare, and dentistry - to give you just a flavour. There is going to be a specific schema for you. If you are a dentist, you'd be silly not to use dentistry schema, to make it clear to Google that you're an official dentist."

Is it important to mark up other content as well, or mainly what you are as a business?

"It's far from just marking up your organisation or address. There are so many different types of schema that may be relevant to your site - from recipe schema to job schema, from schema for videos you are showing to schema for events you are running. There's not much content that you can't mark up. It's also about relating the schema. If you've got a service page, and the schema says what that service is, you can then relate it to the Meet the Team page, where you can say who delivers that service. Then, you can relate it to some of the other services that they deliver. You can also look deeper into the service and look at some of the keywords related to it. There will be other schemas that are deeper that you can relate to that as well. This way, you're painting a strong picture to Google that you're really relevant for that particular service."

How can you measure the success of implementing schema on your website?

"It's really simple. There is a misconception that the only ways that you can measure success are through ranks and traffic. Actually, inside Search Console, you can measure things like rich snippets and structured data, and how many times these have been shown in search. These are some really easy ways to track the impact, and can lead to number of impressions, number of clicks, etc. It can be easy to implement, depending on the site content.

Is there a plugin that will do this automatically for, say, a Wordpress website?

"I was recently looking at Rank Math, which is a competitor for Yoast, and there are some big benefits to it, but I don't think there's a plugin that has the capability to implement the type of schema we're talking about, yet. You're either using custom fields, or you're hard coding to relate all these things together. The issue is that there's so many different types of entities, and types of content, that a plugin would struggle to be able to offer it all."

If schema is hard coded on to a web page, is it something that may have to be removed at some point?

"Potentially. For a very small website, where you're looking at just an address on a contact page, then it's a lot quicker and easier to just hard code the schema than anything else. For a large website that has a significant number of pages and categories, then you would look for a better solution.

Hard coding shows that schema can be implemented quickly and easily. In a small business, it doesn't need to be kept on top of, because you're not changing information like the address, or the Twitter account often. It's information that stays in the footer of your website or sits on your Contact Us page."

In layman's terms, how does Schema work?

"As an example of how schema works: if you Google 'chicken pasta' you will be presented with a number of different recipes. Each one has a picture, the cook time, the ingredients, etc. - and it will show you the reviews as well. Those bits of data are being shown to you because they're marked up on the website using schema. Therefore, Google categorically knows what the official cook time, or number of calories, is and can show it on the search page. Without the schema, you would need a human to actually read the page and categorise those bits of information. Review schema is a good example of something that needs to be marked up, to say to Google what your official reviews are, what your average rating is, etc."

Would the About Us page, and perhaps the footer section of the website, be the best place to get started with this?

"The quickest win is being able to say to Google: this is the official name, the address, and the phone number, and these are social media links. Those things commonly would be on the Contact Us page or in the footer of the site. You also have the ability to mark up the logo to say this is the official organization's logo. Those would be the first things to implement. Then it would depend on the category of the website. If you are a recruitment website, you absolutely need job schema; if you're a recipe website, you absolutely need recipe schema. If you're B2B or providing services, then you need to start thinking about how you can mark up the services. You need to make sure that you are connecting the dots for Google and showing the relevance of your services.

It's all about giving the search engine greater confidence in what your content is about. Schema is one of the few things that all search engines have agreed on using. Whether it's Bing, Google, or Yahoo - it doesn't matter. The format is the same for each search engine so, as long as you focus on schema, you're ticking the boxes for all search."

How does an SEO articulate the commercial value of marking up schema to management?

"If they buy into SEO in the first place, and into how traffic is brought to a website, then breaking down how schema works will make the value fairly obvious. You can also give examples. You might look at featured snippets and look at voice searches based on the top featured snippet, which is based on schema. It's easy to demonstrate schema being used in a lot of different places. You can show what a great listing looks like on a mobile device, for example, with good schema that has additional rich elements. Then compare that to a listing without good schema, that won't show information like reviews and contact details.

Typically, the data will show change within two or three weeks of implementation. The changes will speak for themselves in terms of results in Search Console."

What is the difference, in terms of click-through, for a result that has rich elements on it compared to a standard search listing?

"In the data there is a clear difference, in terms of click-through rates, when you have got rich data around a listing. I have a particular client that dominates in Google for having reviews on their listings. For any search that's related to them, they appear, and 9 times out of 10, they're the only result on the page that has a review listed. That drives a lot of traffic. I haven't got the numbers to share with you, but it's common sense that the eye is drawn to it, and it has a trust factor.

It has a similar impact to Google Authorship, where you were able to put a picture of the author next to the listing, but it's supported by multiple search engines so it's not going away.

The brilliant thing about schema is that it's content that's visible on the page, unlike meta titles and meta descriptions. You're marking up content, we're not talking about something that's hidden."

What's one thing that SEOs should stop doing, to focus more time on schema?

"Google came out this week talking about meta titles, and how they are going to have far less weighting on the headlines that will be used within search. What they are going to be far more interested in is H1s, H2s and H3s on the page. They want to provide content that's more likely to fit the page than what you're trying to tell Google the page is about. This backs up the value of schema because, firstly, Google likes markup and, secondly, it's visible content on the page. The thing to stop focusing on is invisible content like title tags and meta titles."

You can find Jonny Ross over at Fleek.marketing.

Use structured data strategically to build SEO resilience in a rapidly changing SERP - with Crystal Carter from Optix Solutions

Crystal shares a common belief in the importance of structured data and its ability to rapidly, positively impact your site's organic impressions.

Crystal Carter says: "If you are not getting involved with structured data in a big way, then you absolutely should be. If you have invested in structured data, you should be looking at new opportunities to enhance the pages you've already got working for structured data. There are so many different opportunities emerging all the time. They're constantly adding new different schema types and continuously using new iterations in the SERP. This is something that everyone should be keeping on top of, and we're seeing really good SEO results in a fairly swift turnaround - most of the time.

We tend to see that you'll certainly get an increase in impressions as soon as you implement structured data – although it's obviously not a ranking factor. However, it does give you access to certain parts of the SERP that you are not able to access in other ways. It's useful for all verticals, and it's useful for businesses of all sizes. Just adding some structured data to your pages means that people know who you are, and Google can find you and connect all of your different platforms."

How do you prioritise what needs to be done to use structured data strategically?

"From a strategic point of view, I always go for what makes you money. When you think about what to do with SEO, you need to sort out the money pages first. You can't pay the bills with clicks. Clicks are lovely, but if the clicks you're getting aren't actually making money, then you need to think again. If you have an eCommerce website, you need to make sure you've got all the appropriate structured data for the products you're selling - your product pages need to be rock star product pages.

There are some great opportunities for structured data with product structured data, and with the APIs for Google Shopping and Google Merchant that all work together. They're not necessarily dependent upon each other, but they all support each other.

Secondly, make sure it fits with your different strategies. If you need to increase your visibility, consider things that help people know who you are - such as information about your organisation schema and your team pages. If you've got people who are doing talks and going to events, those people should have 'paid people' pages with structured data supporting them. Look at what works with your business, and if you really can't decide where to start, look at your competitors and try to fill the gaps."

What are the main changes in the standard SERP at the moment that SEOs need to be targeting with structured data?

"People talk about plain blue links and being number one or page one of Google, but Google is constantly adding stuff ahead of the plain blue links. A lot of the different elements they are adding are structured-data-enabled. For instance, Google Shopping shows up ahead of the plain blue link. If you're looking for shoes, generally, the structured-data-enabled stuff will show up ahead.

Google's being led by a mobile-first space, and structured data and mobile-first work really well because structured data essentially gives Google the ingredients. If we think about the content on your website like a pizza - previously, you were trying to give them a pizza. Structured data gives Google the ingredients for the pizza. If they start off with a pepperoni pizza, then you give them the ingredients, they can make it a pepperoni pizza, a cheese pizza, or a cheeseless pizza. They can chop and change how they want and make sure the SERP is more consistent for mobile. All of those different things, like recipe cards and shopping cards, are all set up so that they're easy to click with a finger.

Also, they're easy to sort for users because Google is trying to organise the information on your website. They're trying to make the experience very consistent, and structured data allows them to do this because it essentially sorts your website into a spreadsheet.

Structured data gives you more opportunities to chop and change the search in different ways with things like carousels, videos, and articles. Google has said that just because structured data isn't there now, it doesn't mean that it won't be there going forward. A good example is recipes. They used to be a really big space for featured snippets and that sort of stuff, but now it's entirely structured data. That's what they do - they can evolve it via structured data. First, you get the image cards, then you get the video within the structured data, like pre-rolling within the SERP. It just gives Google more tools to do more interesting stuff for users - which is what they want to do."

Is Google Image Search another opportunity for structured data that some SEOs may not have thought of? When I search for 'blue suede shoes' in Google image search, I've noticed that some of the top listings actually say, 'in stock'. Is this structured data being used to tell Google these items are available to click-through and buy?

"That will depend on their configuration. It may or may not be done directly with structured data, as it might be with a product feed. Generally speaking, they work really well together. Google Lens gives you a lot of different tools to talk about what your picture is. Structured data gives you another layer for adding some information about your images within your website, which allows Google to access the images for users in various different ways."

One of the things you say is that structured data builds SEO resilience. What is that, and why is that useful?

"SEO resilience is my way of saying that I don't like having to do things twice. I don't like having to go back again and optimise the same page in the same way for the same thing. If you're doing one-keyword optimisation or aiming for one part of the server at a time, then when things change - which they do all the time - you have to do it again. Structured data allows you to add another bit on to it fairly easily.

You can add structured data to a page that's not optimised for a particular search result yet, and it can just stay there in the background, just waiting for the chance. Then, when Google creates this new Rich Snippet, that page is already for that rich result. All your competitors suddenly don't understand what's happened. They were the top, and now there's this new feature, and you're already there. This is because your structured data was already there.

If you've got pages that are already performing, you can add this on to it, and it gives Google another thing to crawl. It also gives you time to wait and pounce on the latest element - because they're constantly adding things, such as the topic layer. At the moment, it seems to be one of Google's favourite ways of utilising the information on the web.

structured data implementation is great because it works with what's already on the page. It's straightforward in terms of client implementation, and getting permissions or signoffs, because you're reinforcing what's already on the website. You just say, 'We're adding this in the background, and it's exactly the same - we've changed no copy.' It allows you to move at a pace, take advantage of some great opportunities from Google, and get some great results for your clients. It's a no-brainer!"

If an SEO is working in-house and hasn't got any structured data on their site at the moment, what are the most efficient ways to install and manage structured data?

"If you want to see if you have any structured data, Google Search Console has a report that tells you what Google is reading. They don't cover everything, because there's lots of different types, but it will tell you what they're seeing. If you're using Semrush, they also have a structured data report. Screaming Frog also has a crawl you can do - it's a certain configuration - that allows you to see the structured data there. And if you're using WordPress, get Yoast. The free Yoast will give you the very basic structured data, such as organisation schema."

Would you advocate adding structured data manually, or are there good tools out there to do this?

"If you're on WordPress, you can add it with Yoast. There are lots of good ones you can add, and you can add structured data to every different page type.

If you're using Shopify, there's a couple of different plugins you can get that work really well. I haven't used it yet, but I've heard fantastic things about Schema App. The other thing you can do is talk to your lovely developers and tell them what schema you want. If you ply them with sweets and compliments, I'm sure that they'll help you!"

What's one thing an SEO needs to stop doing to focus more time on structured data?

"It's worth dialling down making a bespoke meta description for every single page. I'm not saying that meta descriptions aren't important - it's worth spending time on the meta description for your homepage, your money pages, and particular pages that perform really well. However, if you've got thousands of pages, and you're spending a lot of time and energy writing lots of bespoke pages, this isn't as relevant as it used to be. This activity can be far more automated these days. You don't have to sit there and handcraft like an artisan from the 1800s - life is too short!"

You can find Crystal Carter over at OptixSolutions.co.uk.

Use structured data to highlight the uniqueness and specificity of your content - with Martha van Berkel from Schema App

For Martha, Schema provides a wonderful opportunity to educate Google about the uniqueness and specificity of your content.

Martha van Berkel says: "It's time to get specific. You want to showcase your uniqueness and structured data allows you to articulate that. It's all about specificity."

Should every site be using structured data?

"Everyone needs to be doing it. Back in 2015, when I first started doing this, it was for innovators but it's still here and it's not going away. Google continues to lean into it. In the last year, 52% of the documentation updates were specific to structured data. Google has used structured data to communicate around COVID, for example. We're seeing the different types evolve, and seeing Google participate actively in the conversations around schema.org. Look at what you need to do with it on your site, even if its small. If you want to be understood, and you want the search engines to reward you with traffic, then you should be doing this."

How can you make your site look unique in the SERP?

"It's about who your business is, and what makes your business unique. Who are you? What do you sell? What services do you offer? Then you need to consider how those services or products are different from your competitors. It's not that the structured data needs to be unique, but that you are articulating the things about your business that are unique. You don't need to focus on what makes you different from others, but make sure you're really clear about what you are. You don't just sell blue T-shirts; you sell blue T-shirts made with linen that are manufactured in Canada and have Bugs Bunny on the front."

How would you advise businesses to write about themselves?

"The About Us page is an area where you can articulate deeper things. Where the homepage describes what type of company you are, the About

Us page is where you can decide what else you want to talk about concerning your business. What's most important is that you are not just doing generic markup across everything. You need to know what the page is actually talking about. I always talk about the five key pages in your site: Company, Products and Services, Locations, Key Content, and Q&A.

There should be a tight marriage between the content and the process of writing it. The people writing content are so important because they should not just be thinking about how to attract and engage with the user. They need to consider the title, descriptions, and the actual content, but also how to stand out and make a great first impression - to attract the user in search.

You need to make sure that you capture your uniqueness in the content on your pages and articulate the specificity of what you're offering. However, you also need to architect your content and your pages with markup data, to stand out in that first impression. Utilise the visual real estate in the SERP. Content writers and page architects need to think about that and come together to make a splash in search."

Do SEOs tend to incorporate markup data in their Company, Products, and Locations pages, but neglect their Key Content and their Q&A?

"It's wherever they're not thinking strategically about it or planning for it. Bring it back to the business goal of the website. Often, you need to convert new customers and get new eyes on the site. If you're writing content, and doing webinars and things like that, to drive demand, why aren't you making sure that those are standing out?

The company, the location, and the products are in the consideration phase. Think about what you are doing higher up in the funnel. You should be using structured data to attract people across that journey. You need to think further than the basic pieces. Consider what is strategic for the business and where you are trying to get new eyes and clicks. Those are the things you should be doing structured data on. It's just as important to have structured data on an evergreen blog post that brings in lots of traffic, as it is to have it on a product page, or page about the company."

Where are some of the key places, besides the rich snippets, that

Google uses structured data in their SERP?

"They are thinking about the whole experience, and there are many different areas that they're working on.

FAQ is an area that we've seen Google play a lot with across this year. It's great because it's literally answering the questions that people have, and that's often what's informing content when you're thinking about the buyer journey. I love that Google is providing FAQs on specific questions people are asking. This goes back to the idea of getting super specific. FAQs allow you to not just answer a specific question, with a title description or meta tags, but to also give context. You can identify, and measure, what the user's next question is and what they want to delve into. It's a tool that you can use across any type of content, and you can make sure it is about the super specific area that you're trying to show up for.

Google is also evolving the experience around eCommerce. It's not surprising because more and more people are buying online. In terms of specificity, Google's adding into schema.org things like size, weight, version, and colour."

Is there a way to markup your content to show that a specific piece of text is the answer to a specific question?

"Absolutely, that is where Question and Answer come in. Historically, Google had 'speakable' as a beta, and that hasn't really moved. In 2019, they brought out How To and FAQ, which we're seeing become more specific, and those are the types of rich results that Google is leaning into. They are using natural language processing to extract it. We're seeing that throughout this year, where they started highlighting certain passages of text.

Google is also leaning into NLP for video. John Mueller specifically highlighted this in his Google I/O update. They are looking for clips, as being like a segment of text in a video. They're now saying that you can either highlight interesting clips within your video, or you can tell them how your video URLs are structured. They will then do natural language processing to identify important clips. This is another interesting area where they're using structured data, to allow you to inform their natural language processing.

It's not the first time where structured data has been used to provide guidance or instruction. With logos or images, you can use the structured data to state whether they are licensable. That came out in beta around 2019. Last year it started to include full pieces, where structured data can provide licencing guidance. You can see how Google's connecting their different services together. They're using structured data to instruct their bots. It's about more than just getting a rich result. You can give a broader understanding, make sure that Google understands the specificity, and tie-in to other technologies that Google is offering."

Is it better to always have a video answer as well as a text answer to a question, and if someone finds your answer in a video on YouTube or in the SERP, instead of on your website, is that not as effective for your brand?

"YouTube SEOs would tell you that you can help that by having things in the description that link to your website. With regards to structured data and content, John Mueller talked this year about how you can link things together, but he said that you'll usually only get one rich result. Personally, I've seen evidence that says otherwise - I've seen people get mixes of different rich results. We love that at Schema App because it's something that we can test, measure and be agile with.

Video is the example that Google used in their documentation. If you have recipe markup, and you nest and connect a specific video as being for a specific recipe, they will give you the video rich result, or the recipe rich result, for a search around that recipe. To mix these together, you should have a written answer as well as a video answer. Think about the different ways of engaging your audience. Someone might be looking for a video when looking for a recipe or they might be wanting to read it. Set yourself up, and future-proof yourself, for those different experiences.

This is a landscape where Google's changing very often. We're seeing lots of algorithm changes and lots of testing. You can use structured data to prepare your content to show up for these different types of rich results. Try to combine both video and text where you can and mark it up so that you can be very specific as to what the page is about, and how those elements come together."

What are a few resources for finding what structured data to use and how to implement that structured data?

"There's a gallery in the structured data documentation from Google. The documentation is a bit scary, but the gallery is a way for you to visually start understanding how you want to show up. That's a great place to start. In terms of figuring out your strategy, we have a webinar at Shema App with a step-by-step process on 'How to Develop a Schema Markup Strategy for a Website'. That will help you build your plan. It gives detailed examples for eCommerce, plugins, and WordPress, to help you understand how to start out. At Schema App we're passionate about educating the market about what's possible.

If you're a local business, we have a huge 'How-to Guide for Local Business Schema' that walks you through what's important there, and how to do that. If you're looking for broader, more enterprise case studies, under 'resources' on SchemaApp.com, we have a tonne of case studies that get into more detail on how to be really specific and how to connect your markup etc.

For implementation there are lots of different options. I'm a big proponent of plugins. You just want to understand which plugins do what for you and look for a way to automate the process. Schema App has something for WordPress, Shopify, BigCommerce and Drupal. Yoast has options and there are other options as well. For doing it page-by-page, measuring, and copy-pasting the JSON-LD, look for some different generators. The Schema Markup Generator by Merkle is one that I recommend. They have a great way for you to fill in a form and put it in.

If you're looking at doing it at scale, with nested complexity, and making sure it's done in a robust and manageable way across any platform, checkout SchemaApp.com. That's what we do and what we're passionate about."

What something that an SEO should stop doing to spend more time focusing on schema?

"Stop creating generic pages, like category pages. Don't spend time replicating a certain page with the same content for lots of regions, or just changing a couple of keywords. You need to get more specific. You need to be creating the sort of curated content that's going to answer your users' questions. Look at the big picture. You don't need to be doing generic, basic curation at a category level. Instead, focus your time on using structured data to make that great first impression in search."

You can find Martha van Berkel over at a SchemaApp.com.

Make sure that all your important pages have a square photo near the top of the page - with Joy Hawkins from Sterling Sky

Joy shares a very specific tip about how to use images in your content, and where these images can be displayed in the mobile search results.

Joy Hawkins says: "I am obsessed with images, and a lot of people forget to optimise for what we call 'mobile images'. When you search on a mobile device, a lot of queries will return images right in the search results. We see this a lot with lawyers - if you search for a 'car accident lawyer' you'll get a photo right beside the website. Some sites have them, but some sites don't.

It's a really easy way to capture more real estate, on mobile specifically. All you have to do is make sure that your page has a square image, and that it is somewhere high up in the coding. You want it to be easy for Google to find, right at the top."

Do you need a different version of the image for desktop than you do for mobile?

"I would just use the same image. For a page that gets a lot of traffic, perhaps one that describes the service or product that you offer, then you will want to have an image anyway. You want to have images on your pages, but a lot of people use different dimensions. Google will still pull in an image but, if the dimensions are wrong, it's an image of a person with their head chopped off. A lot of SEOs aren't aware of this because they are looking at search on desktop, where it does not show these images."

How should text be formatted around the image?

"We usually wrap the image, with the text to the left or the right. It doesn't have to be large. We're not talking about a giant image that takes up tonnes of space.

When it comes to the type of image to include, it depends on the industry. For more professional services, like realtors and lawyers, it should be a photo of the individual - something that represents you well. For home services you would try to capitalise on a coupon or an award that you've won – something that highlights your value. That's a great thing to have featured beside your website in the search results.

It doesn't have to be a photograph; however, I don't know if I would use a logo. An award or a badge would go further."

What is the minimum pixel size for the image?

"I've seen a wide range; I don't know if I've found a minimum. Personally, I would never go smaller than 250x250 pixels. There is not one specific dimension that Google is looking for. They are mainly looking for a square. If you don't have a square, sometimes they'll grab one anyway and crop it for you, which is not ideal because you don't know what will be cut off."

Does it help if it's a unique photo, perhaps for your ranking?

"We recently performed a test, that will be coming out on our blog soon, that investigates this. We had a page using a stock photo and we saw the ranking decline. I don't think it was because it was a stock photo specifically, but it wasn't what Google was looking for. The photo didn't match the intent of the search. We then replaced the photo with an original image and ended up winning a featured snippet for that client, just after changing the photo.

Photos definitely have an impact on ranking. Mainly, however, you don't want to use a stock photo for conversion reasons. When we did a study on Google posts earlier this year, we found that original images are four times more likely to get clicks than stock photo images. Just for that reason, I would avoid stock photos."

Is there a particular file type that you should use?

"I don't think so. Our default is always PNG. We're normally dealing with WordPress sites and PNG is what WordPress tends to like. I'm sure JPEGs are fine as well, but we haven't looked deeply into that."

Will this help you to gain traffic through Google Image searches?

"I think it depends. A simple picture of a lawyer is probably not going to draw tonnes of traffic from Google Images. However, we made an infographic for a dentist client - about cracked teeth and the different types of procedures that you might need - and that image got a tonne of traffic from Google Image search. For a client in lawn care, we had an image of a lawn that had been torn up by skunks. Just showing that damage got a lot of Google Images traffic as well.

It depends on the image. You can easily identify the traffic in Search Console by using the Image filter, to specifically look at traffic from Google Images."

Is there an easy WordPress plugin for quickly adding square images to posts?

"If there is, I don't know about it. That would be a great tool for somebody to make if it doesn't exist.

Is this something that should be included in every new piece of content?

"If it's easy to do, definitely. Start by looking at the pages that are really driving leads, those are the ones you want to focus on first. If you're struggling to find where to include images across thousands of pages, look in Google Analytics and see which pages are actually sending leads.

Don't worry about every single blog. For the sites I've audited that have 1000s of blogs, 90% of them don't even get a single visit."

Should businesses encourage their customers to add photos to their local listings?

"Adding photos is always good but it varies based on the industry. If you have a listing for garage door repair, you don't need a hundred photos of a garage door. For a restaurant, however, you will be coming out with new dishes and you want to make sure that your new stuff is added. If you're in travel, having photos of your hotel, your pool and all of your different amenities is huge.

Of course, it doesn't blanket apply to every business type - an insurance agent doesn't need to worry if they don't have lots of photos."

What new aspects of Google My Business should an SEO be aware of?

"It's probably not a known fact that alt tags on images impact ranking in the local results, which is cool. You should be adding those for accessibility anyway but knowing that it is a ranking factor is kind of neat. It's not a new thing, it's been around for a long time, but I think it's often overlooked."

Should you have captions for square images on the page?

"I don't think captions really factor into Google's use of the image itself. In terms of ranking, any text you have on the page is good, and can have an impact."

Does the file name matter for images?

"We tested this. We wanted to know if file names mattered for Google My Business listings, and they don't. We published the study about a year or two ago, you can find it on our blog, and we found that it had no impact."

What's something that you suggest an SEO should spend less time doing, to focus on including square images at the top of their pages?

"Geotagging your photos. My advice is specific to people that work on local SEO, but geotagging photos has been a practice for over a decade and people still claim it works. We recently tested it and geotagging has no impact on organic, or Local Pack rankings. It's a big waste of time."

You can find them Joy Hawkins over at SterlingSky.ca.

How to deal with index bloat - with Marcus Tandler from Ryte

Marcus highlights the importance of managing the content that you want Google to discover – and getting rid of the content that doesn't cut the mustard.

Marcus Tandler says: "Dealing with index bloat is very actionable. A preventive Panda diet is a common recommendation for websites that have gained a lot of fat throughout the years and are now struggling to increase visibility in Google. A large number of irrelevant pages is the equivalent of empty yoghurt containers being kept and stored because you might still need them in the future. Don't get carried away with this kind of digital compulsive hoarding. Instead, keep your website fresh, tidy, and clean.

You should always ask yourself three simple questions for all your pages: Do I need this page for my users? Does this page also need to be indexed by Google? And if yes, what should this page ideally rank for? Of course, you don't need to delete all pages which are not relevant for ranking purposes, and still have a value for your users. Users can still navigate to these pages but be more rigorous about what should get indexed.

For example, you might have a faceted navigation for an online shop for shoes, and the targeted keyword is 'Adidas Superstar'. These trainers are available in ten different colours and ten different sizes, so an interested user can navigate to any variation of these 100 different pages to put them in their virtual shopping basket. However, you don't necessarily want to let those 100 product variations get indexed - only the ones which are explicitly being searched for.

You might end up with a catch-all 'Adidas Superstar' page with displayed trainers in the best-selling colour and size combination. If there's a sufficient amount of Google searches for a specific combination, such as 'black Adidas Superstars', it also makes sense to grant this option its very own indexable page. This way, you can ensure a good ratio of relevant to irrelevant pages, reduce the possibility of cannibalization, and therefore stay safe from Google's Panda.

If your website is already full of these empty yoghurt containers, it's advisable to preventively take out the trash. Ideally, using code 410 Gone instead of the more common 404s, since Google is revisiting 404 pages a couple more times. While with a 410 status code, Google will only revisit this page one more time to make sure the page is really gone. Of course, you will also need to remove any internal links and or references to these 410 pages.

If you have amassed loads of these empty yoghurt containers, which are now 410, and you want to get those out of the index as fast as possible, you can consider using a negative sitemap, which contains only pages that are 410. This way, you can remove large amounts of irrelevant pages out of Google's index very effectively."

How does an SEO find these empty yoghurt containers on their website and define what is useful for users, useful for Google, and a good page to rank for?

"Start by taking Google Search Console data and filter for all pages with clicks=0 within the 12 months timeframe. Then you take this list to Google Analytics and see if those pages are getting traffic besides from organic search. Ideally, as a third step, you should also compare this list with Googlebot behaviour using LockFile data to see if Google is still regularly crawling these pages. Since the scheduler which sends off Googlebot to fetch pages prioritises by importance, you can get a good sense of whether Google is finding any of these pages still important - and therefore relevant. If any of these pages receive no organic traffic, or any other natural or paid traffic, and if Google isn't even crawling these anymore, you can just get rid of them to thin out your website easily."

What is a good ratio of useful pages to these irrelevant pages?

"This always depends on your website. There isn't an ideal ratio you should aim for. If something's relevant - it's relevant. It's about sending out everything which is not relevant. Just let the data talk."

How do you define what a user is likely to like? Is it based upon user behaviour, or do you have to have a group of people analyse that page to ensure it's a relevant and appropriate part of the buying cycle?

"What you're referring to is the long click, and this is Google's main goal. They want somebody to click through to your page and stay on your site - not just be a one-hit-wonder on one page. They want you to surf through to your other pages on your site and not go back to the SERP.

A search completion tells Google that the page really fulfilled the intent. But you've got to start way earlier also with pages, which Google basically promotes in the top ten. To see if users find this page relevant, and before you can even evaluate the long click behaviour, you need to understand if they are clicking through to your site – this is the first sign of relevance. You might think you have the perfect page, and you're getting into the top ten, but if nobody's clicking through to your site, it is a clear indication there might be a different intent here. Your content may be great but it's just not great content for this intent.

You need to be thinking of how you can make the best possible page to fulfil this intent. The most important aspect of modern SEO is not just aspiring to rank in the top ten but being the best possible result for that specific query."

What is the most common cause of index bloat?

"The worst is always online shops. They have all these products going in and out of stock, multiple categories, and tag pages. Just using an out-of-the-box CMS might create index bloat problems by introducing categories, as well as tags. And this can happen even to a blog or any site."

You mentioned having a negative sitemap for 410s, but also removing all links to these pages. If you're struggling to remove so many different links from your website, is it enough to redirect the links to something else?

"If I have an out-of-stock product, the standard recommendation is to redirect users to the corresponding category, so they still have an inventory to choose from. I don't think this will help you in the long run because it's just not as relevant as other online shops with the product in stock. It really won't help you with ranking per se. Instead, I'd just get rid of it.

This is exactly the empty yoghurt container problem. You're keeping something because you might need it in the future. It's better to have a crisp, clean, and compact site. The negative sitemap is speeding everything up and giving Google an indication that this is everything you want out. If you keep these links, Google might be inclined to go to these pages, so I'd remove all references."

If you're training other marketing professionals on the value of dealing with index bloat, would you typically use your empty yoghurt containers analogy?

"I'm always explaining it this way. We tend to keep a lot of stuff on our websites because we think we might still need it. I think SEOs have created this problem. Fifteen years ago, if somebody came to us and said, my site is 1000 pages, what should I do? A lot of SEOs (me included) would have recommended making it 100,000 pages for every possible keyword combination. That's what you needed back then because Google wasn't that good.

Now Google is much smarter, you don't need this anymore. You are also bleeding your link juice because you've distributed to so many pages. These days, it's much more advisable to have a more compact structure. Also, Google had a different objective back then. If you remember, Google was always promoting how many billion pages it has indexed because it was in a rat race with Microsoft and Yahoo.

It's not about the quantity anymore. With social media, they simply can't keep up with the volume of URLs created every day. So now the focus is on quality - and this is why Panda came out."

Suppose an SEO is involved in the original design of a website. Is it better for blog posts and product pages just to have a single category and for any tags associated with each of those pages to be completely non-indexable by Google?

"I would always opt for one indexable structure with categories, but then I would opt out of tags or a structure by dates, such as months. If you also use these things to maximise the internal links to all of your pages, you basically end up linking all over the place, and you don't direct Google to what's really important for you.

As an SEO, I always want to be in control as much as possible. I don't want Google to have to do lots of heavy lifting. I want a structure that tells them what I'm good at and where I provide the most value to the users."

What's one thing an SEO needs to stop doing to spend more time focusing on index bloat?

"Focusing a lot of the time on link building – especially if you are already a big brand with lots of links, and Google already likes you. Any new links are unlikely to have maximum benefit if you have a sub-optimal structure. You don't build a house in the swamp - you need a solid foundation. So always fix the structure before spending a lot of money and time on acquiring new links. With a great structure, these links will have so much more power."

You can find Marcus Tandler over at Ryte.com.

5 KEYWORD RESEARCH

GOOD keyword research has never been more important - with Paige Hobart from ROAST

Paige highlights that even though keyword research isn't anything new, good keyword research is absolutely key to SEO success in 2022.

Paige Hobart says: "Don't lose focus on keyword research. It's going to be as important as it's ever been, and SEOs need to make sure they are not just automating it. I've got a four-step process to ensure that your keyword research is kick-ass."

What's the difference between 'kick-ass' keyword research and poor keyword research?

"At the moment there is too much dependence on tools to do a lot of the work for you. Not everyone is doing great keyword research, it is a skill that you need to train. There is a process you have to go through to make your research effective and relevant. At BrightonSEO, someone was telling me that their client wanted to rank for 'the Olympics'. The issue was that they were a rug company. They felt that, because everybody is searching for 'Olympics', they had to rank for that term. There are so many bad examples out there. I had a household plants brand with 'aloe vera gel' in their keyword list.

It's these sorts of things that tools don't always get right. It makes your performance look bad. If you're using anything like 'average rank', or even 'weighted average rank', it will have an impact. These illogical keywords will make you look bad. Everything we do as SEOs hangs on our keyword research, so it's important that we do it right."

What is your four-step process?

"First, extract your keywords from tools like Search Console. If you're doing paid, make sure that your seed list starts with the keywords that are currently of value to you. That's where you need to start pulling your data from. You can look at your navigation as well. Perhaps crawl the site, see what your anchor text is, or what your H1s are - they should be relevant to you.

Then gather your metrics. Get your search volume, click data, the rank for you and your competitors, and any kind of metric that you can apply to that keyword. Noting the source is particularly helpful. Whether you got the term from Search Console or Keyword Planner will be helpful when it comes to dealing with what's on that list.

Once you have those, start tagging - thematically grouping your keywords. A clever way of doing this is to look at which keywords share the same URLs on the SERP. You will probably end up with some quite uneven buckets of things, some sensible groups and some less so. Expand on the things that need expanding. Try to perfect it, even it all out, and make it make sense.

Lastly, all you need to do is optimise that list. Take out those 'vanity keywords' and set yourself up for success as an SEO. If you're not going to rank for it, it's only going to make your performance look worse in the long run."

When extracting keywords should you look at your own existing paid campaigns or third-party data?

"Use your own, because at that phase you just want to look at what's of value to you. Paid data can give you too much to work with. Cherry-pick the keywords that are good because they drive a lot of traffic. You want to look at conversion data, which you can't really get with Search Console.

From PPC data, like Google Ads data, you can pull your 'exact match' keywords, knowing that they actually convert really well."

Is keyword difficulty still a useful metric?

"There are lots of tools that will give you keyword difficulty and call it something slightly different. It is essentially just the competitiveness of that keyword. As a metric, it can be helpful to filter and sort by, as it gives you a layer of context. However, search volume, and potentially CPC, will give you that competitiveness information anyway.

What you're trying to look for is whether you can rank for that keyword - if you are the kind of business that can compete there. Sometimes you can't, but there will be 1000 other, more niche, terms that are more likely to convert."

How do you know whether you have a chance to rank for a particular keyword phrase?

"It's something that machines can't really do for you. It's about SEO experience. Of course, keyword research is not set in stone. If you are a newcomer to the market you will know if you have Expertise, Authority and Trust in a particular niche - that's what you go for. You can always add the broader terms in later down the line.

That is the human element of the research. Understanding the search landscape, the competitors, the nuances of language, your own business and your USPs is something that tools just can't do."

How do you select your different tags?

"Don't just look at what keywords you have already. Use your well-ranking pages as helpful context but try not to get bogged down in what already exists. You can get too blinkered that way. You want to, ideally at a page level, identify 5-10 keywords what will all rank on a theoretical URL and be grouped to one page. Check that on Google. If most of the URLs on those keywords are the same type of page as yours, then you can probably rank with one piece of content.

Sometimes you will need to separate things out. I was looking at a particular

FAQ yesterday, and seeing if we could put it onto a big page that we are going to create. When we looked at the SERP, it already has a Featured Snippet, and it's doing really well, so we want to preserve that. You need to see what will work for your keywords."

How do you persuade senior executives that are too focussed on vanity keywords?

"Tell them to Google the term. They need to see if they are producing the kind of content that exists on that page. I've got a B2B client that wanted to appear for 'augmented reality', and when you look at that broad term, there's not a single B2B business on the page. Looking at the SERP will show you if the intent behind that keyword isn't relevant to you. However, when you look at a longer-tail keyword phrase, you can see that you could exist on that SERP because it's where your competitors are. Show senior executives the places where the intent matches and where you're actually going to get traffic.

You can also ask your PPC friends to bid on one of those vanity keywords for a bit and prove to them that it's a complete waste of time."

How do you factor in intent when deciding where to use your keyword phrases?

"Keep things simple. Look at the informational versus transactional intent behind keywords. A lot of the time it is common sense – ask 'Who, What, and Why?' for an informational query versus a transactional query. Often you want to have both things, and don't want to just be going after one kind of intent. Usually, your pages will want a bit of informational content about what you're trying to sell, but also hard-hitting transactional content as well.

You also need to know if the intent is the same as what you assume it to be. Check that the SERP is representative of what you think the keyword means. A good example is 'baby doll' vs 'babydoll'. Keyword Planner used to group the search volume together for both of these terms, however one is a child's doll, and one is lingerie. The SERPs are very different. Check that the term is right for you."

How often should you do keyword research?

"It depends. Sometimes you will want to do keyword research every month, with deep dives into different divisions to find new opportunities. Then you can also do performance optimization for work that you've already done. Other times you can start your onboarding with really good keyword research, that forms your strategy because you find a lot of opportunities. Then, you might be working towards that goal throughout a year or six months, depending on how fast the business moves.

Things like seasonality will change the frequency of your research, and how quickly the offering of the business is changing. You will need to consider the rate at which the business is growing and how often they are launching new products."

Where should you put your keywords?

"It's not too complicated. We're still talking about incorporating them into H1s, sub-headings, text on the page, page titles, and internal links. Write naturally is number one. If you're secure on your keyword mapping and tagging, then you know exactly what you're trying to target for each individual page that you create. Make sure to avoid duplicate content - that can be a problem. H1s are great, and I love Question and Answer H2s. Use schema to wrap that up as well, especially if you've got things like FAQ elements on a page.

You need to try to be as relevant as possible to users as well as bots. IBM has a Natural Language Understanding tool which is very useful. You can put your copy, or your link, into it and it will tell you what it thinks your keywords are. Take it with a pinch of salt, as with every tool, but it is helpful. It's a good way of checking your homework if you are doing content writing and optimization."

What's one thing that SEOs should stop doing to focus on good quality keyword research?

"Relying on tools is to our detriment. They are so powerful, and they are helpful, but you've always got to be cherry picking. Keyword research that only consists of Semrush exports doesn't have that human element. If you've done concatenation to find a useful group of words - and you've included locations, or colours for things that you sell - a tool will produce variations on those. It will give you locations where you don't exist, and colours that you don't sell. The tool will think that those terms are relevant.

Search engines are focusing more on user experience as well. If you rank for content that's irrelevant to what you offer, you're offering a poor user experience and that signal will get back to the search engines. Focus on pulling it together manually, then the optimization phase should take a lot less time."

You can find Paige Hobart over at WeAreRoast.com.

Combine keyword research and keyword clusters with your internal linking strategy to increase your page relevancy - with Orit Mutznik, Director of SEO at DataCamp

Orit shares that selecting the right keywords and having great internal linking is a winning combination.

Orit Mutznik says: "Internal linking is the number one strategy, and you just have to be smarter about it in 2022. Keyword clusters is bringing a full set of context onto one page. This is a group of very similar keywords that you can all target in one page. There are tools that can do this, such as Keyword Insights. You plug in a list of keywords and their search volumes, that you can pull up from Semrush or other keyword tools, and the output shows you which cluster would be the most efficient one to use on a specific page. If you create a page using all these cluster keywords together, it's highly likely you will get a boost on your page.

However, it's quite complicated to do because you don't want to get too repetitive and have too much context on the page. This is where internal linking comes in to help you solve this problem. You need to do your keyword research and look at your search volumes relating to the pages you want to create. Then, you take the top searches that are relevant and turn those into your internal links. You create the content based on keyword clusters (the ones you are able to use) but still make the page really accessible, natural-looking, and readable. Everything else you want to add on top of that will be a combination of the remainder of your keyword cluster, and the top searched, most relevant, keywords in that cluster. You will then have the copy written and those internal links.

For an eCommerce site, it's a good idea to have a sort of filter. For example, if you have a page on dresses, you would use context and clusters to create the text in the category page. It's an art because it's something that should be quite short. You don't want to push the products down too much - so you have to prioritise the keywords you use. Additionally, the internal linking complements and creates the filters you want to use. Whatever you couldn't include in the text of the category page, you could include as links to discover more. These links are strategically built based on your keyword research and the clusters you could include. You can do this with every page you link to and have a solid strategy that's very relevant from a clustering and search volume perspective."

I like how you describe it as an art because great SEO is a mixture between art and a science, and the recipe is getting the mixture just right.

"Exactly. Watching Google evolve how it ranks content and evaluates quality over the last decade has been fascinating. It used to be much easier! This is why it has to evolve to the level of art, because we still have the same principles - we want to nail the context and rank. However, now we can't ignore the concept of people as users.

For example, I was frequently pitched by agencies who would tell me to have significantly more content on my category pages to help me rank higher. But I actually disagree with them because the purpose of the content in a category page has to be closely tied to intent - it's a transactional page. The goal of the user is to buy something, so they need context as maybe they found my brand on Google and don't know it. There are a lot of connections and considerations here. Content is also branding, and tone of voice, and other things that maybe are not as often regarded by SEOs.

These are all additional aspects added into tailoring the content. As well as thinking about the most relevant pages for internal links and keywords clusters, consider the user and their intent. They need the right context to tell them they've arrived in the right place and to understand that your brand is trusted. If not, you need very tightly connected contextual links that will get your user to where they want to be. You are effectively tailoring a one-stop-shop."

You said your category pages are transactional - do you not want your transactional pages to be ranked?

"No - I'm just saying the copy doesn't have to be incredibly long. They're already transactional in intent, so just make sure you complete that intent with your copy and include the keyword clusters and internal links that are hyper-relevant to what you're trying to convey."

Is there a maximum number of keywords that should be in a keyword cluster?

"It's very much contextual —I wouldn't put a number on it, especially because it's very dependent on the type of space you have. In a transactional page, you don't have a lot of space, so you don't want to have the products and information down the fold. However, if you have long-form content, you can definitely go wild and use as many keywords clusters as you can. When you have short, limited space, you need to carefully prioritise your clusters and use the ones with the most impact and least effort."

Suppose you've got 10 keyword phrases you want to rank for within your keyword cluster but it's impossible to get them in the conventional areas for SEO. Is it important to have separate pages targeting those keyword phrases? Or is it better to just incorporate them within minor headings and the content further down the page?

"I would refer to this as a developing process. To begin with, I'd attempt to include as many clusters as possible knowing that I haven't included 100% of the clusters. Then, the internal links allow me to have more context without disrupting the flow of the context. You could display them as filters to the page, or as breadcrumbs, for example. This is a way to insert more context into the page and to continue boosting the page. I would also find places to include more parts of the clusters in places like H1s and navigation.

The next stage is to evaluate performance. If the rest of the cluster is important enough, then you could divide that cluster into two and create a different page that you can link from the first page, so the context will remain strong.

Intent is also super important. Both Keyword Insights and Semrush now provide you with the intent – so you have tools to give you all the pieces of the puzzle. This means you can think about taking a different approach to the next page of the cluster. There is a high chance these optimisations will hit the mark because Google is very clever in understanding that even if you only have 10% of the cluster, they'll rank you for the other 90% - especially if the page is technically good."

What does the optimum internal link strategy look like in 2022? You mentioned breadcrumbs as a good way to add internal links and increase page relevancy. What about other internal linking opportunities?

"The ideal would be automation. I'm going to find a way to look at the information architecture of the website and see how I can manage to connect everything together. So internal linking in 2022, for me, is about defining your information architecture in a way that Google would understand. The main weapon of information architecture is internal linking.

It's important to look at the structure of your website. Tools such as Screaming Frog allow you to look at a visual of your hierarchy, so you can see what needs to be improved. Discover which pages don't get enough links inside them, and then do your keyword research to enable you to link to them in a contextually relevant way. Along with the clusters, this approach will help a lot with building your architecture.

Another element of internal linking could be to include lots of automated modules on 'people also like' or 'if you took this course, you might love all of these other courses'. You can slowly cover your entire website in internal linking. Of course, you'll need to have some rules in place, so you don't repeat yourself in every single page to have the same internal linking. There is a way to automate this if the data in the backend has the proper categories and relationships you plan on doing. You can suggest to your readers more relevant content in every place they see.

I'm a big believer in breadcrumbs because I've seen them used as a great way to interconnect your entire website as a whole. Breadcrumbs basically seal the deal and ensure you will never get lost on the website again."

What should an SEO stop doing to spend more time focusing on keyword clusters and internal linking strategy?

"Link building. I'm not saying it's not important - but always prioritise internal linking. No matter how many links you get driving all that link juice, Google will still not fully get your website if it's not interconnected properly. It's not going to discover pages that you don't link to. And no matter how many links you drive into the site, that's not going to help, so focus on having a properly set up architecture with the help of internal linking. Link building can come later to seal the deal."

You can find Orit Mutznik over at DataCamp.com.

Map keywords to personas and user journeys - with Michael King from iPullRank

Mike advises that mapping keywords to personas and user journeys is a way to hyper-personalise your content and maintain the 'stickiness' of your users.

Michael King says: "SEO has not changed dramatically in the last seven years, but Google has changed. They're going down a more hyper-personalised route. The way to account for that in SEO is by mapping keywords to personas, and then mapping those to user journeys. Then, you can create hyper-personalised content at the various stages the user will go through on their process."

How many personas should a typical business have?

"It depends on what the data says and how many business units they have.

Ultimately, it's about what they're trying to target. A given business unit might have 3-4, depending on the data.

If you want to target, say, different populations based on ethnicity then you're going to need a variety of personas. However, if you're trying to target personas based on specific needs you may not need as many. It's dependent on your business goals and your data."

If keywords are quite similar across different personas, would you aim to make one page suit multiple personas?

"It depends on the query. Different user types may have different needs from the same keyword. We're seeing more of that as people's searches evolve. You can get this data directly from Google itself by looking at 'People Also Ask'. Start with a given query, click on the next one in PAA, and you'll see how that journey evolves. You could find specific user needs for specific user types. To that end, you may have to create multiple pages for the same query.

Google is getting very close to being able to identify that if you love video games, but you only love Nintendo, then you don't love PlayStation. Then, it won't show you results for PlayStation when you Google 'video game'. In the future you're going to have hyper-personalised results based on user context and what has been showcased to Google over time.

Google have something they call affinity segments. You can see them in GA and target against them in paid ads. They also have in-market segments, where it predicts potential purchases based on activity across Google. We're thinking about the future of SEO here. The way to account for it is to already be thinking about content in this matrix way, not just aiming for a given keyword like we always do. Google is becoming smarter than just giving iPhone information when someone searches for 'iPhone'. If someone's searching for 'cell phone', and it predicts that they can't afford an iPhone based on their search history, then the results will all be related to Android. They are developing the ability to account for your attitudes, interests, and opinions.

With this happening, you're going to have to create multiple pages targeting the same query, so that you can capture different parts of your target market. Right now, people have one page that's trying to speak to multiple parts of the market. This doesn't work as well because you don't know if they will land on the right section. If the user reads the first blurb and there's no quick link to what they're looking for, then they leave the page.

Google's going to get more specific and you're going to have to create content that speaks to specific personas. It's the same as making landing pages for paid media that speaks to a very specific type of messaging that you want to align with."

Is it possible to target multiple personas on the core purchase funnel, where the buyer journey is more standard?

"Absolutely, but there may still be opportunities to add nuance and have the message match up with the specific person. Let's say you're selling clothing and a user is looking for a maternity dress. Your site will have other types of dresses as well. If you have messaging that speaks to maternity, all throughout the funnel, then that user is going to feel that the business understands their needs. It creates more opportunities to delight them. If you continue to aim for the middle, the experience for that user isn't any different from buying on Amazon, so why wouldn't they go to Amazon?

There are a lot of nuances to think about, beyond just how the content aligns with the targeted keyword. You need to consider how to make sure that the user knows they're in the right place, with a business that is looking to specifically connect with them. It's almost a combination of SEO and CRO, or SEO and branding. It's about more than just getting someone to land on a page because they typed in a broad keyword."

Should you also develop more conventional on-site SEO throughout these pages, to build authority for the keyword phrases?

"Absolutely, those mechanics don't change. That's what I mean when I say that SEO hasn't changed meaningfully in seven years. The mechanics of how to build a page and target keywords is pretty dialled in. When building topic clusters, you now want to look at the keywords that group with your target keyword. Whatever your phrase is, there's going to be a series of topics around it that you want to have content about and have internal links to. It clarifies to Google that you know what you're talking about, because you have what they expect for the topic. You also need to account for co-occurrence and things like that.

It's going to become more complex. It may already be more complex than our tools are presenting it as. When you put a keyword into a tool, it looks at the top 20 results, and the co-occurring entities and phrases, and it tells you to use one phrase more or one phrase less. However, Google is probably already looking across different search phrases to determine that, rather than looking at it in such a linear way."

Should you design your content style based upon persona as well?

"A lot of people think about sticky notes when they think of personas. They see a persona as '18-24 years old, Gen Z', etc. What I'm talking about is a segment of your user base that you're trying to target, which needs to be represented by data. I think of Googlebot as a persona. None of these personas should overpower the others. You need to think about the considerations of any given audience, and those have to be requirements for how you build your content.

You still need copy on the page, for example, but you have to consider how the user will experience it. If short-form copy resonates with a target audience, you might use more expandable divs or accordions, so the page has a sparse experience. Then, users can find more information by opening those up.

There are a lot of ways to solve these problems. However, there are constraints that you need to be mindful of if you want to reach the ultimate goal. If you want search traffic, conversions, and multiple audiences to be targeted, then you need to think about those things while you're creating content."

How do you know whether to target longer-tail phrases that are more specific, and there may be less data for?

"Back in 2011, there was a tool called Trendistic. You could put in a query, and it would show you how that query was trending across Twitter. At the time, I compared the results there to Google Trends, and there was almost a 1-1 correlation between them. That doesn't mean that because something's trending on Twitter it's going to trend on search, but there's a high likelihood that it might. If you're seeing a breakout query, throw it into your social channels and see how much chatter there is around it. You can use that as a proxy for how much organic search traffic you might have.

Beyond that, test using paid media channels. Put the query into Google Ads and do a test on a landing page to see how much traffic it gets. In some cases, it's a leap of faith. Even if you're getting data from a keyword research tool, it's not always a true depiction of the exact number of people that are searching for a term anyway.

At some point, you have to trust your judgement that the data is telling you it's something your audience wants. If it makes sense, in the user journey, then make the content anyway. There's going to be value that you get out of it from an assisted conversion perspective, and a variety of other reasons. There's no reason not to create the targeted content, if you can vet it in other data that you have across your data sets."

What metrics do you look at to measure the success of these kinds of activities?

"You mainly look at conversion rates. It's also increased click-through rates from Google because we're thinking about this as early on as your page title and meta description. Even if you're not in the top three results, when you make adjustments to align with personas, you will see the CTR increase. The metadata is the advertising tagline for the page, so the better that your copy aligns with who you're trying to reach, the more likely they are to click on it. Ultimately, it's more likely that they will convert.

We've had clients see much better conversions from our SEO work than they have from other agencies in the past, and it's largely because of that approach. It's very much measured in how it impacts business objectives and often that's seen in your conversions."

What is something that you suggest SEOs should stop doing to focus more time on targeting personas?

"Stop focussing on content length. So many people are writing blog posts saying content has to be 1500 words long or it's not going to work. That's the wrong approach. Google is getting far better at aligning content with intent, and some intents require shorter content. The better that you align your content with what people actually want, the better it's going to perform. Rather than sitting around trying to squeeze out 1500, 2000 or 4000 Words on a subject, first think about what your audience actually wants. That way you can spend more time on what's going to be more effective."

You can find Michael King over at iPullRank.com.

Stop focusing on keyword research - with Eli Schwartz

Eli advises that you should stop spending quite so much time on keywords and start getting to know your actual users.

Eli Schwartz says: "It's time for everyone in the SEO world to stop focusing on keyword research, keywords in general, and keyword research tools, and start thinking about the users and what they are looking for when they come to a search engine."

Is it not necessary to include keywords in web pages anymore?

"Keywords are absolutely necessary. However, if you think about the feedback loop that comes from keyword research tools, it cuts out the primary focus of the user. If you go to any keyword research tool and plug in the word, 'insurance', they spit back all these ideas around insurance. And it tells you to focus on them, leaving out the fact that insurance on the internet has been around for two decades, so you're unlikely to ever rank on those things.

It's not that keywords aren't necessary. The feedback you should be getting on which keywords to focus on should not be coming from keyword research - it should be coming from topical research from actual users, the founders of the company, or product managers. This will help you understand why they want this website to exist or why they believe search users should be finding this website. You need to discover what the user is going to be searching for because they have a problem that you're going to solve. This is better than the keyword research tool telling you what users search for."

Is there a danger in relying on product managers because their perception of the product is not necessarily aligned with target consumers' needs?

"That only applies to bad product managers. Every product manager should understand their customer and should build accordingly. The product manager is the CEO of a product. This means they're the ones that go to finance to get the money, go to designers to conceptualise how it should look, and go to engineers to get it built. They should understand the users. Now I'm not saying you must get the keywords from that product manager. I'm saying understand who they're building for - and personas are a huge part of this.

Think about SEO personas. Are users on mobile, and what kind of searches would they be doing? Maybe they're doing voice searches, which are really long-tail. Maybe they're doing image searches on their phones. Understand that user and understand how they're going to be searching to solve their problems, instead of going for the highest volume keywords and working your way down. Go for the highest interest and best match keywords. Some of these may not even have any search volume in the keyword research tools. That doesn't matter because you're really homing in on what the user wants, and what the user is going to be looking for."

If you're an SEO working in a smaller firm that doesn't have a product manager, what's the best way to reach out to the users?

"If you're in a smaller firm that doesn't have a product manager, you are the product manager - you own this thing. If you're writing content, you're conceptualising what this content should be because there's a user there. If you don't know there's a user there, take a pause. Maybe you shouldn't be building something if you don't know there's a user. Take a step back and find the user. The best way to understand what the user wants and what they are looking for, is to ask them.

Define an actual user. Use all the data you have within the organisation. This is your treasure trove of information. It could be from street interviews, customer calls, or emails. If you don't have the user to email, then that's not an SEO issue."

Do you target people who have expressed interest in your product or service - so they are just about ready to buy - but haven't purchased it yet?

"It's probably a big lift to have that conversation. I usually work with product managers or product leaders if it's an individual running their own company, as they have access to this kind of data. They understand how to talk to users. Looking for people who might be purchasing may be a little bit further away from their role, and it's certainly not something I'm going to do."

For research purposes, is 25 people an ideal number to aim for?

"Absolutely not. You can do two interviews and find anecdotal information that will provide lightbulb moments. Twenty-five people might just give you the same pattern over and over. It depends on the questions when you're doing a survey. If your questions are fairly tight, and you can get information from them, you don't need that many responses."

What's an example of a great question?

"It's going to be something quantitative, where you know that you fleshed out all the options. And when someone gives you an answer, you need to be confident they're giving you the answer to the question you asked. The question might be, 'Which is more important to you?' and the options could be 'brand', 'price', or 'shipping'. That's a very tight question, and there's no way to manoeuvre around it. If 75% of people say, 'price', you can be fairly confident that they're saying that because it is important to them.

If you ask another question, which isn't as tight, you might start having questions on your questions. If you're doing a small survey, and you have a tight question, and five people tell you 'price' - it's not statistically significant. But you might feel that you should elevate 'price' in your marketing efforts."

In conventional SEO, does that mean incorporating elements such as 'cheap' or 'good value' into your copy?

"Yes, and that's a great point when it comes to keywords. You might find the keyword 'cheap car insurance' from a keyword research tool but if you're marketing to more affluent customers, 'cheap car insurance' may make them feel like they're going to get conned. A more appropriate keyword might be 'value'. You have to talk to users and align your SEO with their preferences."

Can this kind of research be done online, or does it have to involve direct face-to-face or phone conversations with people?

"You don't have to do this over the phone or on Zoom, you could just send an email. It's an easy way to get information - you can welcome them and quickly ask, 'What was most important to you when deciding to purchase from us?' You'll suddenly find information that you would never have found had you not asked."

How can an SEO articulate the value of using a survey-based approach instead of a quantitative keyword-based approach to their boss?

"Why do bosses think that the quantitative keyword approach is any better? It's illogical to me. You need to use logic to convince them to try something else. We believe these are our customers, and we know that our customers are looking for this kind of thing. Allow me to try some content like this and see if it works."

Is this approach more appropriate for product pages and purchase funnels, or is it suitable for every type of content on your website?

"I always explain to clients that SEO is an investment. They're taking away money from other places to put that money into SEO. Therefore, they should be very certain the investment they're making has a customer behind it. If you're writing a blog post just for the sake of getting traffic, why make that investment?

This approach should matter - it's a customer-first approach. Is a search user going to discover this blog post and now have a higher opinion about our company or follow a purchase funnel? Or are they just going to read it? What's the point of having well-read blogs but no sales? I think this approach has worked for everything related to SEO."

What's one thing that an SEO needs to stop doing to focus more on customers and getting the information that's right for them?

"You need to understand the KPIs and metrics that the business is driving towards, which could be sales, dollars, or downloads. SEOs should stop focusing on keyword-level reporting - because it's the wrong metric. When you hand a list of chosen keywords and rankings to your boss or your client, you're judging success based on how you've done on these keywords. This can't be right because the rest of the business is measuring itself based on marketing costs versus revenue. All SEO is doing is measuring keyword performance – and the ones you've chosen might not even matter.

Stop doing the keyword-level reporting and start drilling into the actual attribution reporting. Then you will be far more successful."

You can find Eli Schwartz over at EliSchwartz.co.

6 USER BEHAVIOUR

Focus on user experience and SEO success will follow - with Hellen Benavides from giffgaff.

Hellen shares that SEO success starts with users and if you can't satisfy your users, it's going to be an uphill battle.

Hellen Benavides says: "Focus on what is best for the user and SEO ranking improvements will come naturally. Improve your website experience, listen to the user, and make your content relevant. You will not only make the user happy; you will make Google happy and also improve conversion rates."

What constitutes a good user experience in 2022?

"As we know, in 2021 we had the Google algorithm update called the Page Experience update. Google is telling us that experience is a priority. In order to determine what is best for your users, you need to listen to them and do your research. However, you need to start this research from search, before the point where the user lands on your website. Get to know your user's journey, their pain points, and what kind of content they need. You need to observe what search results your users click on so that you can create pages and content that will rank - because they will get more engagement."

What does high quality user research look like?

"You can look at your Google Analytics data to see which pages people are accessing, and how long they are spending there. You can also use other software to see things like mouse movements for your users. However, the best way to get what you are looking for is through interviews, and video recordings of people going through their searches and trying to find your site. A service like UserTesting.com will give you that kind of data. It is really useful to get several minutes' recording of someone going through your site, and hearing what they're saying when they're experiencing your site for the first time.

Importantly, a recording can also show you what users are doing when they are searching for a product, and doing pricing research in the category of business that you operate in. You can observe what types of results they are clicking on and why - therefore you can see how they interact with your competitors. You can find out what your competitors might be doing better to see what areas you can improve in. Then, you can also see the whole user journey on your own website until, hopefully, they end up buying something. That will help you to optimise your page to make it more user-friendly and you will make Google happy as well."

What signals is Google getting from this optimisation? Are they able to recognise user satisfaction and reward that with SEO rankings?

"Google is a user in a way, but it is also a machine. It's not a human user but it is looking for the user-based signals that are telling it whether your website is good or not. First with the mobile-friendly Google algorithm update, and now with Core Web Vitals, Google has shown that it's mainly focussed on providing the best user experience. Alongside having good content that is relevant, and having a competitive product, you need to provide a good user experience. In that sense, think of Google as a user as well."

How do you measure the impact of improving user experience?

"You should mostly be looking at conversion rates. It's the first signal you can see clearly. You can also observe the impact that your improvements are having on rankings, and on your visibility. Google will see that you are converting more and will therefore recognise that your page is relevant for the search. The result of that will be an impact on rankings.

If you improve the user experience on a certain page, and don't make improvements to the user experience of a very similar page, you can test to see the precise level of impact that the improvements have had. It will be a visible difference. This also makes it easier to get commercial buy-in. Everyone understands user experience, but not everyone understands search engine optimisation. When you have an impact on the bottom line, on revenue and sales, and have an impact on organic traffic – that's ideal."

What are some typical improvements that need to be done, where SEOs and website designers are making mistakes that result in a bad user experience?

"Often the area where users are having trouble, during their interaction with a website, is in filtering the information and being unable find what you have to offer. When a user comes from search, they land on a specific page. Users may not land on the best page for their result straightaway. From there, it can be difficult to see what the best result for their query is within your website. You need to improve the user journey to make sure that they convert.

In the end, we want to sell more. We are on Google because we want more traffic, and we want more conversions. Making sure that your users are able to filter the information on your site, and reach the best result for their query, is a fantastic example of user experience and rankings working together. You need to understand how users interact with the search results in order to do that."

Do you think Google will make more of a formal announcement about precisely how much user experience is going to impact rankings in the future?

"I believe they will keep pushing for improvements to user experience because no user likes to land on a dodgy web page. Users don't like it when they want to click on something, but it moves out of the way, or when the page is slow to load. I believe that Google will continue to show their focus on user experience, step-by-step, as they have done with mobile-friendly and now Core Web Vitals. They will continue to focus on showing the sites that provide the best experience in their results."

How often should SEOs be looking at conversion rates and recommending improvements to the user experience?

"Mainly, it is a one-off major project prior to initiating a major website redesign. Apart from that, it's about incorporating it into your regular checks and keeping an eye open for key changes. I look at it by product and by the important areas of the website. As long as you have first addressed the pain points during the user's journey, you don't need to revisit too often. When you see new things that can be improved, then you can revisit. It is a big job because you need resources to optimise the page: content, design, SEO, and technical SEO behind the pages. Just make sure that you keep listening to the user and tracking your rankings. Whenever you see a group of pages that are not ranking as well as they should, you can revisit and try to understand why."

What's something that SEOs should probably stop doing in order to spend more time focusing in on user experience?

"A lot of SEOs create content just for the sake of creating content. They create many pages which don't get that much traffic, and with time they become out of date. It's a legacy to manage. Whenever you create new content, or a new page, you need to make sure that you are maintaining it - and it is relevant for the user. You need to think about where this page will sit in the user journey, and what purpose it is serving."

Hellen Benavides is eCommerce Experience & SEO Lead at giffgaff.com.

Focus on human behaviour - with Aiala Icaza Gonzalez from Reflect Digital

For Aiala, you need to understand why your users behave the way that they do, in order to build long-term SEO success.

Aiala Icaza Gonzalez says: "Increasing human focus on our SEO strategies through human behaviour and cognitive biases is not as complicated as it sounds."

What kind of cognitive biases might an SEO have?

"Most of these things we already know, we just don't think about them most of the time. Obviously, there are dozens of different behaviours and biases we should be learning from but there are a couple that are super-important. They're key when it comes to SEO - and paid campaigns in general.

The first one to highlight, and one of the most important, is the availability heuristic. This is a mental shortcut that makes things easier to remember and helps us to make a decision. This doesn't mean that what we remember is the right thing. What we recall is based on repetition and recency. It's based on how long ago we heard and saw that information.

For example, you could have seen that robberies in your neighbourhood have increased. Your response could be, 'Where I live isn't safe anymore'. This is not actually true, perhaps it's just a group has been stealing things lately. We tend to think in such ways because we've seen the same information repeating a lot recently."

You're recommending that SEOs help make a brand more memorable, so when someone's ready to buy, they'll go to that brand instead of someone else?

"Yes, it's making the content easy to remember through providing memorable nuggets. With the ongoing rise of mobile and social media, we need to understand that people need to have all the information and grasp the concept quickly. If I'm on Instagram, and I see your ads, I don't want to see numbers or lots of text. I want to see an image showing me precisely what you're selling me.

For instance, if you're selling leggings for the gym, don't tell me that your leggings are made from 50% of a specific fabric. Show me what it looks like in a video or picture. It's the same for content. Show me that content, not 2,000 words. Provide the relevant information in a short way and demonstrate how this is working and how it's beneficial for me."

So, this means giving someone 10 seconds to view a webpage, then

cover it up and ask the person, what's that web page and content about, and why is it relevant for you?

"Yes, exactly - and making that emotional connection. You could use visuals or just highlight some of the text. You need to work with your UX team to make that content come alive, so it makes a connection with the user. Also, you need to understand where the user is in the purchase funnel so you can connect on a deeper level.

For example, identifying that they're looking for something, they're already in the consideration phase, they're thinking about me, and you're the one for them. There's a lot to work there, and it means a lot of synergies with other teams. Obviously, the more we improve the content so that it relates to the user and drives emotional connection, the higher chances we have for that conversion."

How does this impact content style? Is it important to always have snappy paragraphs, or is this dumbing down the effort it takes to understand your message?

"I guess it would depend on where they are in the purchase funnel. If they're in the awareness phase, you need to consider that they might not know much about the product. They just know they have a need, and they want help. For instance, they need leggings, which they usually buy in Zara or H&M. But now they know they need something better, yet don't know much more than that. They will start by looking at the best leggings and come to you in the awareness phase. Then they'll move into the consideration phase, followed by the 'ready to buy' phase. You need to understand and build your site based on these phases.

You need to create content that is related to each stage of the funnel. In the end, this all comes from the keywords, and keyword research will tell you their intent. Agencies struggle with this because all the different channels tend to work in silos. This is not just an SEO thing - all the different channels need to work together to make sure we're sending the right people to the right page.

For instance, if PPC is having an awareness campaign, don't send them directly to the product page. Instead, send them to an awareness page, such as a blog post or a category page. You need everyone to work together and not in silos. This ensures your strategy is fully integrated and works perfectly."

How do you measure the success of doing this from an SEO perspective? Does targeting human behaviours mean people will spend longer on your web pages and go further down your purchase funnel? Or are there better ways of measuring it?

"That's one of the biggest ways to measure it, but you need to understand what engagement is to you. What does engagement mean to you on your page? If it's an awareness page, you want them to spend more time and visit more pages. If it's a product page, you don't want them to spend that much time - you want them to go straight to the conversion. It should be on a case-by-case basis. You need to consider which different engagement metrics are important for you. Ultimately, you're looking to increase conversions because that is why you're doing this."

How do you ensure your page's content is optimised for different personas with different needs, from an SEO perspective?

"That's an interesting one. We actually have a client who is receiving people in totally different life stages to the same page, so we're offering the same service for them. We need to try different things and A/B test everything. We need to learn if one page works for everyone, or if we have to create different landing pages. Here we're working with the UX team really closely and carrying out A/B testing to understand what is working and what isn't. How can we focus this page? Should it be with more visuals and less text, or more text and less visuals?

With all these things, there is a synergy with the UX and CR teams, depending on how you're structured. Then it comes down to A/B testing because, in the end, every audience - like every human - is different. A lot will depend on your sector as well. Some sectors might be more niche, and audiences might need different landing pages for the same product because they have different ways of using it."

How do you define your different audiences? Do you take data from your pay-per-click and paid search campaigns, and then use that as a

way to feed your SEO success to dissect your visitors into different audiences?

"Yes, it could be paid information as well as analytics. If you have enough analytics data, you could also make personas out of it. Then, obviously, there's research on the country or the market. There are different ways to get the information you need. I'm lucky that in my company, we have a team that works on personas, and they know all the resources and sources."

What are your thoughts on how search engines detect changes in human behaviour and deliver different content according to who they think the user is and what they want?

"I think they're getting better. We can see this happening, and they look at what you're doing and what you're looking at. Yes, they might still be slow, but they're machines, not humans, and don't understand trends as fast as we do. I recently saw that Facebook is allowing Google to crawl their pages. I think Google might be able to understand and adapt faster to trends, and discover what users are looking at and how their behaviour is changing, more quickly."

Does this analysis - on different types of audiences to ensure your content immediately resonates - need to be done once every six months, or is it ongoing?

"Ideally, it would be ongoing because you're always creating content, and you always have campaigns going on. You continually need to make sure you're delivering the right message at the right time. This takes you back to recency and everything else we've discussed.

However, I understand that agencies might not have the time to do that but try for as often as possible. It is true what I said earlier - if your organic and non-organic channels don't work together, it might not work. Ultimately, the paid teams and the social teams will bring you the fastest traffic. It's through them that you're going to be able to test if this is working or not as soon as possible, because we know organic takes a little bit of time."

Have you seen organic results being improved by surprising actions?

For instance, driving traffic from email, and demonstrating that the piece of content is very popular, so Google decides to rank it higher?

"I can't say that for sure, and there is nothing specific I can put my finger on. That's because, generally, the clients I have been working with are quite big. There's always something going on, such as emails, paid, and social. I can't definitively say that something specific happened because of a specific action. I have seen organic increasing because of an overall paid campaign. On the other hand, it was about a launch of a famous makeup brand. I can't be 100% sure that it was because of paid"

There was a specific reason I asked that question. A few years ago, I interviewed Rand Fishkin, and he'd decided that the click-through from his Moz email newsletter was potentially impacting SERP rankings for a short period of time. With the increase in traffic, perhaps Google was testing whether it was appropriate to slightly increase that particular listing. It's challenging to tie different channels together, while normal theory suggests the algorithm looks at organic actions and doesn't take into account other sources of traffic. But you never know?

"You never know if it does or if it doesn't. What we need to think about is that ultimately it does not matter, because what the paid teams are doing is actually bringing awareness. It's putting our name out there, so we're in the user's subconscious all the time. Thanks to the paid teams, when users need something, they'll remember what this brand was telling me, so they will come to us organically.

This is why it is so important to work together because we should not be a silo. Whatever they do, and whatever I do, we're going to impact each other - we're an orchestra!"

What do you suggest a busy SEO should stop doing to spend more time understanding and focusing on humans?

"Stop chasing Google so much. Yes, technically speaking, it's really important that we are ready for them - and that you know all the technical stuff like HTML and JavaScript. However, we need to realise that Google is actually fixing their algorithm, so it adapts to humans. Why are we chasing

Google? Let's chase the humans!"

You can find Aiala Icaza Gonzalez over at ReflectDigital.co.uk.

"Intent" is the direction that the search engines are going in - with Mindy Weinstein from Market MindShift

According to Mindy, search engines are also moving towards gaining a better understanding of user intent.

Mindy Weinstein says: "Focus a lot more time and attention into recognising, and identifying, searcher intent. It's not anything new, I've been talking about it for years. However, search engines are always evolving and are using newer technology to try to understand the 'Why' and the 'What' behind searches. From an SEO perspective, we need to dig deep into that. Getting the right traffic is more important than just getting as much traffic as possible."

How do search engines determine intent?

"If you look at some of Google's recent patents, many of them are focussed on Natural Language Processing, and understanding the relationships between words. I believe they're using that to identify intent. They're looking at pages and identifying which specific queries indicate that someone is doing research, and which indicate that someone wants to buy something. There are also what Google calls the 'micro-moments', all the things that happen in between the 'know' intent and the 'buy' intent. They're using AI technology to understand this.

I focus a lot on psychology. We have to try to determine where someone is coming from when they search. It will take a lot longer to do keyword research, but it's about getting the right traffic. I can tell a client that organic search went up 50% but the follow-up question is always: 'How many of those converted?'. We're held responsible for getting the right traffic, so we need to understand intents."

Will developments in Natural Language Processing cause keywords to lose significance?

"They still matter. However now, when you do keyword research, you should be spending time going after more than just one-word phrases. It's great if a shoe company ranks number one for 'shoes', but that's not really quality. You need to be able to target something more specific. You need to develop an understanding of a particular type of searcher. If your marketing department has created personas, go through those. Really try to get into the mindset of the searcher, facing a particular problem or looking for a particular type of solution. Consider what their specific search will be.

Keywords matter even more than before, because we now have to know what someone is actually going to say into their phone, or type. It's more than one or two words; searchers now put in a whole question. As SEOs, we have to become better at the psychological aspect and identifying where the searcher is coming from.

It will even be different within different areas. I've worked with lawyers that service different areas of law and different states. In one state someone's going to describe their car accident differently than someone in another state or, even more so, another country. We're not getting away from keyword research, it's actually even more important. It's a process that you have to spend some time on."

Is there still a place for one or two-word keyword phrases?

Recently I don't think I've worked on a one-word keyword anywhere. It's so broad. However, I'm sure there are scenarios where one word can be very specific and relevant, and it makes sense. I can't say that no-one should be targeting them.

When looking at keywords, focus more on relevancy than just the volume. If you know that a phrase is relevant, and you've taken the time to understand that if someone is searching for it, they are looking for a solution that you offer, then go after that. Even if it's a lower volume, target the intent - understand where they are in their process and focus on getting them to convert. You may not get as many people, because it's a lower volume, but when they get to you, they're really ready to take a desired action."

How do you optimise for the various ways that one concept will be described by different people in different places?

"It's a challenge. It will get better over time but even right now you don't necessarily need to have a separate page for each term or phrase. I had a client that offered boat docks, but in some areas, people refer to them as 'piers'. That is tricky, but within content you can switch out the terms a bit and use those that are most common on one page. It gets to be a bit much if you have them separated into each page. You don't need to have one page per keyword, you can service a lot of phrases in one place. Search engines are getting smarter and are becoming more able to understand what your page is about from the content and context."

Is identifying relevancy a manual task or is there a good tool to help?

"A lot of it is applying wisdom and experience to your data. If you have information about who your target searchers are, look at those and match where a phrase is relevant to them. I don't rely on a tool for that, but it can be a significant time investment. If you've got hundreds of keywords, and you're trying to figure that out, you have to scale it down. Identify which are the higher priority and which of those are the most relevant.

Once you've identified some phrases where you know the right intent is there - and it's relevant - it's important to be aware of what type of pages are showing up at the top the results. Are they government pages or articles? This will help you to determine whether or not you're in the natural realm of what the search engines expect to see and what they're rewarding."

What kind of intent are you looking to map to keywords?

"At the start of a project, when you're looking at your list of keywords, you want to identify the 'know' intent and the 'buy' intent. For 'buy', it doesn't have to be eCommerce - it just means that they want a transaction of some kind. Based on these keywords, you can look at which pages you need to optimise, or maybe create. If it's a 'know' intent you may want to create a guide, a How To, or an article. If you're mapping to the 'buy' intent, you can optimise product pages or service pages, or create new ones. In my keyword research, I have a column where I put the intent so that I know what I'm trying to optimise. If you're going up against pages that are ranking by targeting the 'know' intent, and you've optimised a product page, it's going to be very difficult for you.

That's the groundwork, and on top of it, you need to be thinking about the journey. There are a lot of different journeys, but I focus on the journey of Awareness, Consideration, and Purchase. You need to know, and service, the words and phrases that someone might use at each of those stages. More questions are going to show up in Awareness. Moving into Consideration, you might have more comparisons and by the time they reach Purchase, they're going to be putting in more branded terms. There's also post-purchase. If someone has purchased something and they have an issue, they're likely to search Google. If you can provide the answer, you're much more likely to keep a satisfied customer. At each stage they should keep getting to your website."

How can you make improvements for a page with high traffic but low conversions?

"For that issue you should start with your money pages - the pages that are converting. It could be service pages, category pages, or product pages. Then you need to look at how that page is showing up, and what queries it's showing up for. Go to Google Search Console, see what queries are getting clicks, and consider if those make sense for your page. Sometimes there's a mismatch. Sometimes the page isn't showing for a particular phrase that it was supposed to be optimised for, or for one that would get better traffic. Then you can re-examine the page and start to reverse engineer it.

If your page is not showing up for a phrase that would actually convert, look at the pages that are. Consider the intent of those pages and whether that aligns with the intent of your own page. If not, you're going to have to make adjustments. Perhaps you need to create something that's more article-based and send the user back to a product page through there.

If you're getting a lot of clicks but a really low time on-page, then the page is likely not addressing the user's needs in an obvious way. Make sure your H1 is right there telling them that they're in the right place, break up the content, and have buttons to guide them. You're going to have to do a bit of tweaking. Perform a page-by-page analysis, starting with your money pages."

What is something that SEOs should stop doing to focus more time on mapping intent and getting better traffic?

"Technical SEO can take a lot of time, because if your foundation is not solid nothing else matters. However, a lot of SEOs spend time going through automated audits, getting fixes, and sending them off to the developer, without looking at what is going to move the needle. You need to make sure that these changes are going to make a difference in traffic, not just give busy work for yourself and the developer. Running, sending off, and chasing down reports is not always an effective use of your time. Still focus on technical, but only focus on the things that are going to make a difference, like indexing or crawling. Don't get bogged down in the little things that are taking your time away from something important, like making your keyword research a lot deeper."

You can find Mindy Weinstein over at MarketMindShift.com.

Adopt an "intent-first" mindset - with Chris Green from Torque

Chris believes that 'intent' is something that you should consider prior to carrying out any SEO activity.

Chris Green says: "Adopting an intent-first mindset means using intent to map and guide everything you're doing from an SEO perspective. Primarily that's linking to keyword research, the application of keywords, how you're structuring the website, and the planning and mapping of your content. It's often something that feels quite obvious to a non-SEO. However, anyone that's been engaged with an SEO for any timeframe knows they can often get very constrained around the interface, and they get focused very heavily on pure search volume and what they want to rank. They're not actually concerned about answering the question that someone has, and what is the best content, or the best means, to do that.

The implication of this is not understanding when you cannot compete, or when you should not compete. You should be focusing your efforts where you can make the most gains. And intent - what your customer is trying to achieve - has to be at the centre of everything you do."

Are you suggesting that SEOs should stop thinking about reporting on keywords?

"I'm not saying abandon reporting on keywords, but abandon reporting without the intent lens. Progress and movements in certain keywords may equal commercial success, while others may further your customer awareness, retention, or customer service goals. Assessing which keywords are moving, along with the part of the funnel and what the customers are trying to do, gives a much more nuanced discussion as to what these movements mean. Also, think about what you are actually going to do differently, and what you could achieve with this knowledge."

What about if a keyword could apply at different stages of the funnel? Is it possible to deliver a different experience to people with different intents?

"It is. I think there'll be certain phrases that are always harder to distinguish, or differentiate, as clearly. The hardest ones are those keywords where the intent is really muddled. It's the really generic terms such as 'apple'. Are you looking for technology or a fruit? For these kinds of terms, I would determine the experience you deliver by looking at the SERP and what kind of results other websites are delivering. The specific experience the top-ranked websites are providing makes it very clear what stage in the funnel they are. Broadly speaking, that's a good indicator of what direction you should be moving in.

Now, if you've got split intent, or there's some ambiguity around that, think of your customers and where they are in the process. Which experience do you give first, and then how do you facilitate the second? You've always got to have a dominant target; you can't have your cake and eat it on every single occasion. I'm telling more and more people to look at the SERPs. They are a stronger indicator now of intent than they ever have been. Yes, Google sometimes gets it wrong, but there are a lot of tools out there that can run this kind of analysis. However, a Google search will get you 80-

90% of the way there virtually every time."

What are the areas where SEOs get it wrong when signposting people for a branded search?

"The biggest areas are not owning all of the branded search that's available, or not thinking about what people are actually asking. Brands often say, 'We're not interested in that traffic', or 'We're not interested in answering that question, and therefore, we're not going to provide that'. If you're not owning that - someone else can. This is an issue mainly for larger brands, who have more brand equity and research around this.

There's a degree of being protectionist as much as answering the question. For example, if post-purchase customers are asking questions about your brand, and you're not answering them, you don't have control of that space and you're not going to be able to help them. Owning the brand should be simple in the vast majority of cases, so you need to take the opportunity while you can and get in there early."

What metrics do you use to measure success at different stages in the purchase funnel?

"What really helps with intent is your metrics. Each stage can be appropriate for the goal of that person. We want to measure traffic, but we also want to measure sales. We want to get the 'pound value' that this content is delivering, which is really appropriate at the bottom of the funnel because this is the point where people are ready to purchase. However, if you are judging on 'direct pounds earned' at the top of the funnel, you're going to be using an inappropriate metric. It will tell you that all of your top-funnel content is underperforming.

<u>Top of the funnel</u>

For the really early intent searches, share of voice is a good metric. That says how visible you are. The narrative here is about the likelihood that someone searching around the top funnel will find you. There's a number of tools that will calculate share of voice for you. If you know which keywords you want to rank for, and you know where you're ranked for them, you can establish what that is - and you could even look at average ranking.

Mid to lower funnel

Contacts and interactions on the websites are good metrics. This is about creating an idea of what micro conversions you want to see - such as live chat instigations, contact form fills, document downloads, and add-to-baskets.

Bottom of the funnel

This stage is squarely revenue generated.

You can even create your attribution - you can look at your funnel and not just the last click. You can look at first click, bathtub - or whatever model you want - to see where people are discovering you, and how many times organic is featuring in their journey. That can all be done pretty easily through Google Analytics. It's having an appropriate set of metrics at each stage but also telling people the narrative. You need to know what success looks like, and what you can expect when this content is working well."

Where does an SEO start with matching pages to intent?

"The first place an SEO starts is looking at the top pages that are delivering traffic, googling those phrases, and investigating what the rest of the top 10 are doing. Unless you're in positions 1-3, there's a good chance there are other people on page one who are offering a better experience. What content experience are those pages offering, and does that differ from your own? You need to be really clear on that, because sometimes you won't be ranking because your intent is not right. You're literally not offering what Google thinks is the best response.

It can get cloudy around split intent queries, and you have to be careful what it is you're actually doing there. You need to stress test when looking at those top-ranking pages and explore the queries that are driving traffic to those pages. Are they appropriate? You have to try and remove yourself from the position of working in that company. If you landed on that page, and that was you query, would you be satisfied? If the answer is anything but a resounding yes, then there's potential for work to be done around that.

The other side is if you were working on a massive keywords set, and you could only hope to analyse the top 5% of keywords from a manual perspective. You need to look at some of the tools out there that classify keywords with the intent similar to how Google does. Then you can establish if that page provides knowledge or if that page drives action. At scale, you can see any clear mismatches relatively easily using Excel."

Can it be a challenge to work closely with a content marketing team to ensure the correct content is created to match the intent you've identified?

"Most content teams will come skipping towards you with open arms if you approach them saying that this is how you want to achieve it. I've worked very closely with content teams my whole career, and the biggest objection with SEOs is often that the content doesn't fit, or they're being asked to put keywords in content, and they don't understand why or feel it's correct.

If, as an SEO, you're adopting that intent-first mindset, you can explain that you're doing it for the customer. Most content teams will want to work very closely on that, because your goals should align with theirs. The only times where they might not, is when the content team's KPIs are wrong, or misaligned. Training content teams to use Google Analytics effectively is probably one of your biggest routes to success because they can see what you are measuring."

How do you decide on the type of content that needs to be created?

"That's when I turn back to what the SERP is showing. For example, if they've got a knowledge box with a video embed, or a video carousel, that tells me that video content is what people are looking for. However, I'd also provide a transcript, and text is the best way of getting indexed and returned quickly. Just make sure your content is well-structured with clear headings, good internal linking, and enough textual content to actually explain what's going on in there.

I would always gravitate very heavily to textual content for getting indexed but use the SERP to help establish what other media ranks well, and what content length properly answers that query.

The final consideration is: What is the best piece of content, and how do you make it better? That's where the content team and the customer hat can be really useful because you need to know what good content looks like for this query. This is something that not all SEOs are great at - because that's not their job. You need to rely on a content marketer to work out what the best content is and make sure you have the best result."

How often does this fit into an SEO strategy? Should it be done on an annual basis or more regularly?

"It makes sense to instigate this at key events, such as site migrations and site changes - when you are making lots of changes anyway. Also, the timing will depend on how well you are doing. If 40-60% of your traffic is organic, you've got enough to know that Google is valuing what you write - but there's always room to grow. I'd suggest every three to six months depending on the size of the site."

What's one thing an SEO should stop doing to spend more time adopting an intent-first mindset?

"Stop wringing your hands so much about the vanity terms - the ones that drive high traffic and low intent. It's those really ambiguous queries, where even if you made it into position one, and got thousands of searches a month, what is that going to achieve? From a commercial perspective, the biggest wins mainly come from pivoting to longer-tail terms that convert better, and usually are less competitive. This will free up an awful lot of time."

We can find Chris Green over at TorquePartnership.com.

Employ intent mapping for every core page on your site - with Helen Pollitt from iTech Media

According to Helen, intent mapping is something that you need to be applying for every core page on your site.

Helen Pollitt says: "You need to consider granular intent mapping for every core page on your site. By intent mapping, I mean, making sure you understand what someone landing on your core pages wants to do when they get to them. That should inform the type of content, and how it's displayed and signposted on those pages. Intent mapping should dictate everything about the content, and the user journey through your site from your landing page."

How does an SEO become confident of the intent? Is there a certain place to start gathering information from customers, and how do you translate that into intent?

"I start right at the basics: doing good keyword research - getting yourself a seed list of keywords, and then understanding what someone searching for this particular query might be looking for. Sometimes, it's obvious. If someone is searching for 'karaoke bars near me', you know what they're looking for. If they are searching for "best karaoke bars near me", then you can start to infer that there might be some criteria to set against that list of karaoke bars. Just from reading through the seed keyword list, and whittling that down, you should be able to understand what the intent is.

From there, I look to see what Google thinks the intent is. I put those keywords into Google and see what sort of search results are returned. That helps you to understand what Google might decide the intent is, and that might change over time. It's worth repeating this whilst optimising landing pages if you're doing this over a long period of time. It's also worth looking at some of the conversations that you're having with your customers - your visitors to your site. If you have call logs, or you can speak to your customer service team, you can get an understanding of what your customers are talking about, and what they mean by the language they're using. This helps you start to understand the mindset of your customers."

Where do you draw the line when deciding where it is worthwhile having separate distinct pages on your website?

"It might not be worthwhile having separate pages. Instead, intent mapping informs the type of content you have on your pages. Those pages might not just contain information that is mapped to one intent. It might be that people with slightly different intent are still able to find what they need from that one page.

In my 'karaoke bars' example, you might decide that if someone types 'karaoke bars near me', then their intent is just a list of relevant bars in their geography. You might not optimise for that search phrase at all, because Google Maps has probably swept up most of the traffic there. Instead, you might look at search phrases like 'best karaoke bars near me' or 'what should I do on a night out', where the intent might be slightly different. Then, you would be able to craft content for one page that meets all the needs of those users. It's worth considering whether you can create a really rich page that covers multiple intents that are similar, rather than having individual pages. You might see an overlap of the intent behind those pages."

Would you categorise intents that were quite similar and create H2 heading sections on your page to deal with the different intents you've identified?

"Potentially, yes. If we think about paragraph indexing and how Google is starting to pull out distinct bits of information from pages, we can start to understand how it might be able to deal with pages that have slightly mixed intent. However, as long as you are distinct in mapping the intent against those pages, I don't think that would be an issue."

How do you define what your core pages are?

"It's the pages generating the conversion that you're measuring. It might be the actual revenue, your product pages, or your pages leading to forms being filled in. However, it's not just the pages that convert, it might also be the pages that are attracting people at the top of the marketing funnel. It might be your longer-tail keyword pages, ones that are answering questions, or blog pages, or anything you think is bringing in an attracted audience at the top of the user journey that can be brought down the marketing funnel. It's about the pages that are likely to really engage your audience."

Is this strategy for any type of business?

"Yes - any business that has a website. It's really for anyone wanting to engage users on their website."

Is there a particular frequency with which intent mapping should be carried out?

"It's definitely not 'set and forget', but it's also not necessarily something you would be scheduling in. You need to keep an eye on your data - if you're noticing that click-through, rankings or traffic are dropping, then you need to start auditing those pages. As part of that audit, you need to look at the intent mapping. Has Google started to favour different types of content over the content on your page? Have the search terms changed to an extent whereby the perceived intent behind a keyword is no longer the actual intent behind that keyword?

You may need to change how you are structuring your page as well as the content that's on your page. When you choose to carry out intent mapping needs to be in response to data."

How do you measure the success of your intent mapping?

"You need to measure quality of traffic over quantity of traffic, because quantity of traffic isn't necessarily going to lead to the conversions you want. Intent mapping is about making sure the right people are coming to your page. It's about ensuring that there is a good level of organic traffic coming to your site that is actually converting. You might notice rankings go up for certain keywords and not for others, because your page becomes less relevant for the keywords that don't match the intent of the page. It's a combination of those sorts of metrics.

The focus needs to be on whether the traffic coming to your page is carrying out the activities that you want. That might not be a conversion - it could be click-throughs to other pages, a continuation of the user journey through the website, or a purchase. It depends on what the purpose of that page is, and what you want the user to do."

Is this strategy only suitable for existing content, or can it be implemented in new content?

"Intent mapping is very much suitable for existing content - for optimising and tweaking it to make it more effective. However, it is also a strategy that absolutely has to happen for new content. You should not be putting content on a site unless you know who it is for, and what you want them to do once they've read it. When you're putting new content onto a site, or even when you're building your site from scratch, you need to think: What is the point of this page? What is it trying to do? What sort of user am I trying to attract?

All of that information should be informing your UX, design and content writing teams. Content writers, for instance, need to know who their audience is, what they are looking to do, and what you're looking to guide them to do. Without intent mapping, it's difficult for a content writer to produce something that is going to be effective."

Do you think intent mapping should be led by an SEO, or is it a suitable strategy for someone else within a marketing department?

"That very much depends on the politics within your organisation. I would love to say that an SEO should be spearheading it, because it's something that I think all SEO should be excited to be doing. However, it might be better suited to someone who's been upskilled within the content marketing team to understand keyword research and intent mapping, or perhaps for a product manager to be leading. It very much depends on how your organisation is structured. Regardless, it's definitely something that the SEO should input, and it's something they should be excited to be working on."

What's the one thing that SEOs should stop doing to focus more time on learning and implementing intent mapping?

"Spend less time trying to carefully sculpt your search results - meaning the snippets that are going to be displayed in Google - because Google is probably going to be changing those a lot more in the future. In the past, you may have spent a lot of time trying to craft the perfect meta title or make a perfect meta description, but I can see that kind of activity becoming less and less fruitful. I would suggest your time is better spent making sure the landing pages meet the user's exact needs, because that will make you more likely to rank - despite whatever Google decides to show as your search snippet. With effective intent mapping, you're more likely to convert your visitors when they land on your pages."

You can find Helen Pollitt over at iTech.media.

The user experience trend is getting stronger - with Kristina Azarenko from Marketing Syrup

Kristina shares that the search engine's move towards understanding user experience, and incorporating this signal into its algorithms, is only getting stronger.

Kristina Azarenko says: "We need to start thinking more about user experience and stop thinking that we need to create SEO content. There is no SEO content - there is content that helps people and is also optimised for search engines.

User experience has been an important trend for a long time, but now it's getting even more significant, especially with the introduction of Core Web Vitals. Now, you need to be useful, and not just create content for the sake of creating content. Also - answer the users' questions matching their intent. If you see your users are struggling to find the information about something related to your services, create content about this - even though this content might initially not have a lot of search volume. There will still be users who will be searching for this. I've seen many situations where you create content with zero search, but later end up getting so many impressions, clicks, and visits through these keywords.

Technical SEO should still be a priority if something is going on with your website, especially if you're using some fancy JavaScript framework. You need to make sure that your Core Web Vitals are good, and your pages are accessible and indexable."

How do search engines actually measure user experience?

"Take a holistic approach to user experience. You need to match user intent with your content, and SEO is part of user experience. I'm not just talking about the design and having the right colours, typography, etc. It's about making sure that your content is accessible, and using your website is not hard.

One of the ways Google estimates user experience is through Core Web Vitals and looking at the content - such as interstitials and pop-ups that can be annoying. They also obviously consider user intent. Additionally, you do need to think about semantic SEO. It's much better to answer a question using 50 words if this will be an exact answer to the question. You don't need to beat around the bush and write 500 words answering questions just to get optimised. Google has direct and indirect ways to measure user experience."

Are there any software tools you use to track what users are doing on your website?

"Yes. I sometimes use Yandex.Metrica (Yandex is a Russian search engine), which is very similar to Google Analytics. It's free, maps user clicks, and you can record sessions and watch them afterwards to see how people are looking at your page."

What are the biggest mistakes that web designers or SEOs are making from a UX perspective nowadays?

"Using headings just for styling, instead of properly marking the content. I see designers or SEOs only using H1 tags, where H2 or H3 tags would be more appropriate to create the right structure for your content.

When it comes to getting feedback from session recordings, what's interesting for me is that often people don't actually read the content. You need to have the content in chunks, and make sure the headings are relevant. If you have a page, and people only read the headings, what would they get from this page? What will they understand?"

How do SEOs educate UX people, and make them more knowledgeable and passionate about SEO?

"When I do training for designers, there are two important elements.

155

Firstly, understanding that headings are not for design only - they are also for marking out the content correctly. And the second thing - which is huge - is speed. It would be amazing if designers understood these two themes.

Designers are usually accountable for images and visual content, so they want everything to be really clear and amazing - which makes total sense because they care about their job. However, at some point, it may become counterproductive because uploading the images doesn't help page speed. For example, I've seen websites where only a part of a huge image was used. The page would always load this enormous image - which was something like 4000 by 4000 pixels - and only part of this image will be used. Think about how much bandwidth is used to load this."

How does writing headings with the user in mind impact keywords? Is it still important to incorporate keywords in headings, and all the other traditional places?

"Yes, definitely - keywords are not going anywhere. They're just becoming more sophisticated because you're using semantics, synonyms and variations for these keywords.

For example, if you wanted to rank for 'SEO consultant in Toronto', you could have it as an H1, and use an even wider keyword such as 'I help people with their digital marketing' for your H2. I would still follow the web standards of using H1 for the most important thing you're trying to convey on the website. So 'SEO consultant' rather than 'digital marketing'. Still include keywords - but it's so much easier to do this when you think about semantics, variations, and synonyms."

What does the greater importance of good user experience mean for the SEO role moving forward? Will the SEO in the future be less technical and more creative?

"When I was starting, there was just SEO. There were backlinks, some on-page, and the technical elements. Now, there's so much more, such as international SEO and news SEO. Going forward, the variety in our roles will become even bigger.

There are already signs that SEOs are becoming more specialist. Some are dedicated to the technical parts, and others are obsessed about on-page. If SEOs want to get more creative, they can move into a more content-based role. If you want to migrate pages, or undertake other technical projects, not every single SEO should be an expert in taking on these tasks. You're going to have different people with different skills. Thinking about content and creative - even from an SEO perspective - requires different skills compared to technical SEO. These roles are going to be even more separated in the future."

What's one thing an SEO might be spending a lot of effort on that they should probably stop doing to spend more time focusing on user experience?

"Stop obsessing about keyword rankings. I know it's easy to report on, but it's not the main goal. It can be measured in addition to the main goals, like revenue and important traffic - not just traffic for the sake of traffic. You can also ditch keyword rankings for good, because it's not the main factor to show that your SEO campaign is successful."

Kristina Azarenko is SEO Consultant & Founder at MarketingSyrup.com.

Use intent and user experience to grow revenue and increase success - with Duane Forrester from Yext

Duane believes that user intent allows you to connect the dots - all the way through from research to purchase.

Duane Forrester says: "SEOs need to focus on truly getting down to the nuts and bolts of user intent and user experience. These things are critical. We've been talking about them for years, and everyone thinks they're doing it - but keyword research doesn't give you user intent. It just gives you volume on keyword activity.

User intent comes because you actually connect the dots all the way through, from what somebody is thinking about to their actions, such as researching something on the internet. In addition to the keyword volume, you'll also discover all the things related to the search - when they learned something new on the topic and went slightly to the left, or to the right, to learn a little bit more. These are opportunities for you to pop up again and prove your value to them.

The customer journey, that takes the user into the conversion funnel to complete the transaction, is so incredible. Studies have repeatedly shown that consumers are willing to pay more for a better user experience. They trust brands that give them a better user experience and now expect better user experiences. You can't fail at these things because these people are on the internet, so they will simply click to someone else. Brand loyalty isn't what it used to be.

You have to understand that understanding what this journey looks like is an intrinsic part of the daily life of an SEO. And you won't get a good view of that journey by just looking at keyword data."

Why are user intent and user experience often spoken about but underutilised? What can we do to get SEOs more interested and active in these areas?

"We have a history of siloing things, whether it's topics or teams within an organisation. For example, the UX team may be separate from the SEO team, and they don't really work together. Yes, they try to accommodate each other, but these elements should be intrinsically linked. It should be very clear that you don't build a website and populate it with content without a clear understanding of the best usability.

Does the consumer want video to answer this question? Is it a list of items they want or is it long-form paragraphs? You have to understand these things because it informs the users' experience and the usability of a website. This opens up the entire world of the technical side of the work you have to get done.

Core Web Vitals is right at the top of your priorities here, and you had better make sure you're getting those technical elements nailed down. These are mission-critical today. Every company that scores better than you is ultimately capable of taking your market share. We're talking about the core metrics like page load speeds, time to first contentful paint, and how long it takes a clickable element to load up. These are the key user experience scenarios, and consumers will choose a competitor if you don't get them right.

If you're going to work, you have to be talking about usability and user intent. If you're already doing this, have you truly built programmes that outline how you build a better website to improve usability? Or how you actually define what user intent is? Many don't have an overarching corporate understanding of what this means and how it impacts the work you do. This means you are missing an opportunity to bring more people together.

The importance of your search box

I'm going to dig way back in the archives for a little tip for you because it's still valuable today. We live in a world where consumers have been taught how to search - go to a box, type in your words, you get an answer. It's very straightforward. Now most websites also have a search box. If you're an SEO, and you're not combing through the logs of your website's search box to see what the user's Intent is, you're missing an opportunity. It's huge.

Every website should have a search box. When a consumer shows up to research a problem they have, the first thing they do is ask Google a question. We are trained to do that. I ask Google, I get an answer to my question. Everybody uses a search box because they've been trained by Google. If you put words in the box, you get an answer to your question. People ask for things because they don't want to navigate. That's how we expect to get our answers now. If you don't deliver this, that's a massive missed opportunity.

Get into your search box, dig around and see what consumers are asking you directly. Remember Google filters out a lot of words, puts them in the 'not provided' category, or won't give you the information in your Google Analytics. Yes, you're left with some keywords, but you're unsure if it was a question or a statement. All of this information is available to you directly in your search box."

Many people suggest going for higher authority articles with longer-

form content that solves everything in the same article. Should an SEO optimise for multiple intents or the optimum intent?

"Let's take YouTube as an example here. If you ask for certain things in Google right now, they will give you an answer that is a YouTube video and tell you that the answer is at two minutes and 36 seconds. It's very clear from Google that they're looking for the answer - not the amalgamation of all information that might also include the answer. They're trying to take you directly to the answer you seek.

While there is definitely a place for these larger authoritative articles, because they allow you to demonstrate authority on a topic, that value starts to erode when someone has a quick question that isn't easily consumed. If you're not a featured snippet (you're a link that someone's going to click to) and the answer to their question is difficult to find - you've failed. The user is moving on. For the average consumer with an average question in their daily lives, they are not interested in hunting around and looking for anything."

Can you have longer-form content for the acquisition part but use short-form for the consideration phase, when people are typing in longer keyword phrases and want exact answers straightaway?

"Yes, I like the way you're layering it there. My approach would be to create long-form content because there's value in it for the people who want to do research. Maybe they're not sold on the idea and this walkthrough - with everything to consider - gets them there.

However, for somebody who's asking me a long-tail question with four-plus keywords, they clearly have an understanding of the one thing they want to know. My goal is to get them to the one thing they want to know and answer their question as clearly and cleanly as possible, with my call to action immediately in front of them. You don't necessarily know where they are in the conversion funnel in their own mind. If your answer to that question is the only thing stopping them from buying the new product, then you've got a sale. There's no point trying to get that person to the much longer-form page where you're more likely to lose them to information overload.

There is value in both of these approaches. My foundation is the big, long-form article where I lay everything out. Now I'm going to put up my walls, which are these other smaller pages that will go around it. Eventually, I'm going to put a roof on top and invite people in. That's how I'm building a successful web business today."

Do you think that many pages are like a bad salesperson: they don't see the buying signal when someone's actually ready to purchase and instead direct customers somewhere else?

"Yes, and it's not a formal direction. We're not talking about providing links and telling people to explore on a page that bypasses a call to action or conversion. No. People are simply saying, 'You're not making it easy for me, you're not making it obvious for me - I'm just going to abandon you.'

Google released a white paper called 'The Messy Middle', and it's a really important read. It reveals how we are trained to think that the customer journey is a linear path. Actually, it's a crazy ball of yarn that kittens have been playing with for a week. The consumer comes in at one point, and they pop out at a number of different places. Then they come back in again, and eventually, they convert.

Your job is to orbit around this scrum and literally provide value anytime the consumer pops up. That is your goal. By doing so, when they come out, instead of forgetting who you were because you confused them, you are the thing they remember as being most useful on this journey. This means they'll immediately go deep with you, and you own them. It's very eye-opening."

What's one thing that SEOs should stop doing to spend more time on user experience and Intent?

"Stop blindly doing keyword research. I believe in keyword research, and believe it's foundational, but if all you're doing is keyword research every week trying to discover the next phrase to wrap inside some content to produce another page - you're doing it all wrong. There should be no metrics for success around how many pages you produced, and how many keywords you targeted. It's all about bottom-line revenue and conversions. If you're an SEO, and you're not focused on that, make it your focus, even if it's not formally your remit. Make it your business to know that side of the business and understand how you're impacting it.

Get cosy with all the information available to you, including reviews. You're going to find competing products that people have mentioned because they were upset with you. They might say, 'I should have bought X', and then you'll know exactly what the intent is. The intent for you becomes making sure your product is better positioned than the competing product that was mentioned.

If you're daily SEO is Core Web Vitals, technical SEO, keyword research, and all the basic tenants of historical SEO, you need to broaden that. You need to find at least 30 minutes a day where you're taking information from the review management team, and you're working with the content team to figure things out. Find out who owns access to your search box on your website and get access to it. Now you're starting to see a real-time thread of what the actual commentary is that you're seeing. Now you can start unlocking some of those keyword research mysteries, which helps you prioritise what you're going to be telling the content team to work on. Now all of these pieces start to become interlinked."

You can find Duane Forrester over at Yext.com.

The debate is over - mobile UX is officially now part of SEO - with Pam Aungst Cronin from Pam Ann Marketing

Pam wishes to highlight that mobile user experience can't be forgotten about in 2022 – now that Google's Core Web Vitals incorporate mobile UX elements.

Pam Aungst Cronin says: "Mobile user experience is officially part of SEO. Google's Core Web Vitals initiative is all the evidence we need, to say that UX metrics are finally part of our SEO goals. What was missing before was that it wasn't quantified, so it could be debated all day long. Now, Google has quantified it and made it measurable. It's here to stay."

Does mobile UX have a different set of standards compared to desktop?

"Absolutely. Usability overall should be important. As with most things, Google is thinking mobile-first with page speed and indexing as well. The large majority of searches occur on mobile, it's not that these things are not important on desktop, but it's more important on mobile. That's where most searches are happening, and what Google's getting pickier about.

It's also a lot more challenging. I tried to resell some concert tickets on my phone today, and it took me three or four times longer than it should have. There were issues with browser compatibility, and things moving around that I was trying to click on. Mobile is innately difficult. I'm glad they're forcing the issue because it shouldn't be this frustrating - after we've been a mobile-first world for so long."

What elements of Google's Core Web Vitals are most important to focus on for mobile UX?

"Right now, there are three that you want to focus on. The first is Largest Contentful Paint (LCP), then First Input Delay (FID), and finally Cumulative Layout Shift (CLS). Those are the three that matter right now, that Google has officially made measurable and set benchmarks to. I wouldn't doubt at all that there are more to come down the pipeline, but those are the first three to focus on for 2022.

Largest Contentful Paint is fancy wording for the biggest thing on the page, and it's about perceived load time. It can take the rest of the page longer to render and load, but Google wants the user to feel like it's happening fast by putting the biggest thing in front of them first.

First Input Delay is how long it takes for your first button to do something. If the browser has rendered the code and displayed a button, but it's not yet clickable, that's an example of FID. It's the delay between the user seeing the first input they may want to make, and actually being able to interact with it.

Cumulative Layout Shift is the amount of movement that you get on a page as it is continuing to load. It's the really annoying effect you have on a mobile website, when you're about to click a button, but something suddenly loads in and moves everything around and you miss the click."

What's something that an SEO can do to help to improve the LCP time?

"First you want to identify what the Largest Contentful Paint item is, according to Google. You may have several large images, hero images, and background images that are similar. Head over to PageSpeed Insights, the Google PageSpeed tool (which is essentially also the Google UX testing tool), run your site through there and look for the Largest Contentful Paint part of the report. It will tell you exactly which it is. It may not even be an image - it's whatever the largest element may be.

Then, since it usually is a very large image, it's pretty simple to optimise the file size, and maybe the dimensions. Don't upload a 4000-pixel wide image into a 40-pixel wide space - it's not going to load fast. Also optimise the weight of the file - make sure it's not four megabytes if it can be condensed down to 40 kilobytes."

Can the LCP element be below the fold, and would that impact the metric and user experience?

"The metric isn't focussed on elements above the fold, although theoretically it should be. If the LCP element is below the fold it is still important for that to load fast because whatever is above the fold may be waiting on that piece to paint. As far as page structure goes, the largest things need to be loaded first. Other divs, and nested elements within them, will load afterwards."

Can CLS only be improved by the UX team, or are there SEO elements to that?

"This is the first time we've needed front-end designers to be involved, to this degree, within the SEO optimization process. Page speed included front-end, but it was mainly back-end developer tasks like server speed optimization. Cumulative Layout Shift is about how the page is painted, and in what order things are loaded. A lot of that has to do with the CSS, and that's where the front-end designers come in.

It's something that SEOs and front-end haven't had to deal with before. It's almost the newest territory to figure out: navigating how to be more helpful to those front-end CSS designers. SEOs have to be managers now - managing content teams, front-end developers, and also back-end developers.

With Google's emphasis on mobile page speed over the last year and a half, we've become more heavily involved than ever with back-end developers. Dealing with First Input Delay is a continued discussion with them as well. It's more of a functionality issue than a design one."

How important a part of the algorithms is UX? Are you going to be de-ranked because Google perceives your UX to be poorer than your competitors'?

"There are hundreds of things that matter when it comes to SEO. Google, and other search engines, evaluate so many different things when trying to decide how high to rank a page. These three metrics are new ones, but they are among probably 300 that matter.

Think of it like playing a game, where you have to earn as many 'points' as you can to beat out your competitors. Use the cards in your deck to deal with the cards they have in theirs. If you're a leading brand in your space already, you may have an Ace of Spades in your hand - with a tonne of relevant and reputable inbound links. That is giving you 'points' in the game. If you're already earning a lot of 'points' in one category, you probably don't have to worry about losing 'points' in one of the others.

Think of it like a percentage. Consider the percentage of things that you're not tending to, or doing poorly, and how that relates to the percentage of things you're doing well."

Do you need to ensure that your UX is good on old versions of mobile operating systems as well as on current versions?

"This applies equally to page speed optimization efforts, as well as to new UX efforts. Google gives us several testing tools, but they only produce simulated data. They pretend to be a user. They will try to emulate slow mobile connections on old CPUs, operating systems, and browsers. They will pretend to be on a Moto 4, with a 1.6Mbps 3G connection. They try to be tough on you with the testing tools.

However, what matters is the field data, and what users actually experience. Google doesn't get that data from their testing tools or from Googlebot, but from Chrome user experience data. Google owns Chrome, one of the largest browsers in the world, and they collect data about what users actually experience on your site from there. That's how you're ultimately judged."

What is the frequency with which an SEO should be checking their mobile UX?

"It does need to be checked regularly, as with most things in SEO. You could optimise a single page, like your homepage, and maybe consider it good for a couple months before checking in. However, there will be all the other pages on your website that you should be testing and looking through. By the time you've finished fixing one, like Whac-A-Mole, there'll be another one that's misbehaving.

You should budget a little bit of time every month to digging through the mobile UX of your pages. The PageSpeed Insights tool is a place to get your metrics for a quick test, but Search Console is really where you will get the data for every page. It will separate the data for you into the pages that need a lot of work, and those that are doing fine. Every SEO should budget time every month to dig through issues that come up in Search Console."

What is something that SEOs should stop doing to spend more time on improving their mobile UX?

"Google's algorithms are getting smarter year after year. Now, we can spend a bit less time agonising over exact data analysis when it comes to things like keyword research. Don't worry as much about picking the version of the phrase that has 2000 searches a month, or the one that has 2500, but is a bit more competitive. That's where you're able to save time because Google's algorithms are beginning to understand that 'red sneakers' has the same user intent as 'sneakers that are red'. You hit a point of diminishing returns agonising over specific wording. The time spent on that kind of deep-dive analysis should be shifted over to improving the experience of mobile users."

You can find Pam Aungst Cronin over at PamAnnMarketing.com.

Stop reacting to each Google update and instead, pay attention to local audiences - with Motoko Hunt from AJPR

When you run a big, international website, it's easy to forget about the specific requirements and desires of local audiences – however, if you don't personalise experiences enough for local audiences, you could be leaving a lot of money on the table.

Motoko Hunt says: "Stop reacting to every single Google update. It is important to monitor the updates, and how they might impact your website's performance, but you need to step back and consider your audience. Don't worry so much about what Google is doing or what Google wants. Make sure that you are not overlooking how your customer base is responding to the changes you make, and whether those changes are actually helping to grow the business. At the end of the day, the SEO work that gets put into a website is there to grow the business for the company. That's the ultimate goal. We need to rethink what we are prioritising, and make sure that it's translating into business growth."

Should you focus on the way that users interact with websites, and the signals that get back to Google because of that?

"Google's perception is important, but the key is not just ranking number one in search results – it's that whatever changes you make are helping to grow the business. Your changes need to be translating into sales, conversion, or whichever measurements are important to your KPIs.

Many people have been focusing on adding more content to their websites, and in content optimization, which is a good thing. However, often companies are pumping out new content, focussed on keywords with high volume, that only slightly relate to their business. You might rank number one there, but if it's not something that is closely related to your business, and your audience, it's not going to immediately translate into business growth. Content creation requires a lot of resources, manpower, and money. After a while, not translating that significant cost into business growth is just not sustainable.

When you do keyword or topic research, organise the terms and the content topics into different groups and then prioritise those that are closer to conversion. You might see a broad, high-volume term, but if you don't think it's going to convert, put it as a low priority. Focus on high-priority keywords, where adding content will help to grow the business. We see good conversion from articles that may not have product, or service, information directly on the page. That information already exists on other pages on the website, but by adding supportive content around the product or service, you can target the different needs of your audience. People that are interested in your products might be trying to solve a specific problem, or find additional information related to the product. Content that targets these user needs can turn a potential customer into a customer."

How do you decide if a keyword phrase is likely to convert?

"You need to do extensive research on a content topic. Look at search volume, keyword tools and things like that - but mainly you should listen to your customers. Pay attention to feedback from events that you have for your customer base, or from conferences. Gather information on what your potential customers want to know, what kind of concerns they have, and what additional products they are interested in. Customer support feedback will be helpful too.

When you have new clients, particularly B2B, you should sign up for newsletters in that industry. Start reading articles to see what kind of information the engineers, manufacturers, or owners are interested in. You should be stepping forward and looking ahead. Try to see what content the customer is looking for and put that content onto your websites before your competitors do. Let them keep chasing high search volume keywords. You need to do high level market research, instead of just relying on keyword information out of a tool.

Also, create additional supportive articles, so that you can start to build a content area with multiple pieces of information that support each other. That will help sell products and services because it's what potential customers are interested in - they want to understand and learn about what is new with the business."

What's your definition of a local audience that you should be

researching and targeting?

"Your local audience is your target market. SEOs work with global businesses and global websites. A local audience, in this context, could be in multiple countries, or even multiple markets - it is the niche audience to which you are highly relevant.

Companies often do extensive research on the markets that they already know, but don't think far enough when targeting new audiences. Especially when Western businesses are trying to tap into the Asian market. They may translate the content into the right language, but they don't do any additional research to localise the content. You need to understand how your audience in Korea, China, or Japan, might be different from your audience in France or Germany. An American business may do well in Europe but fail miserably when they try to tap into an Asian market because they just copy and paste their content.

You cannot just translate the keywords you want to rank for and then optimise the content for what you find. That might not be the keyword that people in another market are interested in. The articles, topics, and information that interests that audience will be different - even the industry regulations or laws will change across countries. The market will therefore be seeking different resources."

Is it a mistake to spend time working on short keywords before you have targeted the phrases that will resonate with the local marketplace?

"Generally, you already have the content for short-tail keyword phrases and translating that content will be the first step when reaching out to new countries or new markets. The next step will be optimising that existing content, and this is when you can invest the time to target the local audience. Add other resources and new content and start thinking about additional articles for the local market. That's the right time to also carry out your local keyword research.

The localization process will especially make a big difference for a large site, where you may not be able to translate 100% of your content at once. Even a small amount of local interest research will help you to prioritise which content you should be localising first. Of course, you should start with your product and service pages, but the market research will help you to identify what supporting content is important to focus on next. You want to be localising the content that is going to have the most impact for your business."

What's something that SEOs should stop doing to focus more time on high-quality research into their target market, and identifying relevant keywords?

"When you are planning to create content strategies, don't just find new keywords with high search volume and create new content based on that. Sit back and develop a plan. Make sure that your content creation is not just based on search volume, or popular keywords, but prioritises the goals of the business. It should be based on the likelihood of the user converting, or on helping and supporting a customer to convert. Reallocate resources and budget into determining what will have the right impact. Otherwise, you spend the money and resources on generating large amounts of new content, for its own sake, that doesn't help the business to grow. This will help you to spend your time and your budget much more effectively."

You can find Motoko Hunt over at AJPR.com.

SECTION 3:

DELIVER

7 CONTENT CREATION

Create topic clusters that talk to each other - with Maret Reutelingsperger from Mobe Digital

Maret wishes to emphasise the importance of forming relationships between the different content pieces that you publish.

Maret Reutelingsperger says: "Create topic clusters which are useful for the people visiting your website, and make sure that they talk to each other."

How do you define topic clusters?

"Topic cluster is quite a loaded term. It's a phrase that people like to throw around in digital marketing and SEO quite often. All it really means is creating content that's useful for your potential buyers - the people visiting your website - and categorising it, so that search engines can easily understand that all of the different pieces of content are linked."

What's the optimum way of forming a topic cluster?

"The traditional way of creating a topic cluster is to start with a big, evergreen long-form page that is about the overall topic. That page can then bring together a lot of information and link out to many different articles that go into more detail about the topic. You will then have a long, authoritative piece of content, and lots of smaller articles about subtopics that point to the larger one. Often people feel that creating topic clusters requires a complicated strategy, and a well-thought-out plan. However, most companies that have done keyword research have essentially already created some topic clusters, by categorising keywords into different tabs."

How do you decide on the most rewarding topic cluster to start building?

"Part of that will come back to keyword research. See whether there is a lot of search volume for a particular overall topic that you want to share with your audience. Something that can also really help is understanding whether there is a lot of competition, and a lot of other companies writing about the topic. Even if search volume is lower, the content being relevant to your audience is what is most important."

How do you define relevance, and can that process be automated?

"There are ways of automating, but mainly it's a case of knowing the business that you're working with, or for. You need to understand what the goal of the company is. If the goal of the company is to sell red shoes, you can write about 'tea' as much as you like, but it's not going to help you sell red shoes. Knowing the company will help you understand what information they want to share.

Keyword research can also help focus your mind on what types of content people are looking for. In doing this research, make sure to use tools like AlsoAsked and AnswerThePublic to really find the best topics."

How do you predict the topics that people are going to be looking for in the future?

"Seasonality is definitely trackable. You can use Google Trends, for example, or you can see how certain pages on your website have performed in the past. You can also keep track of new product releases in a sector, look at different serial numbers that have been released, and think about what is going to be successful at some point in the future."

How do you make topic clusters that talk to each other?

"Often people portray topic clusters as a big page in the middle, with lots of subpages, articles, FAQs, and blogs around it. You need to make sure that it's not just a spiderweb of that big topic linking out to all these separate articles. You want to link in between the articles, where relevant, as well. If you have three different articles about trainers, on 'Best Trainers for On-the-Road', 'My Trainers Are Not Giving Me the Support I Need', and 'Best Places for Running Off-Road' for example, they will all sit under the topic cluster of 'running trainers'. They can also link to each other.

Topic clusters talking to each other is the next step. You can take the topic cluster of 'running trainers', and a second topic cluster of 'fancy shoes', and link them. It's like a Venn diagram. Although they might not seem to have that much in common, you could use some articles like 'Shoes for Any Occasion', or 'How to Go from Daywear to Nightwear', to bring them together. You don't need many articles like these, but they can overlap and link both topic clusters. That's how they can start talking to each other."

Should you be aiming to have all of your articles link with other content within their own topic clusters, and to other topic clusters as well?

"Not every article has to necessarily link to another topic. Just make sure that there are some articles in each topic cluster linking to articles in a different topic cluster - where it fits. It's better if it's not on every page, and in every article, but where it makes sense. You want to be creating a beautiful internal linking structure. Then, if you're introducing a new product, you have an existing topic cluster that you can utilise, which is already strong and already internally linking to other clusters. Even if your new products are in a different topic cluster, having that infrastructure internally might help boost them up in the rankings faster."

Is it more important to link from existing clusters to new ones, as opposed to the other way around?

"If you're talking about a new product, then yes, because it's the existing authority for each page that can help rank the new product quicker. Overall, it's something that should be reviewed relatively regularly, maybe every quarter, to make sure it's being done effectively. It's not just a case of making sure that the infrastructure keeps growing, but also that the internal links are all still right, and you're not ending up with 404 pages or 301s."

Do you have any other rules about where links are located?

"Search engines get quite clever nowadays. The main thing is to make sure that you give a contextual anchor text, so that it makes sense within the article, and it makes sense to the article you are taking them to. You should be more concerned with the context than with the keywords in the link or the position on the page."

Will content writers need to be given a lot of guidance to optimise the topic clusters effectively?

"It depends. I have some clients that are very rigorous with their briefing. You might use a template, which is great because it's always the same. That can include things like the overall topic keywords to focus on in the page, and the internal links to push to. The only danger with that strategy is that you will only ever link to already existing pages, which means that newer pages will always be behind. This is why you need to make sure that you are regularly reviewing your clusters."

What is something that SEOs should be doing less of to focus more on building their topic clusters, and getting them to talk to each other?

"One of the areas where you can save some time is very well-known: 'keyword stuffing'. It's the situation where you have extensive documents with keyword research, and you try to fit all the different relevant keywords into a page. Search engines nowadays are more than clever enough to understand the semantics, and that different phrases fall into the same bucket. Don't waste time forcing as many relevant keywords into one page as you can. When you are convinced that topic clusters that talk to each other are the way forward, and if you have any questions, please feel free to come and find me."

You can find Maret over at MOBEdigital.com.

Combine Tech SEO and Topic Clusters for maximum results - with Jo Juliana Turnbull from SEO Jo Blogs

Jo shares that, even if you happen to be a content-orientated SEO, you can't afford to ignore the technical side of things.

Jo Juliana Turnbull says: "Have a TOP site, that is Tech and On-Page together. I find that, to achieve maximum results, it's about having both elements combined. When I was working on just on-page only, I found that some sites had very poor Tech SEO, which meant that they weren't able to achieve the results that they wanted."

What are the specific aspects of Tech SEO that typically stop sites from having the success that they should?

"The main problem areas are around indexation. You may have pages that are not being indexed, but need to be indexed and crawled, or pages that are indexed and crawled that you do not want. Another issue is what we call "index bloat". This is when there are too many pages from the site being indexed and it makes your site bigger than it actually is. For example, filter URLs or internal search URLs are crawled and indexed, which we would not want. You may also have sites that have product pages taking the category URL, and if that product is found in many categories this can lead to duplicate content issues."

Does this mean that you are confusing search engines, so that they don't know what pages to rank and are not confident that you are an authority in your niche?

"Yes. You want to make it as easy as possible for all search engines to crawl and index your site."

What are topic clusters?

"Topic clusters are the way we should be doing on-page SEO in 2021 and focuses more on topics instead of keywords. HubSpot Research talked about it back in 2017, but it seems to have gained more traction these past couple of years - with others talking about it in detail. Maret Reutelingsperger spoke about it at Turn Digi, and Authoritas' Tea Time SEO.

Topic clusters are a group of pages on your site around a certain topic.

These pages link to a pillar page, which is the broad (and high search volume) topic. The topic cluster goes into deeper analysis and contain content that focusses on the longer-tail terms.

For example, if you have a site about baking cookies, one of your pillar pages would be 'chocolate chip cookies'. That's where you'll talk about the ingredients, the different types of chocolate chips - white chocolate, plain chocolate, dark chocolate, etc.

Then you will have the topic clusters that support that pillar page. The clusters are subtopics that offshoot from the pillar page and focus on the more specific, and longer-tail, areas around chocolate chip cookies. Those could be how to make the white chocolate chip cookies, how long they take, the ingredients involved, and so on. These cluster pages, or blog posts, interlink back to the pillar page."

Is this content all an early part of the customer journey, or could elements of a topic cluster target a customer further along in their buying journey?

"The pillar page is the broad topic, and it is supported by the subtopics that are written on the blog (or news section) of the site. These cluster pages focus on the longer-tail keywords. The 'top of funnel' terms are more informational queries, whereas the bottom of the funnel is further along the customer journey and will have transactional intent."

Can the issue of confusing the search engines occur on smaller sites, or is it most commonly found in big eCommerce-type sites with millions of pages?

"It can also be an issue for small sites with hundreds of pages. I think the main difference between the two is that with smaller sites it can feel a bit less overwhelming. It's easier for you to organise content more quickly on a small site than it is on a big eCommerce site."

What are the typical problems for smaller sites powered by WordPress?

"The issue with some smaller sites is the fact that not enough time has been given to the URL structures. Perhaps, for example, the products fit under the product page, but they also sit under the category page. There's a risk of duplicate content - although that can be found in big sites as well."

Can it be an issue of navigation with WordPress, where you've got tags as well as categories, as opposed to duplicate versions of pages or posts?

"Yes. One of the issues with tags is that many people thought that simply using tags would help the site, but actually you can be putting the same content under tags, categories, and products too. You can end up in a position where it's taking the URL from each tag, category, and product, which could result in duplicate content."

How do you build your topic cluster to begin with, and how do you identify what keyword phrases to focus on?

"If the site is already live, you should run it through a tool or platform. There are many such tools in the marketplace - like Semrush, Ahrefs, or Authoritas - where you can see what pages are ranking, and for what terms. This gives you a good vision of where you need to go next.

I like the keyword gap analysis in Semrush, it really helps you to see where the content gaps are. If you do not have a website, and you're starting from scratch, then you can start by looking at some of your competitors - what they are doing well and where they are not doing well. I also like to look at Google's search suggestions for specific terms.

Google Trends is a good one to use too, especially for new terms because you won't always find search volume for them. Whether it is for a new or current site, before starting the research, you need to decide as a business what topics you want to be known for and, in particular, what are the key pillar pages going to be for those terms."

Is it still important to focus on search volume when identifying keyword phrases to target, or do you need to use instinct and knowledge from within the business?

"It's important to find out what the business wants, and what they want to be known for. However, if there is no search volume, and there is a new product, then look at Google Trends and Google Suggest.

We work in an industry that is always changing – when the first iPhone was released there was no search volume for "iPhone". It's the same for a lot of new products that are coming out, and you will still want to rank for those terms even if there is no search volume at the moment. If the site is already live, look and see what the queries are, and where you have impressions and clicks within Google Search Console. If you have Google Ads running, see what the impressions and clicks are there, too."

Is it easier to try to rank for phrases that do not already have search volume, because there is less competition?

"It can be easier to rank if there is less competition and your site is a TOP site (tech and on-page SEO optimised). You should look for the longer-tail search terms, where people may be searching for something specific - and therefore may be in more of a position to buy.

If we take the chocolate chip cookies example, I might recommend targeting phrases like: "order your chocolate chip cookies" or "order homemade cookies" if you are offering home-made deliveries.

You can be more specific with the phases because it's not just about driving traffic, it's about driving the right traffic - the people that are going to convert on your site."

What sort of content do you recommend for these pillar pages?

"The pillar page is a broad topic. When coming up with the content for the pillar pages, you need to also think about the topic clusters as they will be interlinking with one another.

If we take the example of a SaaS product (We have seen an increase in the number of SaaS products over the past few years): you may want each pillar page to be a feature of that SaaS product and include a video of that feature, images, and written content for that feature.

The key is that you want to have as much information as possible for the consumer to then follow up with the next step, whether that's to sign up to the newsletter, to make a purchase, or to drill further into the site. The pillar page should link to the relevant individual topic cluster pages. These can sometimes sit under your blog or news section."

What can SEO consider moving away from to focus more time on their Technical and On-Page SEO?

"Some people want to be able to know where they're ranking on a daily basis, and they just want to tick that off the box. There's a lot more to SEO than just ranking."

In your experience, who do you find is too focused on daily ranking?

"It's a mix and it really depends on the team. There are some clients that focus too much on it because they don't know that much about SEO. It's when the clients don't know the different elements of SEO that they end up constantly asking for these ranking reports. You need to focus more on TOP SEO, which is Technical and On-Page."

You can find Jo Juliana Turnbull over at SeoJoBlogs.com.

Create something of value that your competitors can't replicate - with Barry Adams from Polemic Digital

Barry advises that you need to be creating content that is difficult for your competitors to replicate.

Barry Adams says: "It's hard to stand out nowadays in a very crowded internet, where everybody is doing the exact same thing over and over. It is about finding something that sets you apart from your competitors, makes you different, and attaches people to your brand. For example, I work with a lot of news publishers, and news is a bit of a commodity nowadays - you can read it everywhere. My UK clients ask me how they can compete with the BBC, because they are everywhere. My answer is: don't compete with the BBC.

The BBC does what they do extremely well. They produce neutral tone news at a huge scale, which you can't replicate. You have to find a different angle, and present your content in a way, that differentiates you from the BBC. Maybe it's a certain tone of voice. Maybe it's a slightly different perspective on current affairs. Perhaps it's covering things that the BBC doesn't necessarily cover.

I think you can extrapolate this example to pretty much any industry out there. It's about creating something that your competitors can't replicate, that is unique to your business, and your corporate personality. This gives you something that sets you apart."

How do you determine what that difference should be? Do you create

content for purpose-built personas, undertake some customer research, look at the SERP or just decide internally?

"This can be fairly hard to define. Some companies find it very easy because they have an internal persona, and a personality as a business. It's about translating that personality into content on a website and social media channels that engage with the audience. You don't want to necessarily force this too much. If a company like Vodafone is suddenly starting to go 'cool and hip' - that won't jibe.

It has to be authentic, or appear to be authentic, to what you do as a business. I have seen companies specifically create sub-brands for that purpose, and you'd be surprised to know who actually owns some of the brands you think are really cool. They're often spinoff brands from big established companies so they can adopt a specific persona.

I think it's very easy to get lost in building personas and doing market research. The problem is that you end up with recommendations based on stereotypes, which don't accurately reflect the people in your actual market, or you end up with an artificial personality. You have to be wary about this. It's better to see what you are like as a company, rather than trying to fit what your market is trying to do.

Look at your own organisation and try to determine what you want to achieve as a business. Nowadays, corporations are expected to be more than just personality vacuums - and pure capitalist enterprises. They should have a social and fundamental purpose. It's about trying to be confident enough as a business to adopt that purpose and use it as your external personality in everything you do. SEO and content are just one facet of this."

How do you encourage more people within the organisation to be better promoters of your brand?

"I don't think we should be obliged to do this, and a lot of employees just want to do their work and go home – which is fine. Companies shouldn't always try to encourage employees to be more than employees. However, every organisation has leaders, and they don't have to be senior managers. Leaders are people who take ownership of specific things and carry a certain message. It's important the business listens to these leaders at all levels of the organisation, because they set the corporate personality and the corporate culture.

Sometimes you find these leaders may not be the right fit for your company, in which case you have a different problem to solve. You don't want to let people carry on unchecked. On the other hand, you will have people who represent you on social media who have a very strong voice. This voice can be a benefit to your business because it aligns with what you as a company. However, they can also do something you don't want them to do.

Do politics and SEO mix?

Politics is very polarising nowadays. I have a nuanced perspective on this because I don't think that companies should always be activist organisations. It's okay for a company to not be political. You can have a corporate personality without having a political stance on current social issues. It's okay for you to draw boundaries. As a business, you can have a certain personality and culture you want to promote - that makes you unique from other companies doing the same thing - but stay within your boundaries.

Basecamp is a good example here. They've made a very strong position and said, 'We're not going to talk politics and only talk about issues that affect us directly. We'll talk about IT and internet regulation, but we're not going to be internally talking about politics.' At the time, there was a big backlash, but it was fairly brave and probably the right thing to do. They knew exactly what their position and personality was, and they knew what they didn't want it to become. They drew a line in the sand and made it very clear to their employees where that line was. Some of them disagreed and left the company, but others felt relieved as they knew what they can do and what they can't do.

It's probably an exercise that a lot of companies should be doing, so that they don't run into that problem later down the line. You don't want to suddenly discover your company has morphed into something the employees don't recognise anymore. You don't want to end up like Enron, where fraud and deceit were part and parcel of the company culture because that's what they've been doing for decades. They never took that step to look at themselves and ask, 'What do we want to become?' This is because nobody was monitoring what was happening with the business."

Brand value is extremely important, but how do you select content that's likely to resonate with your target market? Should it be long-form, video-based, or something else? How should you launch your piece of content?

"A lot of this is trial and error. You'd be surprised sometimes about what works and what doesn't. As an example, I work with news publishers, and I have strong opinions on news and publishing, and how Google works in the news ecosystem. A couple of years ago, Donald Trump was tweeting about how Google News was biased against him, and I thought that was nuts. I wrote a detailed 2,500-word post about potential bias in Google's news algorithms and how it might impact what they say, and what they don't show me.

I was really proud of that piece of work. I published it literally within a day of Donald Trump's accusations, but it didn't really get any traction. This surprised me because I thought that it tapped into my target market. It was what people wanted to read, and what I do as a consultant. That was lesson one.

Google ranked my Google rant

A couple of weeks later, I got triggered again. This time, by Google sending out announcements about Accelerated Mobile Pages via Search Console: Google thought the AMP version of an article didn't match up to the real version of an article. I wrote a very angry blog about Google AMP – it was really just for therapy, getting something out of my system that made me angry. I had no real expectations for the blog.

Unexpectedly, this post went mental. It got posted on Hacker News, it went viral on Reddit - it crashed my hosting for a short period of time and I had to upgrade to a better hosting package. It even ranked first for 'what is Google AMP'! I was totally surprised, and it was a lesson learned as well. It told me that people expect that contrarianism from me - which I've always done. That's why I named my business 'Polemic Digital'.

Both examples were an educational experience, both for myself as a business and for how I advise my clients. Just try stuff out, see what does and doesn't resonate. Sometimes you'd be surprised, maybe it's video content or long-form content. Maybe the type of content will surprise you – whether it's educational, inspirational, or argumentative. You can never be sure what will gain traction in your target market and what makes people resonate with your business."

Can you formalise this trying-out process?

"Probably not, because it will become artificial. You can have a content calendar, of course, and have a structure to how you produce content, but there needs to be flexibility built into it so you can react to stuff that happens. Ultimately, your content needs to come from the heart. This is why you need a corporate personality. It has to mean something to the content creators, or it's not going to have the same impact, and could feel like a PR stunt.

You have to be open to taking a risk as a business and sometimes putting the wrong message out, as long as you say it from the heart and with emotion. Too many companies are too focused on avoiding potential Twitter storms, and they become very insulated and bland. There are so many bland companies that, by taking that risk, you will automatically stand out from your competitors. It's okay to court a little bit of controversy. Have the confidence to step outside of your comfort zone as a company, take those risks, learn from your mistakes. Be more open and honest about what you are, and what you're not, as a company."

What's then one thing an SEO can stop doing to spend more time taking risks and creating content your competitors can't replicate?

"A lot of the standard tasks are just treading water, or even a total waste of effort and resources that has no meaningful impact on the website's performance in search. I'm talking about everything on the monthly checklist: writing one blog post a week, fixing the internal redirects, and making sure every page has a proper title tag.

The big impact stuff is the difficult stuff. That's what you should spend your effort and your resources on. All the smaller, standard stuff doesn't really do anything. It doesn't actually improve the website or traffic. You need to put those things in context. Yes, you need to write content, but make sure it's great content that's actually worth reading. Yes, your website needs to be technically sound, but nobody cares about those last two dozen internal redirects. Google doesn't care about them either. Focus on the stuff that has an impact and actually moves the needle."

You can find Barry Adams over at PolemicDigital.com.

Never forget that your job is to help searchers get the answers that they're looking for - with SEO Specialist Freelancer & Consultant, Heba Said

Heba shares a reminder: that your job as an SEO is to help searchers get the answers that they're looking for.

Heba Said says: "Never forget that you're doing SEO for the user, or searcher, to find their answer. When you're looking at the website, you need to know what this website is about and how it's helped users when they search for it."

What does it mean in practice, to help searchers get the answer that they're looking for?

"It means that you need to make it easy for a user to find your website, by making it easy for the search engine to find your website. I look at every project from the perspective of a customer, who needs to know how this website will help them in their life - or answer their query. You need to know how your website can reach your users. At the same time, you need your client to get revenue from what you're doing. You need your user to come to your website, and then convert. Before thinking about SEO on its own, you need to know that SEO is part of a marketing funnel that ends in sales. Look at every step of the customer buying journey when you're determining the questions they are likely to ask, the answers you should be optimising for, and the call to action to end this journey."

How do you determine which questions are the right ones?

"Always look at the SERP; it answers everything. From this, you know how the customer is reacting, what they are asking, and what they need to know. Always put yourself in the customer's shoes.

Keyword research is also still very important. It is not just about looking at individual words, it can be questions and everything about the website. Your keyword research will come from the SERP, your tools, People Also Ask, Google Suggest, etc."

How do you decide which phrases are the best to start with if you don't have high search volume?

"I often just go for it. Even if it's low search volume, after a while the impression gets higher because the content itself is full of the information that people are searching for. You don't need the title to be 100% high-volume keywords. The content itself is very important and can contain a lot of good answers for questions. Even a volume of 10 is worthwhile. Those 10 people are your important clients, because they can become 10 Customers."

How do you financially measure the success of this?

"Include CTAs and track them on Google Analytics. That's a very good way to measure how much revenue you are making for a website; how many users are signing up or making a purchase. You can measure the return on investment from there."

How do you decide what type of content you should be publishing?

"Stalk your competitors. First, look at your competitors in the SERP to find out where they are ranking, and how they are ranking - what they are writing about. You need to see if it is informative, clear, transactional, etc., and then you can imitate this in your own way. If your competitor has a video answer to a particular question, then that would be a good signal that that's what you should be providing as well.

You can determine your competitors based on the SERP, and by looking at who is ranking for your target keyword phrases. It can also be other businesses that do a similar thing to yours. It depends on the queries that are relevant to the project."

Should answering questions be the only part of your content marketing strategy?

"Sometimes people don't ask questions because they don't yet know enough about your service to ask questions about it. You need to write about your service as information, and then answer questions as well. It should be 50/50."

Answering questions within your content can also work for pillar pages. If you're looking to create a big, authoritative piece of content about a particular topic, you can link smaller pages to it that answer questions around that topic. I have done this before and received a 1000% traffic increase. I started with my pillar page and I made a blog. Then I wrote about that page but in smaller pieces of content, Questions and Answers for example, and linked them to the pillar page. We got much higher traffic and went from ranking on page five or six to ranking in the top three."

How regularly should SEOs be researching the types of questions to be answering on their sites?

"You should be planning for three months ahead, so it should be done quarterly. You might find that old content on your website needs to be optimised, or re-optimised. It doesn't always have to be new content. You need to check every three months to consider what you're doing with your old content and what you need to add."

What do you think about the current trend of search engines trying to answer questions directly on the SERP?

"It is definitely increasing, and it's going to continue into 2022 and beyond. As SEOs, we can take advantage of that. It's possible to generate some traffic by branding those answers. Some people need more than just an answer, they need to know more information. When you provide that initial answer for them, you can generate a lot of traffic. Also, if Google is starting to write an answer for something, that's mean that people are asking that question.

There are a lot of opportunities. You can see what questions exist on the SERP, click through, and see if the answers are truly relevant. If they link to articles that just don't provide the right answer to the question, that's a great opportunity for content in your niche."

Once you've optimised your pages for answering user questions, how do you go about linking those pages to get them to rank higher?

"You need to find high-quality links. It's been a struggle for two years now to get very high-quality links. You need to have a good relationship with people - you can't just post anywhere, because of Spam Score and the updates that Google is doing regarding linking. You need to find a website with a good reputation and Spam Score, that's high quality and is writing good content for people, so they are drawing high levels of organic traffic for keywords. When you reach out to them, reach out with your own quality content, so they will want to share with you. The SERP is good for findings those high-value websites, but you can use tools as well. Ahrefs is particularly useful for looking at backlinks."

Why is Google Search Central so helpful and what can you learn?

"Seven years ago, it was very hard to be an SEO, but now everyone is talking about it. Even Google has a video channel that tells you what to do to rank. It didn't used to be like this. You need to take advantage and pay attention to them. Follow Google Search Centre, on Twitter and on YouTube, to see what's happening with SEO.

Google can actually help you to do SEO. You need to put your own thoughts into it, but they will give you good pointers and explain the guidelines that you have to follow. You do need to be educated enough to know what advice to take, and where you can be clever and play with the guidelines. Although, they will always be sensitive with some of their information.

Twitter is particularly helpful because it's very up to date. There are also many SEO twitter chats that you can get into, like the #SemrushChat on Mondays. This is a great way to get ideas about what you're doing. They talk about content, keyword research, technical tips, and much more. The SEOFOMO newsletter by Aleyda Solis is also very good. It's gives the latest updates on SEO and will keep you on track."

What's something that SEOs should stop doing to spend more time making sure that their content is answering the questions of their users?

"You don't need to spend as much time link building. Stop trying to get as much links as possible because sometimes content can win over a link."

You can find Heba Said at Twitter.com/HebaSaidSEO.

Answer your customers' questions efficiently - with Brianna Anderson from BEAST Analytics

Brianna advises that it's essential to answer your customer's questions efficiently – it's not about the volume of content!

Brianna Anderson says: "To answer your customers' questions efficiently, you first need to figure out what questions your audience is asking. There's a lot of different ways to do this, and you can use a lot of different tools to help you. The best way to figure out what questions your customers have is to ask them. SEOs actually skip this step a lot and think that it's not totally necessary, but there are a lot of ways to crowdsource what questions your customers really want answered.

You can do this on social media. You can ask on Twitter, or maybe you have a Facebook group with a lot of your top customers in. This is a great place to go in and ask them what information you can provide that will actually be beneficial."

Is it important how you phrase the question or the heading and the initial text? Are you targeting keyword phrases within your answers, or is it simply about providing great UX and service to your customers?

"At the end of the day, our job as SEOs is to make sure we are creating content that's good for buyers first, and then the bots second. If your

190

customers ask, 'How do I get my microphone to work on my computer?' You don't need to go to Google and say, 'How do people look this up?' - your customer just told you how they ask the question!

Have more faith in the customer. Yes, you're going to track this over time, and maybe do a little A/B testing, but always lean on the customer's words whenever possible to create content that actually helps them. Long gone are the days where you can just decide on the keyword, throw it into a blog post with similar keywords, and hope that it's helpful. You need to focus on actually answering the questions that your customers have."

Historically, we used to have one page for all FAQs with just a few line answers to each question. From an SEO and usability perspective, is it better to have distinct pages for each answer that you're going for?

"All of this goes back to answering questions efficiently. If you think it's going to be too convoluted for the user, then that question needs to have its own page. Maybe make a blog post providing the answer, or a guide. You don't want your customer to have to scroll to find an answer or sort through other information. FAQ pages get a little dicey, especially if they don't have a search function built into them. I tend to stay away from FAQ pages, and try and build those questions into pages that make the most sense for the answers."

Are we aiming for these answers to be indexed by search engines? Is that the second reason for doing this, or is it solely for users?

"Yes, that is the secondary reason. You want to be indexed, and this is where we get into answering customers' questions efficiently. The goal of Google, or any search engine, is to get a searcher to their answer as quickly as possible and help them get on with their life. That's what people are doing. 80% of the time, they're Googling on their phone because they're on the go, and are trying to figure something out quickly. If you answer questions efficiently, Google's going to see that users come to your page. They get their answer, and they're able to move on with their day."

Does it matter where this content resides? Is it important that Google displays the answer on their SERP, and the user is satisfied without

actually visiting your website?

"There are pros and cons to each. I'm trying to encourage people to look at the featured snippets, or the rich features, that make the most sense for them. So, if it's a How To guide, make sure you have a video in there, because you're still able to brand that. If Google just puts your video in front of people on the search engine result page, you might not have the same branding power as you would if your URL was under there, but you're able to start building that relationship with the customer."

In his book, 'They Ask You Answer', Marcus Sheridan advocates forming your whole content marketing strategy around answering questions from customers and creating videos and other long-form content to achieve this. Do you agree with this approach?

"Absolutely. The process that works for me is starting with that long-form piece of content, such as a video or a blog post, and using that to create additional content. You can create tweets of quotes from the video, make shorter clips out of it, make a blog post out of a video, quote graphics - there are so many opportunities.

Remember, SEO was a piece of a puzzle, and it all goes together. When you create tweets that link to this video later on, you're still getting users to that video - whether it lives on your website or YouTube. All this, in turn, will lead people to your website. So, if you really think the process all the way through, it's going to help your SEO."

Should we ideally be looking to create videos for every single one of these questions? Or is there a better way of determining what answers should be video or text?

"I look at the SERP. If you look at the search engine result page, and Google is showing you a carousel of videos, or even just one huge video and then the carousel underneath, you know that Google has done the research. They've watched the query long enough to decide that they should be throwing videos into this search engine result page. This is a very good cue telling you that you need to create a video to answer the questions efficiently, because that's what Google is looking for.

If you don't get tons of searches for a specific query, consider how easy it is to convey your message through written word. Sometimes it is easier to show people how to do something. If it's not a very mature query, you might make that decision yourself - make the video and hope for the best. The worst you're going to do is create more content that you can distribute. That's not a bad place to be."

Is it a good thing to have all this duplicate content in many different places? Should the content be published on social media or your chatbot?

"I would encourage people to share the content in multiple places. You do need to have a home base, and in most cases that's your websites, as this is the only thing you actually own. It's unlikely, but YouTube or Google could go away tomorrow, so it's a good idea to have all your content in a home base that you own.

I don't worry so much about duplicate content when it comes to videos. Facebook videos are being indexed and shown in the search engine result page. Obviously not as much as YouTube videos, because Google doesn't own Facebook - so they're not going give them the same priority. Also, I don't really worry about tweeting quotes from blogs and then sending people to the blog post, as duplicate content, either.

The big one we see a lot is people publishing a blog post and then going to Medium and publishing the same blog post. Personally, I wouldn't go that route. Your best bet is making chunks, so maybe publishing a guide on your website and then publishing a chunk of that on Medium. You should at least delay publishing on Medium by a couple of weeks, just to make sure that Google knows who the original publisher was. Even still, I veer on the side of having your home base, and really focusing on that."

Is there a good general way to funnel people asking questions towards becoming a prospect or a customer? Could this put them off, as they're not actively looking to buy?

"Marcus Sheridan tells the story about how one of the first people to come into his shop, after he created all of that content, had visited almost 100 pages before they walked in. They knew exactly what they wanted, how much it was going to cost, had all the information they needed to make the decision, and were completely ready to buy.

Your content is going to build trust and authority with your audience. The next step is to eventually try and get them closer to the funnel. One of the best ways to do this is to have the related articles underneath the original blog post. Once you do that, you're pushing them down the funnel with every article. Call to actions should naturally be within your article, without being salesy, but you definitely want to have those CTAs in there. A cool way to do it is having a chat bot on your site that can welcome back returning visitors, and remind them they can get in contact with sales if they need anything."

What if your boss starts questioning why you are targeting keyword phrases with hardly any volume?

"I would tell them that it's definitely quality over quantity. Also, it's looking at quick wins. The people asking questions that only get 50 searches a month might be closer to the buying stage than those using a keyword that's looked up thousands of times a month. You have to look at the intent of each keyword as well."

What's something that SEOs should stop doing to spend more time focusing on the quality questions that you suggest?

"We are currently seeing Google rewrite title tags, and we know they rewrite meta descriptions a lot as well. I would encourage people to lean into automation in places that take up a lot of time. Handwriting title tags and meta descriptions for each page can be very time-consuming. Instead, find a structure that works for your website and let automation do the bulk of your work. Of course, you still need to go in and check to make sure everything's looking good - but this will free up a lot of time."

You can find Brianna Anderson over at BeastAnalyticsCo.com.

Originality is overrated, don't force it if it doesn't come naturally - with Rejoice Ojiaku from Incubeta

Rejoice highlights that you don't have to be completely original with the content that you produce.

Rejoice Ojiaku says: "You don't have to constantly think of new, innovative ideas around content, especially in SEO. There is so much content out there that you can repurpose, or focus on different aspects of, to take further. You don't have to constantly be creating brand new, amazing ideas for your website. It can be a waste of time, especially if you're not that creative. You don't have to be creative; you just have to think differently.

Look at what the competitors have, and how you can recreate it. Perhaps you can repurpose one of your articles with a different subject matter from the same topic, or in a different format. If you presented it as a blog, you could repurpose it as an infographic and add a bit more actionable information. You're still engaging with your consumers with the same content, just from a different angle."

How would you convince enthusiastic content teams to focus on existing content?

"Look at what's doing well on your website and what's not. If it's not broken, don't fix it. Your content isn't broken, you just have some content performing well, and some that's not. Look at the content that's not performing well. See what keywords you're using, and how you've presented that content.

Your content team may be excited to pursue creating new content but channel this excitement into looking at what you already have and using it differently. Think about how to engage a different side of the consumers. Perhaps your content is targeting consumers that are in the awareness phase of the buyer's journey and you could repurpose it for users in the consideration phase. By making small tweaks, you can make it more relevant for people further down the purchase funnel and start increasing conversion rates.

Think about the intent of your content and how you can target a new demographic or audience. That can still be exciting, because now you have to research. Look at what's currently happening, what consumers are doing, and what content is already out there. Feed that excitement into your own content and get your team excited to think about things differently."

How does an SEO decide on what content provides the best opportunity to focus in on?

"Go to the site and look at what's ranking on other pages besides the first and second. As an SEO, you're lucky to get first and second page but look at the ones that are maybe third and fourth. Those pages can often be linked to your high-performing pages. If you have an article that's coming up on the third or fourth page, look for ways to refer to those through things like internal linking. I love seeing 'related posts', 'you may be thinking of', or 'more on this topic' underneath a blog post. That's how you interlink your content together.

To find these opportunities, you can also think about keywords that are doing quite well and can be linked to those pages. Find where you are missing those key words in your blog posts. If you have a new set of keywords for an idea you have, look to utilise your existing content, and start linking your pages together. Make your content relatable to the pages that are already performing."

Can you use a plugin to do that linking for you, or is it better to manually decide what content is related?

"It's better to do it manually because that shows a bit of thought. Plugins are great, but they often just make links based on the title, or general topic. If you do it manually, you're actually looking at the body of the content. Different topics might be related to different posts that a plugin won't pick up on.

I always say that any task will be done better if you go in manually and give it some thought. You will be able to see when one paragraph links to an entire article that you have on a particular topic. Your consumers will appreciate it. They may want to find more information on a tiny insert that you spoke about in one article, and you can link to a whole article talking about just that."

What type of content should people be looking to publish nowadays?

"The long-winded content form makes it harder for consumers to read. Break it up. You might be able to embed videos and things like that into it as well. Consumers love tutorials; they love watching people explain things. It's hard for a consumer to engage with content that will take 30 minutes to read, no one really wants that. If you have long-form posts, with tables of contents, break those up. Have several different blog posts, that are related to a generic topic and go into more detail elsewhere. Then start linking these posts together. You will start to build your authority and the trustworthiness of your site. It will also keep consumers on your website, because they will want to continue and learn more."

Would having 10 linked blog posts of 500 words be better than having one 5000-word article that contains the same information?

"In my experience, yes. A lot of consumers will leave the page if the content is too long. As a consumer, you don't want to spend your time reading a 5000-word blog post just to find one particular answer, on one particular aspect of the topic. Your website can make it easy for your consumers - break that information up into 10 different articles and take them directly to the sub-topic they're looking for. Even though it's separated, you can still link it together and have nice interlinking going on."

What KPIs do you use to measure the success of this?

"It depends on the type of website you have. If you are selling a service or a product that you want people to purchase, then you will focus on conversion. Look at whether or not your articles are leading to a purchase. If your website is more informative, then you want to look at traffic and retention - how many people are landing on your page and how long they are staying. That will give a good indication of whether this information is being received well. Embedded sharing helps to keep track of whether your content is being shared to other people, and how. These metrics will allow you to gauge the interest of your consumers."

Should you be thinking about managing where your content is published, and aiming for it to appear directly on the SERP?

"You can target SERP features like knowledge cards or the carousel, but I don't always advise to focus on this. You have to think about the experience first, before you think about the search engine. If you're trying to always hit SERP features, your content may not appear organic, because those features have been your sole focus.

Ultimately, you need to focus on your consumers: are they going to appreciate this content? Are they going to find the answers they are looking for? When consumers do find answers, the algorithm will pick up on that and factor it in. You do still want to structure your content. Use schemas and great linking, so that Google can see the structure and understand the content. Eventually it will happen. However, your focus should be on trying to answer the questions of your consumers."

Is Google not looking for original content over updated content that's been around for a couple of years?

"I don't think Google always focuses on fresh and new content. There is still a value in repurposed content that is different. Your old content might not be answering the questions that users have now. Change up what you're talking about. Think consumer first, and Google second. Counterintuitively, Google will find value in that. Google doesn't look at it as fresh content vs repurposed content - it looks at what content is answering the user's question. That's the best content you're going to serve, whether it's fresh or not. Serve the most relevant, purposeful, and valuable content. That value can come from repurposing what you already have."

What is something that SEOs should stop doing to focus on auditing and repurposing their existing content?

"A lot of SEOs want to focus on very high keyword volume. They're not bad keywords but stop fixating on them. I know it can be daunting because clients will always push you towards those keywords. Understand that long-tail keywords may not carry that volume, but they still carry purpose, intent, and great visibility. You can know the intent of keywords better when it's long-tail than when it's short-tail. The 'When', 'What' and 'How to' phrases tell you exactly what your users are trying to do. When focussing on high-volume keywords, you might struggle to think about what content to create. With more specific keywords, the user is telling you exactly what to create, because they are telling you exactly what they want to know."

You can find Rejoice over at Incubeta.com.

Focus on actual expertise as part of your content strategy - with Lily Ray

Lily advises that it can be very effective to incorporate your own personal experience into the content that you create.

Lily Ray says: "It's more important than ever for SEOs to focus on actual expertise when it comes to creating content on their websites.

By this, I mean the expertise of whoever is involved in producing or reviewing the content, to make sure it's demonstrating to Google that it comes from people who have the proper credentials to write about these topics. As opposed to, perhaps, copywriters or freelancers who don't actually have the real subject matter expertise."

A few years ago, Google highlighted authors of different articles and gave you an opportunity to add a little snippet within the code to demonstrate that you are the author. What are they doing now?

"I think they are trying to bring back something similar, but not necessarily in the same search features that they've had in the past. For example, 'rel=author' was deprecated. Now, however, they're launching some new features surrounding who's in the Knowledge Graph, and potentially linking up those Knowledge Graph experts or authors with content they've written in organic search. That's one interesting area.

Also, pay attention to projects like Google Cameos, where experts can contribute short videos in the Knowledge Graph. They've also published some documents lately that make it very clear you should list your authors for transparency purposes and have a dedicated bio page for them. They're clearly going down this mission of enhancing expertise, authority, and trust."

What are some of the best ways to give you an opportunity to appear as a knowledge panel?

"Generally speaking, it's best to have some type of creative work that you've been associated with, such as publishing a book or music album, or have some type of very noteworthy events taking place. Google My Business is a great starting point for a lot of businesses. There is a whole running list of the different databases that Google pulls from. Some of them you wouldn't expect, but it's a way to shoehorn your way into the Knowledge Graph. I would recommend looking at Jason Barnard's work to help you with this."

Is this a strategy that SEOs working in large organisations should be thinking about, and maybe research the potential authors within the business to ensure all of the authority is taken back to the website?

"Yes. It's the job of an SEO team to ensure that whoever's producing content, and has their name associated to the content, has proven expertise in that area - that's conveyed properly throughout the website. There's not always an opportunity to use every author as a dedicated expert, but maybe there are experts you have on staff, or expert reviewers that you can hire. It's also really important to bridge the gap between the SEO team, who might work with this set of content writers, and the actual experts at the business - who should probably be more involved in the content creation process. Some of the more effective and successful SEO campaigns in the past couple of years have the expert's name associated to the content they're creating, even if they've just reviewed what other people have written."

What does this mean for the type of content the expert is able to write? Is the expert pigeonholed into just one niche type of content, or are they able to write about different forms of content freely and easily, and still take authoritativeness from Google?

"It's becoming increasingly difficult to be a jack of all trades. You should focus on the areas where you're an actual expert and produce content that stems from your own experiences, and your own real expertise. For example, some of the best performing content on gardening was from a guy that does gardening all day. He has a podcast, and the company transcribes his podcast - and that's the content.

You didn't have to do any keyword research for that, you are just using what the expert's encountering in his day-to-day life. That content does very well because it adds a lot of value and comes from a real place of expertise. There are so many people doing SEO and content creation nowadays that are reverse engineering search volumes, topics, and everything else based on the existing data. That doesn't account for the real contributions experts can provide in the content."

If you need to reach out to people outside of your organisation, is there a way of ranking authorities to get the best possible person writing for you?

"There are tools that basically surface those types of insights. If you're using one of these tools, that has a database of expert writers and contributors, it'll say what areas they're experts in, where they've gone to school, and what their credentials are. It's obviously very important to pick the ones that have expertise in your category.

It can depend on the topic. For example, if you're doing 'Your Money or Your Life' pages (YMYL), you do want to look for people who are willing to put their name behind it, and maybe link to the other places they've been cited. You want them to have built a personal brand for themselves and to be trusted as experts. If you encounter a writer who's not comfortable using their name, you have to be careful. Google's made it very clear they care about transparency regarding who's writing content. The more sensitive the topic, the more important it is to work with somebody with a clear brand and expertise."

Does this mean you'd be better off working with just one or two people, and getting them to write multiple articles, instead of reaching out to lots of different people to write just one article for your site?

"Yes. One of the analyses that my team works on is overlaying author names on top of SEO performance. A lot of the time, you'll see a small subset of authors outperforming the rest, and they write on certain topics. There might be some other authors not performing as well, writings about other topics. Maybe this is not necessarily only because of their writing, but because your website could be perceived as authoritative in certain areas. If you venture too far outside of those areas, I think Google has a perceived authoritativeness that it assigns to certain sites. You're not necessarily able to write about finances and internet security on the same website - unless you've been doing that for a very long time. It's becoming increasingly clear that Google's focused on these niche areas of expertise at the domain level."

What about frequency? If you've got someone writing for you, are you better off going for 5,000-10,000-word articles, or is it better to have a more frequent publishing cadence?

"I don't think it's one or the other. It really depends. If you're a news publisher, or someone trying to get lots of traffic from somewhere like Google Discover, then frequency is very important. Those areas of search are pretty short-lived in terms of how long you can rank.

On the other hand, if you're writing science or health content, frequency is perhaps not as important as the accuracy and quality of the content. One of the big mistakes SEOs make is arbitrarily creating the cadence of how often new content needs to be created. In reality, maybe 80% of your content is not doing anything for the site. Why not double down on the 20% that's doing well and make improvements to it with updates? This might result in less content than we're used to, but Google's already not indexing and not ranking a lot of content that's already out there."

If a writer's personal brand gets associated with a business, but moves on somewhere else, will the authority they build up for the website stay?

"As long as they're willing to keep their name associated to the content after they leave, it should be fine. Writers come and go, but their brand doesn't - especially if that's what they do. If you have a chef contributing to your recipe website, they could have contributed 20 great articles with a lot of links and social media signals, and they've done well for the site. Just because that chef left and now contributes to other sites, it won't work against you in any way. It just shows you work with high-quality content contributors."

To measure success, is it a case of looking at conventional SEO metrics - at organic traffic for the created articles - or is there some other way?

"It's getting tricky. We should look at the rankings of the content and how much traffic it drives, but it's becoming more challenging to evaluate the performance of content. Google is getting so much better at determining intent. In some cases, people are too focused on rankings. You might have moved down three positions, but that's not to say your content writer is no good. It could be because Google determined there's a different type of intent for the query. It's really important to make sure that the keywords you're focusing on are actually associated with the type of keywords that matter for your business."

How does this fit in with your overall SEO strategy? Is this something that should be planned on a quarterly basis, or does it need regular tweaking?

"This is an ongoing work. We do this type of work ongoing for a lot of our clients. One of the biggest problems we see is that they've produced too much content over the years, and many of these sites have been doing SEO a certain way for so long. The result is that 80% of their content is not performing, which could equate to tens of thousands of articles – and Google's grappling with having too much content. There's always work to be done to ensure you're focusing on the right areas."

What should you do if an article isn't getting any traffic? Get rid of it, or redirect it to a more relevant page?

"It's a decision you have to make based on the data. If there's an applicable article or category that makes sense to redirect it to, then it's probably better for SEO. Don't fake it just for the sake of trying to redirect it somewhere if you don't have that corresponding piece of content.

Another thing we run into is when a publisher wrote about way too many topics in the beginning. They might have some sensitive, political or emotionally charged content that is not going to do well in search. In those cases, you don't always want to redirect it somewhere else, because this doesn't get rid of the problem. We have examples where clients don't want to be associated with certain content anymore, and we just let it 404 and get rid of it."

What should an SEO stop doing to focus more time on creating highly relevant content

"SEOs tend to build out a process where they produce X number of articles per month, using the same keyword research tools as everybody else to determine the highest volume version of the keyword. This is how they write that article. They are not thinking about whether they have anything new or unique to say on the topic.

Google's going to see your content as the same as everybody else's. Can you change your content creation process to consider what you are doing that's different? You can be at the forefront of leading this conversation, and this might involve working with people you're not used to talking to, such as customer service. Using these resources to curate a content strategy is going to be far more effective than trying to reverse engineer what will drive the most traffic - it's just too competitive. Nowadays, there are too many SEOs doing the same thing."

You can find Lily Ray over at LilyRay.NYC.

Focus on semantic SEO and natural language processing - with Koray Tuğberk GÜBÜR from Holistic SEO & Digital

For Koray, we've already got to a point where we can trust the machines to be producing at least some of the content for us.

Koray Tuğberk GÜBÜR says: "Natural language generation is a new concept that basically means generating text through AI, and the next step of this will be natural language optimization. At the moment, a lot of people are using the GPT-3 model for natural language generation. GPT-3 is an AI that is able to generate highly convincing text, and incorporate keywords into the copy. However, as more of the text online is becoming automatically generated, it will decrease the quality threshold for search engines - because the web will become more bloated. 70% of the content on the web in the last three years has been generated by AI, and this percentage will only increase in the future. Because of this, semantics is becoming even more important in content creation. You need to be giving clear context, using clear sentence structure, and communicating the relationships between entities using attributes."

How does an SEO add meaning to their content? Are you suggesting that they use AI to generate more content?

"I would suggest using our own brains first, because any kind of tool can prevent you from learning about semantic SEO (SEO with meaning built into the words used in content). Projecting meaning, creating a contextual vector, or giving a contextual relevance between entities, can't be done naturally, because we are also semantic creatures. I suggest that every SEO creates proper content briefs for the authors first. Then, they can start to perform tests for question generation, answers matching that question, and fact extraction. There are a lot of algorithms you can use, like RoBERTa or BERT, or data sets and free language models for text generation, at the moment."

Do you think AI is at a stage where it can produce the type of content that users will love and think a real human being has written it?

"Yes. It might not be perfect, but in the near future - maybe one or two years - it will get better and better. I still believe there will be a human need for organising the content. If you don't create proper parameters in your function, and if you don't use your parameters in a proper way, AI might also generate irrelevant text. They might not know some answers like humans do, especially when it comes to reviewing a reviewable entity - sometimes it is a product, sometimes it is a kind of service. AI might be biased, based on language, the data set they use, or on the human feedback. I believe there will always be a need for human assistance. Soon the content writers could be the assistants for AI, and they will use AI for generating more text."

Is Google getting better at understanding the context of everything that's written on a webpage?

"Definitely. Google have announced two different algorithms, MUM and LaMDA, and they also have some other language models they didn't announce, like SMITH, KELM and REALM. Since they are able to understand human language in a much better way, they have started to explore new contexts - the contexts that are not answered yet. That's why they also created the Question Hub that has been integrated into the Google Search Console because there are lots of questions that are not answered yet. The other thing is that some questions are not answered in different languages – so they're trying to make all of the information accessible for all the languages.

When it comes to semantic SEO, people should focus on the concepts and the meanings, not the phrases or the languages. If you focus on one language, you will just get that entity's one-sided feature or profile. Search engines gather their information from all geographies, audiences, and languages. If you unite this information, you will be able to understand a concept in a better way.

This view leads to a second phase, which is the search activity, or search behaviour, of the users. When you start to understand them in a better way, it means there will be a lot of different contextual layers. You can use variable portions in the questions to explore these new contexts. There are lots of different subtopics in every area, and at the moment, they are starting to organise all of these contextual domains with an idea."

What does this mean for keyword research - is it still relevant in 2022?

"It is, but it's about how we use it. To be honest, I don't use it for my content briefs, I usually use it for improving relevance. When it comes to semantic SEO, using synonyms, or different variations of a phrase, is important. Let's say we have a query with two million documents with different levels of relevance. When you have millions of documents for a query, you will see different types of co-occurrence matrices, and you will start to realise there is a query document template, and different types of pure clusters.

Once you're able to extract entities and concepts, you will start to realise there is a user behaviour pattern. When you extract all of these themes, it will start to be about actual entities, concepts, interest areas, or search behaviours, more than keywords. You can still use keywords but try to use them to improve relevance, instead of creating the content brief. If you want to create a content brief that can rank in Google SERP, you should use these types of connections based on entities, attributes, semantic role labelling, or lexical relations - there are lots of other terms that can be used."

If an SEO was responsible for creating this content brief for each new article on the website, how do they decide the length, and what needs to be included in the content, to deliver the ultimate answer to the question being asked?

"When it comes to creating a content brief, you should try to understand the prominent attributes of an entity. Semantic search engines will start to parse entities, and their queries, and recognise that there are some attributes. These attributes are mutual for some certain types of entities. For instance, countries have capitals, presidents, regimes, populations, and currencies. These are the root attributes. Based on your question, and your source's context, everything can change.

Let me give you an example from Google's MUM announcement. If you search for 'hiking mountain Fuji', they will start to give your possible contexts there. If you ask me, there are three main contexts. One is hiking on Mount Fuji. The second is hiking. And the third is hiking on a mountain. Based on your source's context, you will need to create different types of topical maps and content groups. If it's about hiking mountains, you will need to include all the mountains in Asia or Europe. If it's just hiking, it will include all sorts, like, hiking books, backpacks, shoes, podcasts, and tips. If it is about Mount Fuji, the context will be entirely different, as will your topical maps and content groups. When it comes to creating a design, it's actually about your topical map and your source's context."

Does this work equally well for product pages, when you just want to talk about something very specific that you're selling?

"It definitely works. When it comes to SEO semantics, it's not just about one type of content. At the moment search engines are SEO semantic. For products, the search engine creates a line of products and related brands.

When it comes to reviewing or explaining how to use a product, these types of questions can be used in the content section. When I try to create content for a product, I usually check off the popular eCommerce sites because I can extract dimensions and attributes for the product from there. Furthermore, I can extract angry rants from the reviews themselves. All of this product information can be used within the product page.

ECommerce SEO should also be about the layout of the webpage, as well as reviews and product explanations. This should also be included within the semantic SEO, because Google talks about how meaning can change based on the layout of the webpage. If a product page doesn't have a proper order, or placement of components, the context can be shifted - even if the content is perfect."

What's one thing that SEOs can stop doing to focus more time on semantic SEO?

"I see lots of SEOs who add random leads into content. They usually add internal links for the sake of adding them and think: 'the more, the better'. They use links just for referencing other pages, so that search engines will think it is endorsed and reliable content that can be related to its sources. I suggest you stop doing this.

If you want to use internal links, create a contextual bridge between two pages - internal links should have relevance between two pages. They need to have a connection. Try to use your internal links within the main content, and do not add extra links just for the sake of it. Also, only link to other sources if it makes sense. Be very careful about this too. If you link to an external website that mentions or links to your competitor, you might end up losing your competitor in an indirect way. Majestic's Link Graph can really help with this, as they will show you the millions of indirect links within the pages."

You can find Koray Tuğberk GÜBÜR over at HolisticSEO.digital.

8 LINKS

Review the tiered links to your website, and the tiered links to your competitors - with Bill Hartzer

Bill shares that you should be aware of the links that point to your links, not just the ones that point to you.

Bill Hartzer says: "We need to get past the fact that we've just been analysing who is linking to us. We need to open our eyes and understand that the internet is not just one link, or a few 1,000 links, but literally billions of web pages. How do we find not just the links that are linking directly to us, but also links that are part of the overall web, that are influencing the majority of websites? There's a whole network of websites out there, it's not just one website, linking to another, then another. There's a path that we can follow. The internet is a very complex place with lots of links - that's what we should focus on going forward.

Try to get past that time where you're only focusing on getting a link from one particular website. In a lot of cases, you should be looking at your competitors' links and thinking, 'I need a link from that website because my competitor has that link.' Let's look at Tier 2 links - who's linking to whom. Let's think bigger picture,e and think about the internet as a whole."

Are you talking about multiple tiers of links - who's linking to your competitors' sites and who's linking to them - or are you talking

about going even deeper than that?

"There are 100 or so major influencer websites, such as New York Times, Wikipedia, Google, and Yahoo, and they link to other websites. You need to understand who they're linking to, and how they're influencing the web. Why is Wikipedia such a powerful website? Why are they getting links from other influential websites? There are so many other opportunities, even if you narrow it down to your particular topic or niche. Sure, there are standard links in your industry you'd like to get - but let's start to look beyond just the influential links you're getting. Let's talk about who's influencing the influencers."

If you can't get a link from the top 100 sites, should you then get a link from someone they are linking to?

"Exactly. If you can't get the Wikipedia link, get the next best thing - which would be a link from someone who is linked from Wikipedia. You can go to the Wikipedia page, where you would like to have the link, and find the existing external links on that page. Then, investigate who is linking to those websites that are linked from that Wikipedia page.

When we talk about tiered links, Tier 1 would be a link from Wikipedia directly to you. The next best thing is Wikipedia linking to another website that then links to you. That would be Tier 2. You're in the link chain, so you're still essentially linked to Wikipedia, because they are linking to somebody that is linking to you."

How might you determine the authority value that Wikipedia is passing on to you via the other website?

"You could look at Trust Flow numbers and try and figure that out, but I don't think that's necessarily something to spend a lot of time obsessing over. Lately, I've been more concerned with whether the web page that's linking to me is on topic and appropriate. For example, if it's a news website, is it about news? If they wrote an article about digital marketing, then I'd want to be linked from that article, rather than a page about football linking to me. It's not necessarily the website - it's the actual page and copy that has more value at this point. It needs to be an on-topic link rather than having a certain authority number on that particular page."

Have you looked at Trust Flow or some other metric as a way of determining how much of it flowed from second to third-tier links?

"When I think of these numbers, I remember how many people manipulated those PageRank values. There was an old trick you needed to be aware of as an SEO. If you redirected a page for a certain period of time to a higher PageRank page, such as a news website, your PageRank number authority score would improve, and remained better even after you removed the redirect. I've always questioned authority numbers. Nowadays, you can't do this level of manipulation, but we have to understand that the number may not be completely correct.

There are all sorts of other considerations as well, such as location of the link. Does it matter whether the link is buried in the footer or is right there in the middle of the article? I'd rather have a good prominent link in an article, with a Trust Flow of 50, rather than have a link from a 78 that's buried in a list of 100 other links on the page. There are all sorts of what-ifs, and other factors we have to consider."

How often should an SEO be deep diving, using a tool like Majestic, to analyse who their second and third-tier links are, and determine their link acquisition strategy?

"It comes down to how often you are working on your link strategy. I recommend a thorough link audit every six months, or at least every year for smaller or non-competitive websites, to understand what's going on. If there are major ranking changes, you're going to need to dig in and see what's going on. For a regular process of looking at your link profile, I would recommend at least once a month. You need to look at links in general, not only the links you've acquired, but Tier 2, Tier 3, and Tier 4 links at the same time. This has actually become part of my daily routine."

What's something that SEOs can stop doing to spend time on improving their own second, third, and fourth-tier links?

One of the biggest changes in the past five years has been search engines understanding a lot more about natural language. For example, 'attorney', 'lawyer', and 'solicitor', are essentially three different versions of the same word. In old-style SEO, we would create additional pages for each term, which takes up valuable time. Now, you don't need to be doing that - you can create content that will basically be one page.

This same concept for keywords flows into the anchor text of links. If you want to rank for 'London lawyer', you might want to get some other links with other versions of the same word. Making this change is going to free up a lot of time. You don't have to spend all this time creating a page for every single keyword, and every version of it, including the singular and the plural. Stop creating pages for every single keyword that you uncover, and start trusting Google to actually deliver your page - even though it might not be traditionally optimised for that keyword phrase."

You can find Bill over at Hartzer.com.

Focus on businesses, not content creators, when it comes to link building - with Bibi Raven, aka Bibi, the link builder

For Bibi, it's important to build relationships with other businesses, when it comes to building links.

Bibi Raven says: "A lot of people focus on content creators, bloggers, and influencers when they're creating prospect lists. These specific types of prospects have been outreached so much. It makes more sense to look at businesses that share a part of your audience and make a connection with them. Reach out to them, build relationships, and create content that serves their audience - and helps them engage with their potential customers."

Many businesses will already have partnerships with other businesses, is the best approach to leverage the existing contacts you already have?

"Yes, people leave those on a table a lot. However, if you do some lateral thinking and think about your audience's motivations and triggers, you can also find new angles to your prospect list. I think a lot of people already have connections with other businesses directly related to their products. If you do a bit of more creative thinking, you can find even more businesses you can connect with."

Should SEOs reach out and make these connections?

"I would focus on marketers or the founders of the business. I wouldn't go to support or tech; I'd just focus on the people responsible for the site's content, or the people who lead the company."

Are business leaders generally receptive to what you're trying to say? Do you lead with a link-building discussion, or are there better ways to secure the link you're looking for?

"You need to be transparent about your intentions because you don't want to waste people's time. If they fully understand your motivation, you can save a lot of time and just mutually collaborate with each other. This is a good thing for both parties. However, you do have to think about their goals. Instead of just thinking of your needs, you have to be a step ahead and think about what's in it for them. This is where a lot of SEOs make a mistake and only focus on getting the link. Your starting point should be what's in it for the other business."

How do you build a mutually beneficial partnership without simply just exchanging links?

"I'm not against link exchanges if they make sense, but it shouldn't be your whole backlink profile. Put it this way, I wouldn't turn down a reciprocal link. However, if you look for other ways to do it, then you have to think about their goals. If you're reaching out to a marketing provider, you have to think about their objectives and offer content they can use to help sell to their audience."

Can you provide some examples you've seen of building a great quality link as a result of reaching out to a business founder?

"Let's say I'm a garden furniture site, and I want to get links from other sites that are relevant to gardening. However, I don't want to reach out to bloggers, because they're all going to ask for money. Instead, I can build a prospect list consisting entirely of people that provide water sprinklers. Then, on my site, I create a resource about water usage in a garden. This is something the water sprinkler system manufacturer can link out to for their audience – so it's mutually beneficial for both parties."

One approach is to interview the top 10 water sprinkler experts and create content to generate links. Is this still an effective strategy?

"I've only done three expert roundups - and they all bombed!"

Do you mean people weren't willing to link because they're interviewed in so many other places?

"Yes, they weren't linking back at all. Maybe at the time, it was such an overused tactic that people weren't impressed by being mentioned somewhere. It could also be the way I executed it. I know other people are still using expert roundups, so there must be some good in it because they must be getting links back. I'm not against a lot of link-building strategies, I just think you have to take the approach that's closest to your own skills and personality. A strategy is only as good as its execution."

Why do you not want to focus so much on content creators for linking building nowadays?

"It can still work if you find a right angle, and you are very persuasive, but the problem is that link builders have reached out to so many content creators and influencers that they've become very jaded. These prospects will now ask you for money. That can be okay, but it can be risky if your whole backlink profile is built on paid links, and those people are selling left and right to everyone. It won't be a very competitive backlink profile because you're not getting the links that your competitors aren't getting. Shift your focus to look into places where not everyone is looking."

Is it a concern that you're reaching out to people who might not be comfortable with creating a link, or what a link means in terms of value?

"It's not a huge problem. You may have a couple of unlinked mentions, but you can always go back and hunt after that link. At the same time, so many brick-and-mortar businesses now have a website - especially after the impact of COVID. Business owners are now more likely to understand the value of SEO - so they understand more about links. Even if they don't, you can educate them and explain how this will help them."

How often should link building happen? Weekly, quarterly, or bigger projects every six months that can be forgotten about for a while?

"I have clients where we paused link building for a period of time. For others, we ramped up the link building. We also do the same number of links continually for other clients. The results are so varied that I don't really have a good answer to this question. It's dependent on so many other factors. If you have decided to do link building, you should probably do it continually, because you will learn so much about link building if you do it consistently.

Doing it all the time also allows you to start seeing great opportunities around seasonal things, current topics, and developments in your niche. Don't just do link building at the moments you feel you need to give your site a boost."

Is it not important that link building matches the cadence of content publishing? Is there a danger that getting lots of links, despite not publishing content for six months, might look artificial to Google?

"I don't know if this is a danger. I either do link building for content that already exists on your sites, or I do guest posts, so it's not dependent on your site. It's just dependent on the quality of the content in the guest post. A guest post is an extension of your own content, it's just on another domain - so it's still part of content marketing.

I try and use my common sense. If you have evergreen content, then you might be picking up links all the time after you start ranking for a keyword. We did a piece on the science of kissing for a client last year - but now it's suddenly starting to pick up links. Is that going to look unnatural? I have no idea - but that's what's happening naturally."

Absolutely. I'm aware of pieces of content that have been published five-plus years ago that are still exceptionally popular, because they're great pieces of content. It's completely natural for people to still be recommending them to their readers.

"Yes. The only issue is that you don't know what is going to become popular. You need to create 20 pieces, and only two of them are going to get these results. You've got to be okay with taking risks."

If an SEO wants to spend more time on higher quality link building, what's one thing they can stop doing to free up some resource?

"Stop just finding link-building prospects based on keywords. Many SEOs build their list by looking for sites that are ranking on the same keyword they want to rank for. Use a couple of different prospect angles. You could look at businesses that are catering to your audience in a similar customer journey. Let's say you have people that are interested in gaming, so they might also be interested in VPN. You can reach out to VPN sites to get links from them.

Another angle is to look for people that have a correlated interest. If you're looking at people who are interested in keto diets, they might also be interested in gardening or sustainability. It's not your direct customer, because they don't have the same search intent you're trying to rank for, but they are in the same realm. Explore relevancy and don't just go directly for your main keyword. Stop building up the same type of links and start thinking outside of the box."

You can find Bibi Raven over at BibiBuzz.com.

Cut reliance on cold outreach and start thinking about assets that drive inbound links - with Stacey MacNaught from MacNaught Digital

Stacey recommends that you build high quality, original content assets - *before* you try to build links.

Stacey MacNaught says: "Stop relying so much on cold outreach. Invest more time in assets that generate their own links over time and can run in the background, while you crack on with something else.

Cold outreach does still work, and people can use it to great effect for landing links. However, with every month that passes, it becomes less and less efficient. Everybody's sick of having inboxes full of it, it's only a matter of time before you're having to send 1000 emails to land one or two decent links. It has diminishing returns as a tactic."

What kind of assets are ideal for driving great links?

"Researching what to produce is very much an SEO task. You need to do keyword research and find out what people are looking for. Statistics content, templates, and free downloadables are particularly effective. In this instance, we're not looking for people who are going to come to the website and buy something, the search intent is different. We're looking for keywords where the search intent implies that they are looking for a resource, or a source to cite. In many areas, those are statistics queries: 'obesity statistics', 'basketball statistics' - pretty much, pick a word and add 'statistics'. You'll find that the top three results for those keywords have natural links pointing back to them, because 'statistics' is the type of keyword that somebody looking for a source to cite is typing in.

It's the same with templates and downloads, and every niche has its own keywords. You need to find keywords where you think the user's intent is to find a source to cite, and then go off and improve it. Look for the keywords that sites already rank for and look at their backlink profiles. That's how you can verify it. A lot of statistics, data pieces, research templates, and things like that are great for driving links."

What specifically does that type of content look like?

"It depends. We just launched an 'insomnia statistics' piece three months ago for a client centred on the UK. We looked at the current top five in the UK for 'insomnia statistics' and analysed their strengths and weaknesses. They were all very in-depth, so we thought ours should be in-depth. Four of them were using US datasets, so we then knew that we could improve relevance by focusing on a UK dataset. Also, the most recent data set was three years old, so we could make ours better by being current. That piece was 1600 words or so, with three different data points, but we've done these with as few as 800 words and as many as 7000. The length of the content will vary from topic to topic.

Eyeball-test the SERPs. We all fall back on tools a lot, but the output of any tool is only as good as what you put in. When analysing content that you're trying to compete with, if it's only a few pages, you need to look up. There's no substitute for a human being looking at what's good, what's not so good, and what you can improve.

It's worth investing time in. Our 'insomnia statistics' piece now has 52 referring domains and it's only three months old. Our first link was from The Times and was established within two weeks with no outreach whatsoever. The initial time investment saves you from time spent on cold outreach later."

Is Google getting better at distinguishing whether data fits a user in a specific country?

"In some areas it's getting better. However, what we see from Search Console for these pieces is that many people search for the location specifically. When the Times journalist found us, our only impressions were from very niche queries, like 'insomnia statistics UK 2021' and 'how many people in the UK have insomnia in 2021'. For users like journalists writing for a UK audience, they will specify that they want UK data. Google is getting better at surfacing local data, where it thinks that might be a requirement, but it's often the user that specifies. For some data the location doesn't matter as much.

It does come down to how much data is available. What we were competing with from the UK was an Aviva study from a few years ago. It had geographical relevance, but it hadn't been updated in years. That was what we had available to us."

Do you do some initial outreach to try and make journalists aware of your content?

"If a site has enough history, it will typically start ranking by itself. You start to rank for long-tail, obscure versions of keywords, build the first few links, then those will help to cement the bigger rankings for headline statistics queries.

For a brand-new site, or one where things are not ranking particularly well, then there are a few options. You can do PPC on big 'statistics' keywords - just until you have the first few links. You can also pull a list of everybody who links to the page you're competing with and contact them. For business websites, or smaller websites, that have published an article more recently that links to older data, get in touch. Tell them you've got a brand-new dataset that answers the question in a different sort of way or has a new take on it. If it's a news website, it's often not worth it – it's okay for them to have archived news using old data on the site, so the chances of them updating a four-year-old article are negligible.

You only really need a couple of links. Give it a couple of weeks to rank by itself. If you come back and it hasn't established any visibility, then try PPC and getting in contact with people."

Should PPC be hyper-targeted to individuals or are you targeting traffic that's relevant to your keyword phrases?

"Mostly we focus on keyword-centric targeting. If someone was typing in 'travel statistics' or 'UK staycation statistics' you've already established that those keywords imply somebody has the intention of finding a resource. You can literally 'Exact Match' target a handful of statistics queries.

Advertisers who are looking for sales, and are potentially negative matching, are using non-commercial queries. Someone typing in 'skiing statistics' is unlikely to be booking a ski holiday tomorrow. Therefore, these are typically low-cost keywords. If there's enough volume to 'Exact Match' on it, then you may only need to do the PPC for a week or two before you've built up a couple of links. Then you can switch it off."

What's an ideal link nowadays?

"Try and replicate what might happen in a natural link building scenario. Google still advises against doing anything with the sole purpose of link building, and we can assume that a Natural Link Profile would be a site that doesn't have to link build. Look at big sites, market leaders and brand leaders like publishing companies. Look at where they're establishing links from.

Consider a market leader in supplements, like Holland and Barrett. From their link profile over the last two years, you can see that they're naturally building links from press for product, press where they give expert commentary, health information assets on their website, and from other business and health websites. Their links are typically international as well.

To compete with a brand like that, you need a link profile that is as diverse. You need links to product (usually achieved by PR), links to content assets (usually achieved by statistics work) and links to the homepage (where it's been covered because of something that's been said or done within the business).

Look to replicate what the market leader has, in terms of where links are coming from and what type they are. Mainly, think diversity. What looks like a giant red flag is having all your links coming from a subsection of mum bloggers on a Facebook group running any old content for $30 a time."

Is there an ideal number of statistics-based articles that you would want to publish per year?

"For most of the campaigns that we work on, we're doing anything from three to twelve a year, rarely more than that. Sometimes it comes down to how much scope there is. If you're in healthcare, you could write a statistics or research piece on millions of things. If you're in a more niche sector, there may only be five or six obvious areas with link building opportunity.

Once you've got an established bank, even if it's only five or six pieces, you can invest your time in going back and updating them annually - as opposed to starting again. If you're starting entirely new, you don't need many. A handful of really good pieces will have you covered in most cases."

What is something SEOs should be doing less of to focus on driving inbound links?

"Stop writing posts for random guest spots on random sites. Even if you get an email back from someone saying they'll run your content, think of the time that goes into producing that article to get published on someone else's website, for a link that could be negligible. Stop writing content for small outlets you've reached through cold outreach. Too many companies are spending significant amounts of their copywriting resource doing that. That same copywriting resource could be producing bigger, better assets for your own website."

You can find Stacey over at StaceyMacNaught.co.uk.

9 KEEP AN EYE ON THE SERP

Use the SERPs as your best and most up-to-date SEO tool - with Omi Sido from Canon Europe

Omi shares that the SERP isn't just the place that sends you traffic – it can also be a wonderful source of competitive intelligence.

Omi Sido says: "Use the SERPs as your best and most up-to-date SEO tool. Obviously, we all want to rank well in the SERPs, but we often confuse rankings with SERP visibility. Ranking number one doesn't automatically mean that your website is visible to the user, or even in the number one position in the SERPs. Imagine you're searching for 'running shoes'. First, you're probably going to have adverts in the Shopping slider, then 3-4 traditional PPC adverts, then the Google Map with local stores highlighted, and then the opening times and ratings for 3-4 local stores below that. Your tools might be telling you that you rank number one for running shoes, but your position in the SERP is more like 9 or 10. That situation is even worse on mobile."

Is it still worthwhile trying to rank number one in organic search results?

"Ranking number one is still worthwhile, but you need to know the SERPs, and target what the user is actually seeing. If you want to compete for 'running shoes', that user is unlikely to scroll all the way to position 8 or 9 - they will hit something before that. They are more likely to click on a slider advert or on one of the local shops. Instead of just trying to rank number one, think about what the best position will be for that keyword and target the SERP instead. You need to decide whether you just want to rank number one, or if you also need to target slider ads, rich snippets, or local shops."

Do you need to regularly check the SERPs, or are there tools to help you decide which elements to target in each SERP?

"Tools can help you but at the end of the day, you still need to manually check the SERPs. There's no way around it. It's not just keywords that you need to consider, there are a lot more elements that can only be seen when you're looking at the SERP itself.

Imagine you're on page two and you want to rank well on page one. You check the backlinks of the pages ranking well on page one and see that they have an average of 20 links. Only looking at this information, you might assume that acquiring 50 links will automatically jump your page to number one in the SERP. However, just looking at the number of links is misleading. The companies that rank well in your niche may actually be ranking because they have good authority. If you don't look at the SERP, and you don't see that authority, acquiring 50 links will not help you in the rankings. A bot will compare your page with your competitors and see that there is something wrong. In this case, it may be the content, the performance, or the technical health of your site that is stopping you from ranking well. Of course, you can't check every single SERP manually, but you can definitely check for your top 10 keywords.

I was working for a travel company a few years ago, and we were trying to rank pages in South American countries. We started by acquiring national links for a page in Brazil, but we were not ranking. The only reason for this was because our links were from all over the place, and our competitors had acquired local links. The companies linking back to them were local companies with local pages. There is no way to see this kind of information in the tools, you have to go and see for yourself.

SEOs are always unsure as to whether they should have short or long text on the page. Neither of the answers will be correct without looking at the SERPs. If the first five pages have short text on the page, it's unlikely that you will rank well with long-format text. If the first five pages have well-written long articles, it's almost impossible to for you to outrank them with short and direct answers. It's a manual process, but the only way to truly know whether your page will rank well is to go to the SERPs."

Should you check the SERPs in Incognito, or should you be looking at how it appears for different users?

"Both ways are valuable. If you're in London, and you want to know how a page will appear in London, then check it while you are logged in. If you're in Ealing, and you want to rank a web page in Ealing, check the SERP on your mobile. This will help you to see what the user you are targeting may be seeing. However, Incognito is, in some ways, the best view of the SERP - because it's neutral."

How often do you need to analyse the SERP results?

"For your top 10-20 keywords you want to be doing SERP analysis every six months. You can get a lot of inspiration from this analysis too. If you're trying to write an article on 'How to Run the London Marathon', a tool can give you keywords that are ranking well, but the SERPs can tell you a lot more. Check the People Also Ask questions and answer them all in your article. Even better, use those questions as your H2s. You can get so much information about what people want to know for your topic, that no tool can give you.

If you're analysing the SERPs every six months, you're going to know exactly what the people in your niche are talking about, not just what the tools are telling you. The keywords from your tools may or may not be good for you because they are only telling you the search volume per month. A lot of tools don't even tell you if it's an informational query or a transactional query. Companies will invest a lot of money and expect a 3000-word informational article to rank in a SERP that is transactional. They cover all the key words from the tools and are surprised that it doesn't appear. All they had to do was check the SERP.

You have to understand Google's point of view. We are not the customers; we are just SEOs. We're trying to push our pages, but it's the people who click on those pages who are Google's customers. Google is thinking about them, not us. Google doesn't care if you've included a search keyword in your copy that has a massive search volume, it's deciding whether your page belongs in the SERP. You need to look and see if it does. You're not catering for Google; you're catering for the people who are your target market on the SERP. Their actions determine how the algorithms perceive your site to be relevant or irrelevant for those queries. However, you need to know how Google sees those potential customers, and what the different SERPs will look like for different searches."

What is something that SEOs should stop doing to spend more time looking at SERPs?

"At the end of the day, we are all guilty of talking about rankings as if it's the ultimate goal. The ultimate goal is to bring in revenue. You may be ranked number one, but with 10 adverts above you in the slider - the normal ads and everything else - your page may not be bringing any revenue. Ranking number one can be almost pointless in that regard - people will still not hit your page if it doesn't suit the SERP. As SEOs, we often spend too much time reporting on ranking every day, thinking that if we manage to rank all our pages in position number one, then we've won. You may be ranking well, but you need to know that what you are doing is actually good for revenue.

I'm not advising anyone to stop what they are doing, but I am asking SEOs to start looking at the big picture. Looking at SERPs will take more time, but it is time well spent. You need to see things from Google's points of view in order to see that your efforts will have the result that you're looking for. Remember that the end goal of SEO is actually to bring value to the business rather than just to report on rankings."

Omi Sido is Senior Technical SEO at Canon Europe.

Brand will become a more important part of the user journey, as well as Google's understanding of your company - with Gus Pelogia from Teamwork

Gus implores you to incorporate brand building as part of your SEO activities, to maximize the number of clicks you receive from the SERP.

Gus Pelogia says: "It's getting more complicated to rank on Google; there are more ads and fewer opportunities to get the click. This is why it's so important to focus on your brand. Even if you're not the number one rank, the more that people that recognise you, the more clicks you're going to get."

Why is brand more important? Is it because there's more competition, it improves conversion rates, or other reasons?

"It's both of these reasons. Competition is getting higher, and we now see brands competing on terms that are not really commercially related. You need to be at the top, even when people are doing that 'top of funnel' research. Protecting your brand, and being there every step of the journey, will become increasingly important. Google's also looking at entities more and more now. If you can connect your brand to a specific topic, that will help you rank and help users recognise you as the proper answer."

What are some of the key reasons for focusing on a brand?

"You're going to get better CTRs and you're going to get your knowledge panel. I would start by researching your own brand and seeing what type of results you're getting back. Look at people's questions and the reviews that you have. Are you replying to them – even on other websites? Are you listed on the places where people are doing their searches? It's important to be visible in all of the steps of the journey. Now that it's getting harder to rank, as Google shows less results and more featured snippets, you don't want to just rank with your own website - you want to be present even when people are looking at a different blog or website."

Do you believe that a brand should be actively asking for reviews?

"I see no problem in actively asking for reviews, and it's an important thing to do. You may you have an automated process so you can ask everybody. It is also important to protect the reviews you already have. If people are unhappy about something, how did you deal with it, and were you honest? Bad reviews are the ones that matter the most, because they show how the company handles these issues. If you see businesses that only have a five-star review. or everything's great, that can look a bit dodgy."

Is it potentially useful to include reviews on your own website, or are you only talking about reviews from a third-party website perspective?

"I would have more belief in reviews from a third-party - but you can integrate this on your website. If a review looks dodgy, but you can validate it through a link to an external website, then you'll be provided with enough trust. It's good to look at other reviews as well, and not just the angle the company's trying to give it to you."

Is there much SEO value using things like schema to mark up review information on your website, to hopefully get some additional Rich Snippets, search results and a higher click-through rate?

"There's definitely value in these things, although a lot of people do it wrong - they just toss a number there and try to manipulate them. The right way is being honest and having an automated system. Even if your reviews went down, just pull up the most up-to-date information. Don't just say, 'five stars' for everything. That sounds fake. Every company will have some unhappy customers, and not all happy customers will give you a five-star rating. Being realistic is the key."

How do you use content on your website to help educate Google about what your brand does, and what it represents?

"There are lots of directions you can take. Your homepage is a great place to explain who you are, along with your Wikipedia profiles. Yes, they are hard to manage, but at least make sure the information is actually correct. Google is also looking into lots of external websites, such as Crunchbase, or LinkedIn. Make sure that all your bios across the web are up-to-date, and don't contain conflicting information.

I like to map all of the social profiles that I have, and a good starting point is to Google yourself, or your company. You'll be surprised at the number of websites that have your name, bio, picture, email, and social handles. There are tonnes of places beyond Facebook, Instagram, and Google My Business where information lives. Do your best to connect all of these places and make sure the information is correct. With more evidence, Google can increase its level of trust in who you are and the topic you belong to."

Is it important to use exactly the same sentences in each social channel, to give Google more confidence?

"There are mixed opinions on this. I'm fine with using the same text, as long as it accurately reflects how you want to position yourself. You don't need to duplicate your content across all the channels exactly, but be consistent about who you are and what you do, and link all the social platforms as much as you can."

How does this drive measurable SEO success? As brand isn't quite so tangible, how does an SEO explain the value of what they're doing?

"It's not as straightforward as the clicks that you get, but you can measure this by looking at your branded searches - are they increasing? You can also show if you have your knowledge panel, and if your social channels are there, and whether you are seeing more conversions on your blog. If your company's on position five or six, but people started recognising the brand, CTR starts increasing across the board as well.

It's not as straightforward as measuring leads or clicks, but there are ways to measure it. You could look at the referral links as well - are you getting more traffic and conversions through these? It's not going to show up directly as SEO perhaps - but you know it's a consequence of your good SEO work."

Do you think it's good practice to incorporate your brand name at the beginning or end of page titles, or meta descriptions?

"Yes, it's always a good test to do. I always put it at the end, but I've seen cases where people decided to put in the front and their CTR improved. As with everything in SEO, I would not just take the word from someone else. You need to do your own test. Change the titles, put your brand in front and see if you start getting more clicks. Although, it can be difficult to isolate things if Google is changing titles."

Is this focus on the brand something an SEO should be doing every week or as a one-off project?

"Not every single week, that's for sure, but there is always an iteration you can do. Maybe there's a new structured data type you can include, or a new page that doesn't include all the elements you need. Keep monitoring the panels, and Google's understanding of you as a brand connected to your competitors.

This is all easy to test. Search for your brand. or your competitors' brand. and see if they show similar brands below your knowledge panel. There's some ongoing work to be done, but not as much as you do for links or content.

I really like to do research on my own brand and see what type of results are out there. It's hard to own all of the space, and sometimes Google will put other websites on the list. Make sure that what's in there actually reflects your company. Sometimes it could be something simple. Maybe your YouTube profile is showing on your top five, but you forgot about that profile ages ago, you're not posting videos, and your company description there is incorrect. Make sure you are presenting yourself the way you want in all those places.

Even when people know your brand, they will research in lots of other lost places, such as Reddit and Amazon. Think about the journey they will take and take note of the steps they'll make, and the things that matter for them. Do lots of research here, but not with an old-school SEO mindset of thinking about ranking."

What's one thing SEOs need to stop doing to spend more time focusing on brand?

"SEO should stop bothering to follow links to save PageRank. Firstly, you're losing that PageRank regardless of whether the link has been followed or not. Secondly, Google is making their mind up about the value of links anyway. Perhaps you shouldn't spend a lot of time trying to save that information if you're leaking out anyway. Also, I wouldn't waste time bothering to 'nofollow' my internal links - even if it's a page that doesn't have a reason to rank, or wouldn't show up in searches."

You can find Gus Pelogia over at Pelogia.it.

Educate Google about your brand - with Jason Barnard from Kalicube

Jason agrees with Gus that brand is key – and shares that you need to communicate what you do to Google as clearly as possible.

Jason Barnard says: "You need to educate Google about who you are, what you do, and who your audience is. That is the fundamental building block, on which everything else can be built."

How do you let Google know who you are?

"An important factor to consider is that Google has probably already gathered information on who you are from what you have on your site, your profile pages, and your LinkedIn page. However, you probably haven't communicated that information sufficiently, or consistently enough, for the machine to truly have a grasp of it. Not only does Google need to understand who you are, what you do, and who your audience is - but it needs to be confident in that understanding."

How do you ensure Google has that confidence?

"Think of it like educating a child. A child doesn't understand a concept when you teach it straight away. Education requires multiple elements, one of which is repetition. However, repeating the same thing in different ways can be quite confusing, and the same is true for a machine. The trick to getting the machine to become confident in its understanding, is to repeat the same thing on multiple platforms in the same manner. If you say one thing on your website, you need to say the same thing on Crunchbase and LinkedIn.

Another important factor is language. If you speak to a child using words it doesn't understand, or in a language it doesn't understand, there are going to be problems. Google's native language is schema markup. You want to repeat the information on your website using schema markup, because this explicitly restates what you're already saying, but in Google's native language. That's phenomenally important. However, schema markup is only repeating it once. You need that repetition from all sources that Google is listening to."

Is it important to have schema markup on other pages, as well as the About Us page, or is that the most important by far?

"It depends. Google is trying to identify the Entity Home. John Mueller talks about this problem as reconciliation. It's a very simple problem that we, as the 'responsible adults', can help to solve. The information about you around the web is fragmented and contradictory, so it's very confusing. You need to identify where you can allow this machine to see the defragmented version. Google is actively looking for this Entity Home to reconcile the contradictory information to the version from your site.

Google will tend to go to the homepage, because the homepage is the most powerful, but that's not your best bet. You want to attract Google's attention and drag it away to the About Us page. There, you can be factual about your key information in a way a machine can understand. On the About Us page, you don't need to try and impress, or direct, a human audience in the same way you do on the homepage. There, you can state your key information on the page, and in the schema markup, and you can point to all the corroborative sources such as, LinkedIn, Crunchbase, and Wikipedia. All of these places will confirm who you are, what you're doing and who your audience is."

When it comes to giving Google confidence about what you do, will you need to bring in other content sources outside the About Us page?

"You can state what you do in simple terms. For example, Kalicube is a company that provides consulting services in the SaaS platform for brands who want to optimise their brand SERP and improve their knowledge panel. That states the basics, but what I actually do is much more detailed and nuanced. Kalicube is part of SEO, it's got the brand SERP, it has different rich elements like video boxes, Twitter boxes, and knowledge panels. There are a lot of nuanced details. That is what the rest of the site will describe, where you might potentially provide a solution to Google's users - which is the trick for SEO.

On your About Us page, you are giving the basic core message of what you do. The rest of the site gives the detailed messages that inform where Google might be offering individual specific solutions. John Mueller recently said that your content that doesn't drive traffic is still useful, because it helps Google to understand what you do. Informative pages, like large FAQ sections, may or may not drive traffic, but I'm fundamentally convinced the existence of these pages is supporting evidence for Google. It is evidence that you are experts, you're authoritative, you're trustworthy within your industry and that Google can trust you."

Should you maintain pages in your site, that don't get traffic or have any external links pointing to them, because they could still provide a useful service to Google?

"We have a client called Ubigi, who do an eSIM offer. We built up an FAQ section for them and we did no link building at all. Now, we outrank Apple for the short head term 'eSIM' with no links at all. That indicates that we serve Google's audience with answers to questions around eSIMs, in a way that shows we are truly an authority. Apple, on the other hand, is hedging their bets because they do a lot of other, different things. You can definitely rank for short head terms with no links."

How do you get Google to know who your audience is, and can that be done on-site?

"You start by stating what it is that you want the Google 'child' to understand. The 'child' will then get the corroborating information, to understand and become confident it has understood. If I state who I am to a child, then the teacher says it, and then the policewoman says it, the child has understood and is confident. I'm coming at the same idea from a brand perspective. If you want to build a solid SEO strategy, or even a digital marketing strategy, you need that fundamental understanding from these machines.

It is Google principally, but it's also Facebook, Apple, and Amazon. These machines are all trying to understand the world, and they're all going about it in a similar manner. You need to make sure they know that you are the authority, and you are telling the truth about yourself. That will apply to everything you're doing, on every page. If the machine understands what's on the page, what it offers to the user, and who the audience is going to be, then it can offer you up as a solution to its users when they're searching relevant terms."

What is the process that leads to Google adding your information to the Knowledge Graph and triggering a knowledge panel, and what is the value of getting one for your business?

"The knowledge panel, from a human perspective, is significant because when somebody searches your brand name, they see a big panel full of information - you look impressive. You look more impressive than if you don't have one. You can consider it to be part of your 'Google business card', which is what your audience sees when they search your brand name.

Google's reason for putting up a knowledge panel is that they bring information together from all around web, they defragment it, and they put it up as a reconciled version that they have built themselves. The panel shows the information that Google has understood about a company, and it is being presented so that a user can read it. The user doesn't need to click through to multiple results to get all that information. For Google, the panel simply makes their users' experience better.

Your aim is for Google to represent your brand in a manner you think is relevant, helpful, and valuable to your audience - and is truthful about who you are and what you do. You need to take control, you need to manage it, and you need to educate Google. The Knowledge Graph is Google's understanding of the world - its 'education'. Your responsibility is to look after your tiny corner of the internet. Once Google is confident it's understood what you are teaching it, then it will trigger the knowledge panel.

Another factor is probability. If you have an ambiguous brand name, then getting that knowledge panel to appear becomes quite difficult, because the probability that a user is searching for you, specifically, is not as clear as it is when you've got a completely unambiguous name.

For the Knowledge Graph, you are looking at understanding and confidence. For the knowledge panel, you are looking at understanding, confidence, and probability."

How do you go from being a recognisable brand to being a brand leader? What takes Google from being confident about who you are to thinking you're one of the best at what you do?

"I've noticed that confidence in understanding is a big driving force for Google. If a child is learning something new, they don't go into the playground and shout about it if they are unsure. However, if they're incredibly confident about what they've learned, then they shout it out so the whole world can hear. Developing Google's confidence in its understanding will already put you a step ahead of the competition.

Another factor is what I call credibility, and what Google are calling expertise, authority, and trust. For any SEO, expertise, authority, and trust makes a lot of sense. For most people, credibility makes more sense. Are you a credible solution for Google's user or, more crucially, for the subset of Google's users who are your audience? Google is trying to match that subset to the audience you can actually serve. If it's confident that it's understood who your audience is, and what you can offer them, that's already a big plus. If it's confident that you are a more credible solution for its users than the competition, you've won the game."

What can an SEO consider moving away from to focus more time on educating Google?

"When I tell brands to write a description about their company, stick to it, and repeat it until it is understood by the Google 'child', they see it as duplicate content. They insist they need to write different versions to avoid duplication. However, the problem with duplicate content was plagiarism, and attributing the correct source. Google always wanted to rank the original source and not the copies. In this case, you are the original source, and you're copying yourself. From an education point of view, if you're saying something in one way in one place, and then reiterating it differently in another, the child will get confused.

I did an experiment about a year ago where I took the same exact text, and I spread it across the entire web - probably 100 references to me, personally. One of the things that I thought might happen would be that Google would then demote some of the results on my brand SERP because it was repetitive. It didn't, it kept the same results. It just pulled different chunks out of the pages, put them in the meta description, and moved the title around. Google recognises that these are good representations of you as a brand and they are helpful, valuable, and useful to your audience. It will look through the different things that you do, and that you represent to your audience, and determine what feels most relevant for each of its results. Let Google do the work - why waste your time?"

You can find Jason Barnard over at JasonBarnard.com.

Create semantic content using the Google SERPs - with Paul Andre de Vera from Workday

Paul follows on from Omi's tip at the beginning of this chapter, by sharing that you can use the Google SERP to design your semantic content strategy.

Paul Andre de Vera says: "Create semantic content, it's really easy. You can just use Google SERPs to figure it out."

How do you find the SERP that is right for you, and what do you do when you find it?

"SEOs are too caught up on ranking for just one term. Semantic content is all about ranking for intents and multiple terms or queries. You can get more, better quality traffic than just ranking for just one term. Why rank for one term, when you can rank for hundreds?

Take your head term, the one that you really want to rank for, and put it into search. On the SERP you'll see People Also Ask questions - use those as your subheadings, and as questions or answers. Then, scroll to the bottom and you'll see some related keywords, which you want to sprinkle in as well. To make it more semantically related, and have more density, click on one of the related keywords and go to the next page. You'll see another set of keywords at the bottom of that SERP. You can do this at least three times.

SEOs get caught up on page one, but page two and page three are like emerging topics and trends. This is how to find key semantic terms and create semantic content. To be more current, change your Google settings to 'searches within the past year'. That way, you'll be catering to what's trending right now, and what people are actually searching."

Should you add these relevant keywords to your existing page, or create new pages?

"You shouldn't need to create new pages. I'm in the B2B space, in enterprise SEO. I think about this when I'm creating SEO briefs for writers. When I'm asked how we can rank for a certain term, I'm not thinking about that term on its own. I'm thinking about the terms, intents, and queries that would come up using the strategy I just mentioned.

Keep it simple. There are four places to hit first: the meta title, the URL, the H1, and within the first 100 words. From there, write naturally, answer the People Always Ask questions, and keep including those keywords. I've seen a lot of my content that's been done this way rank for 1000s of keywords. That includes different queries and long-tail phrases. Having hundreds of relevant terms on the first page is a better way of showing value than just showing up for one keyword.

This method is also less competitive, you're more likely to retain your rankings over the long-term and build authority for your broad subject."

How do you justify the value of seeking out phrases that may have lower search volume?

"Search volume is a good indicator, but not a hard source of truth. People are always searching for new things. You can look at this within your Google Search Console and see how many times these things show up in the impressions.

On Google, if you use 'within the past year' or 'within the past month' and these keywords are showing up, it shows that people are searching it. They may not be appearing on some tools because they are new. Using these settings will let you see the keywords that are actually being searched for right now."

What type of business is this strategy most appropriate for?

"I've seen it work most effectively for bigger brands. If you have brand recognition, it's going to work really well - it definitely suits for enterprise companies. At enterprise companies you can use great writers, link out to your sources, and design a really semantically-created page. Semantic content works best when it is well written, annotated, and resourced."

How long does it take before you can measure success?

"It will be at least three weeks after you start publishing before you start seeing anything publicly. I used this strategy to target the term 'financial management system'. It's a fairly well-used term that we're now on the first page for. There are thousands of other keywords on that page that are ranking as well. When going for those big terms it can take longer. It depends on your brand recognition, and the amount of data you already have on your website. If you are known in your niche it will really help."

Is this strategy best for standard blog articles on your website, or is it effective for other content as well, like YouTube titles?

"This is a strategy I'm testing on YouTube right now, and I think it's going to be effective on a lot of different platforms. It almost feels like I'm spilling secrets. Try it. I'm trying it and I'm getting good results. It will give you a head start against competitors that aren't using it yet. It works because the same person that searches something on Google, is also searching on YouTube. People use similar search terms on multiple platforms. The title of a video, for example, is very important. Doing that research beforehand, and incorporating the phrases that people are looking for, is a big opportunity. If you're going to use this strategy on YouTube, make sure you say your keywords in the video as well."

How does this strategy fit in with other tactics and tasks that SEOs are doing?

"I am doing this all the time. For every campaign that comes out, you will have as SEO portion. You may be doing content syndication and a paid search campaign attached to it, for a whole omni-channel approach. Organic search work should be a part of this. Whether you have campaigns quarterly or yearly, it's something that you should be doing for all of them."

How do you convince corporate to support this strategy without high search volume data?

"I've had to do this before, and I used the results to prove its value. I had to convince corporate to give me a budget, so I could get some content created, and come back to them with the results.

Once you've got your content written in the right way, you can prove the value by showing which keywords are ranking. Throw those into a tool and see what the cost per click is for them. Take the value of the keywords and multiply that by the actual visits from organic clicks. This gives a value of how much the page has saved you in contrast to using paid search. That's a metric I always share with leadership - the value of all the keywords that a page is ranking for, added up monthly. That's how much you're saving from paid search."

What type of content should you be creating with these keywords, is it necessary to have images or videos?

"You should add images for sure, though videos tend to slow down the page. You can have certain sections of your website where you put your videos.

You also need to identify what the SERP is looking for. You might think you need a minimum of 1500 words but look at the SERP to gauge it before you start writing. Observe the SERPs, and even competitors as well. Dig through the top 10 pages, see what the average word count is and use that as your guide. You can always tweak it afterwards. Let it be concise for the user to begin with, then see what you can do after you've completed some reports.

I only really use SEO tools for research, search volume, and maybe seeing backlinks. If you want to get ranking, the answers are right in front of you on the SERPs. You can also see the featured snippets, copy what's working, and then make it a little bit better. You might be able to steal that as well."

What should an SEO stop doing to spend more time looking at SERPs and creating semantic content?

"Stop trying to find a shortcut. Don't get hung up on putting blog comments or forum comments all over the place - the sorts of things that used to work back in the day. It may work if it's targeted in a certain niche, but it doesn't have broad value, especially if it's going all over the place. If you want to get great links, use tools, and find the links that your competitors have. Look for places where you can capture and have your links used instead.

With the emphasis on social media, blog comments have become much less important, even if the signals of social may not be a direct ranking factor. Whether it's Twitter, Tumblr, or other Web 2.0 properties, I love to include social in my SEO strategies. For some companies I've developed their own Medium page to get some equity from there. Social provides a great mixture of benefits over seeking a shortcut through blogs."

You can find Paul Andre De Vera at Dre.me.

Do not ignore Passage Indexing - with Dixon Jones, CEO of InLinks and Majestic Brand Ambassador

Dixon shares the importance of Passage Indexing – understanding which content from your web page is being featured on the SERP, by Google.

Dixon Jones says: "In 2021, Google started talking about passage indexing as something they were going to be working on, but they've not been very specific about what this is going to be. Even though all the headline SEO places are saying passage indexing is coming, Google is simply not doing a good job of talking about it. Let me try and explain my understanding of this concept.

What makes up knowledge is interesting, because it's lots of different ideas or topics around a subject. For example, if you have an encyclopaedia on gardening, you've got lots of really interesting elements, and different articles that are all equally valid. When you try and put all that onto one page, you've got expertise all throughout, with different bits of information and ideas. Passage indexing is the understanding from Google that a good page of content is probably talking about many different ideas and topics, in the same corpus of content.

Trying to understand those bits separately probably makes more sense. Looking at things by passages and sections, rather than the text as a whole, is generally much better. A good example of this is if you wanted to find out what eBay was about: it is made up of so many different products and every single page is a different idea. If you can take that concept and bring it down to a page level, even each page is about all sorts of different things - so all of a sudden, it's about nothing.

Chunking

One sentence, or a block of text, may absolutely answer a user's question - so it's a way of looking at a needle in a haystack. What's really interesting is that Majestic came up with this idea of breaking a web page down into chunks, or sections, back in 2019. Earlier research suggests that analysing the content of a page in chunks is better than analysing the whole, to get the meaning of that page.

Measuring chunks and passage indexing sound like similar concepts to me, and passage indexing probably describes it better than chunking. Majestic divides a web page into 40 different sections and looks at the angle, and the links in context, within those sections. It's great that Majestic does this, and it is both interesting and useful. Understanding these sections of text might be much more valuable in the future, and it will probably change the way we write content."

Research from Google suggests that 7% of search queries will be affected by this - which is relatively significant. Are there any particular types of businesses that are more likely to take advantage of passage indexing?

"It may be very useful for products that have a high spec. For example, you might want a certain width screw - so you have a very detailed need for a product that is very specific. If a supplier has filled out their product specs for thousands of different screw types, then Google can pick that up and understand that this particular product will fit this particular user's needs.

Google are saying they're trying to fix a very unique user requirement that's unlikely to be needed again. The problem here is that you could spend all your time doing SEO for one person that may or may ever come along. You've got to get that balance right, between putting everything into a way that Google can understand at a passage level, and time.

I suspect data sets and how you display them will be important. I think the downside for us is that people who've written things in bullet points may have a disadvantage. Bullet points used to be a quick way of covering all the key ideas. However, they are unlikely to do well in Google's meritocracy-based system that wants to return the best content. Also, you would assume that long-form content is now broken up into more meaningful subsections as Google is trying to understand a little section of that web page. It might be that long-form starts to lose some of its influence on SERPs, although it's difficult to say how it will pan out."

Bullet points often appear in featured snippets, so what's the main difference between featured snippets and passage indexing?

"I think it's the stage at which Google is analysing the information. Featured snippets are really done at the reveal stage for Google. When you've typed something into a search engine, it's already indexed absolutely everything, and it knows what's where - what's an FAQ, what's an event, and who's a person. Google can then use featured snippets to better display its already organised, understood, and indexed content.

Passage indexing is at a much earlier stage - it's about how it's going to store that information in the first place. It's about how it reads your page, and where it puts it in Google's huge machine of databases and structured data. You could think of passage indexing as being passages of rich snippets. I expect Rich Snippets to start showing passages of text better than they did before. I suspect that a passage could easily be shown as a rich snippet, but the fact it's indexed in a different way means they'll have this magic sentence that hopefully is going to answer a very specific user's requirement.

I reckon this is going to be mainly driven by Voice Search. You're going to say, 'Google, where can I find a bolt with a flange of 2.3 centimetres and a length of 4 centimetres?' and it'll find a passage with that exact bolt somewhere and read it back to you. Bullet points will cover a lot of different ideas in a very short period of time, so they don't make a very good passage index. A good passage index is a well-formed couple of sentences that very much explain an answer to a super-specific query."

One scary situation for SEOs is the thought of appearing in a search result, but not getting a click through to a web page. Is passage indexing, and more content appearing in the SERP, likely to result in more people staying on the SERP and not visiting web pages?

"Yes. Your business has to cope with this being a positive, not a negative. If you're the person selling the 2.3 centimetre flange screw, then you're not going to have a problem. The problem arises if you're trying to monetise the information - this is a challenge. Google wants to be the world leader in monetising information itself. You are basically a competitor to Google. One solution is to put your stuff behind a walled garden and try and make people pay for that information, but Google wants to show it and charge somebody else to advertise for a 2.3 centimetre flange.

Moving forward, Google is certainly aware that we're starting to search in different ways. We're no longer looking at the homepage of Google for our search. We're starting to use voice and all manner of devices that don't have a keyboard or mouse. We have to make sure our businesses are able to cope with this."

If an SEO wants to start taking advantage of passage indexing, what are the steps they need to take to restructure, reorganise, and rewrite existing content?

"I would imagine that writing paragraphs rather than bullet points is probably helpful, but the paragraphs don't have to be hugely long. What may well help is page indexes —links within the page to the different sections. You could have all the things you're about to talk about with little hyperlinks at the top of the page. That would certainly help Google identify which sections are about specific ideas or concepts. You could use the bullet points at the top as a table of contents in this content-driven approach.

You can use schema in paragraphs and text as well. 'How To' schema is quite complicated because it requires an image for each section to be properly formed. However, having each section in your How To process properly marked-up with an image is going to help. Google is going to be able to see where the individual steps are in a long process of learning. This will really help Google to dive in and not just give the answers to generic questions."

If an SEO is struggling for time, what's one thing they should stop doing, so they can spend more time focusing on passage indexing?

I would stop trying to write the same thing on your website in 20 different ways. Instead, cover more topics in smaller amounts. You can still do it in long-form content, but these paragraphs have got to make sense on their own. Make sure your paragraphs stand up on their own two feet. If that paragraph was the only thing on your website, or that came back in the search result, would it make sense? Does it answer a particular question, have a call to action, and monetise that information?

We've become lazy as human beings, writing content and understanding the importance of a paragraph, but machines are going to understand the paragraph. You need to consider a paragraph and a passage as the same thing - and make sure they are self-contained."

You can find Dixon Jones over at DixonJones.com.

Optimize your business for Google My Business - with Greg Gifford from SearchLab Digital

Greg highlights the importance of optimizing your Google My Business profile (now called Google Business Profile.)

Greg Gifford says: "If you do face-to-face business with customers, optimising the heck out of your Google My Business (GMB) listing is probably the most important thing you can do to get found in search. Yet so many people ignore it, or put minimal effort into it"

What does an SEO need to do to optimise the heck out of Google My Business in 2022?

"Get into the GMB dashboard and fill out everything you possibly can. You'd be surprised how many people will choose a single category - and it's probably not even the best category to choose. They'll drop their phone number and their website in, and they're done. They move on, and they never come back and touch it again.

There are so many fields there, and you need to fill out all the appropriate categories. There's a really cool, interactive category list at PlePer.com that shows you all of the similar categories you should also choose. When you put in your website address, make sure that you've got UTM tracking on that website link, because mobile traffic doesn't get attributed correctly in Analytics. It gets sent over as direct traffic, but you want to make sure you're getting credit for all the organic visibility you're getting as a boost.

You need to put in awesome photos of your business and change them regularly. You've got to preload questions into the Q&A section. This part is not in the GMB dashboard - it's actually a community discussion feature of Google Maps. A lot of people don't realise that the Q&A is there. You've got to go in and interact with it on your profile, preload your questions, monitor it, and answer new questions that come in.

Also, you've got to have Google posts going because they are basically free advertising. There's so much to GMB that so many people don't do. It makes a massive difference into how well you show up in searches, and how well you convert people that see you when you do show up."

I've seen that you can be a service area business, which means you don't actually need to have a physical address anymore. What does this mean for businesses?

"It's actually been around for a while for anybody that does face-to-face business with customers. If that's at a brick-and-mortar location, you will show your address, and everything is standard. However, if you're a service business, like a plumber, or electrician, where you still do face-to-face business but at the customer's location - that's a service area business. Typically, you need to tick the little box that says 'hide your address', which you need to get verified, but it's just not going to appear in search results. I'm sure you probably don't want random people showing up at your house in the middle of the day when you're not there.

When you're a service area business, you hide your address, and then you can enter in service areas. Now, a lot of people think that's going to affect how you show up in search results, but where you rank is based on the address, not your service area. What it does, is draw that little line around your service area – so people up North won't call you if you only serve London. It's important to understand the distinction that filling out as much as you can doesn't necessarily mean you will rank in lots of places. It's more about conversion, and letting people know where you actually serve customers."

What do SEOs do if they are independent SEO consultants with a virtual business address?

"You can't actually use a virtual office - it's against the rules. Google doesn't allow co-working spaces and PO boxes. This is because a lot of attorneys in the United States got a bunch of Regis offices to try to rank in places where they didn't actually have an office - so they ruined it for everybody else. It's like all SEOs ruin things for everybody else when you find something, exploit it, and use it too much.

However, you can solve this problem by using your home address and ticking the button to tell Google that you don't want your home address to be displayed."

How long should posts be, and what do they need to incorporate?

"Posts can be 1,500 characters and a big giant image, but the key to success with posts is not what's in your post - it's what shows up in the thumbnail. This is because Google will crop your big image down to a thumbnail image and truncate your text to just show the first few words. You really have to approach it like an ad in AdWords. If you don't do AdWords, just watch a couple of videos to learn how to do it.

If the thumbnail isn't compelling, nobody's going to click on it and see the full post. This is why a lot of people do posts, and they don't work. Also, it's because they share the same content they share on Facebook. It's not a social post - it's literally an advertisement. You need something that's enticing, compelling, and will make people want to click through.

However, the image cropping is really wonky. You have to pay attention to what shows when it's cropped down into that thumbnail with just a few lines of text. Make sure it's optimised, so it's going to make people want to click."

How often should you be posting?

"We still typically recommend going once a week so that you've got something fresh there every week. You've got several different post types to use. The main one is the 'What's New' post, that used to only show up for seven days and then disappear. That's now changed, and it's live for six months. The other post types are the 'offering' and the 'event'. They have a date range and will only be visible for the length of that range.

You don't want to post five or six a week. I've seen some businesses do three or four a day because they're approaching it like social media. That doesn't work, because it gives you a carousel that you have to swipe through to see all of them. Typically, people aren't going to swipe through and look at all your posts. Be strategic in what you're putting there. Don't put too much information there but post often enough. Also, only post something compelling – otherwise, you are wasting your time."

What questions should you be asking and answering in your Q&A section?

"A lot of people don't realise you can load your own questions in - and that's the key thing here. Take all the questions off your FAQ page on your site and throw them in there. In addition to including all the common questions on your site, talk to the people answering the phones and put their common questions in. Also, look at the questions that people ask your competitors.

The really cool thing is that Google autocompletes the answer. As you type your question, the answer will pop up if it's already been asked, or if an answer exists in a customer review. It's all about conversion here, and it doesn't matter for ranking but if someone's got a question, you want to have those answers already packed in - to demonstrate authority. You can have 30 or 40 questions in there - there's no limit. I've seen places with hundreds of questions, and you're making it more likely that someone's going to click through and contact you if you've got the answer for them already."

If I'm based in the middle of the UK, and I offer SEO services, is it better to be highly targeted to local customers or offer services to anyone in the British Isles?

"That's a lot more about your content strategy and your standard SEO stuff than what you're selecting in GMB. The area you enter as a service area doesn't really have any effect on your visibility in a wider and narrower radius. It's more about how dense the competition is, and what your content is. If you're trying to say that you serve the entirety of the UK, then you've got to optimise correctly to show up for that and understand that you'll have a lot more competition. You're probably not as likely to show up unless you SEO the heck out of it."

What insights are available, and how can you optimise further by checking out this data?

"One of the great things to pay attention to in insights is phone calls and website clicks, because it's not always going to match up with what shows in Google Analytics. Clearly, phone calls from GMB are not going to show in Google Analytics. To get them to show on your call tracking, Google allows you to enter a call tracking number on GMB. It's best practice to put a call tracking number as the primary number and your actual number as an alternate number – but as the primary number that is displayed to the public.

Make sure you're taking advantage of all the data you can to show that you're getting more visibility, as you do your SEO and optimization, which results in more impressions, website traffic, leads, and calls.

The two important things to pay attention to in the insights are your

246

branded impressions and your discovery impressions. The brand impressions are the ones where people are looking specifically for your business. Whereas the discovery impressions are when you show up when people are not explicitly looking for your business. That's important because as you go for the various keyword phrases, and get more visibility, you should see your discovery impressions ramp up.

Discovery impressions are registered every time you show up in the map pack - the map of the three results underneath - or when you show up in a result in Google Maps. It's really helpful to show this over time, especially if you're an agency-side or a solo contractor. You can prove to your clients that they're getting more visibility, phone calls, and impressions."

What is something that an SEO should stop doing to spend more time focusing on Google My Business?

"In reality, Google cares more about the quality of your content, not the quantity. There are so many SEOs out there churning out blog posts and content. Dial that back a little bit, and worry more about putting up a couple of great pieces instead of a lot of 'just okay' pieces.

This will give you more time to do GMB, and it's not something you have to spend a lot of regular time on. You just need one chunk of time to optimise everything. After this, you only need to monitor the Q&A section and do a weekly post on an ongoing basis. There's no excuse not to stay on top of it."

You can find Greg Gifford over at SearchLabDigital.com.

Align your Google Business Profile with SERP features to better serve user search intent - with Maria White from Kurt Geiger

Maria follows on from Greg's tips to share the importance of checking the SERP, at the same time as optimizing your Google Business Profile.

Maria White says: "Include alternative content strategies in your SEO. That can be Google Business Profile (formerly Google My Business), SERP features, image optimization, featured snippets, and much more. It's not possible to add them all into an SEO strategy but try to include the SERP features that are aligned to the search intent of your users, and with your brand and consumers. For example, if you're a large brand, Google Business Profile is helpful but might not be the number one feature to focus on. You could instead aim for a creative piece to become a featured snippet. However, if you are a small business, Google Business Profile could be one of your main sources of traffic, and leads, in 2022."

Should SEOs focus on the content that is used on the SERP, how it looks there, and what kind of user action is encouraged by it?

"Definitely. I used to focus my SEO strategies on technical links, internal content, external content, etc., because that's what everyone else said was the thing to do. It was like a race to gain positions on the search engines. However, as the search result list has evolved with time, we are noticing the SERPs changing, and adapting results to align with search intent. Those results are mostly changing based on the ways that consumers prefer to consume content, and the way they behave online.

If one of my clients is looking for a bouquet, and they search 'flower bouquets Clapham' or 'flower bouquet Burgess Hill', they will have localised results. For this type of search, the results will show a local pack, followed by social media posts, and then organic search listings. If a small business has a good Google Business Profile strategy in place, then they can attract more relevant traffic, and more leads, than by investing a lot of time trying to target an influencer to increase traffic through organic results. That kind of visibility doesn't necessarily translate into sales for local clients, or into improved visibility in the local pack."

What pieces of content do you recommend SEOs focus on for taking advantage of the SERP? Is there anything special to do so that your content starts appearing in the SERP features?

"To win a SERP feature or have visibility in the local pack as a small business, you need to know your audience. A good place to start is with keyword research. Look at the most popular search phrases, and then divide your research into categories - informational, educational, etc. Alongside informing your Google Business Profile strategy, that information, plus your data from Google Analytics, can help you to think about the pieces of content you can create to answer the questions your audience asks.

For a small business, you obviously want to have your product in a product section in Google Business Profile. Remember, you don't have to put all of your website, your categories, and your products in there. That will overwhelm your visitor and they may end up leaving. People mostly use Google Business Profile to find opening hours, delivery information, or your address. However, within that profile you have the opportunity to offer products that they are looking for, based on keyword research and information on Google Analytics. If you add those products in the product sections, you have a higher chance of a customer seeing the product, seeing that it's easy to buy, and purchasing straightaway. Many times, customers that were mostly looking for information about the business, will end up buying.

I had a client that, before Valentine's Day in 2021, had zero sales through Google Business Profile because they did not have a strategy in place. At the end of October 2021, they had made €53,000 from Google Business Profile alone, not including website or social media sales. That was just from putting the most popular products into categories in Google Business Profile.

I recently saw a case study on a large, global brand that sells trainers, where they created a piece of content with the aim of earning links. It was based on one of the most common conditions in runners, called 'pronation'. They were looking to answer one of the most common questions asked by runners: 'What is pronation?'. The piece of content they created not only answered what the customer was asking, but also showed, at the end of the piece, how a product could help with that condition. This piece, that was originally designed for link acquisition, is still one of the main sources of traffic to that global brand a couple of years later. It is the answer to one of the most common customer questions, but it puts the product in there and shows how that product can be the answer to the question as well. An alternative content strategy, for a small business or a large brand, can be more productive than obsessing over some of the more conventional SEO strategies out there."

Are people going to start buying on the SERP and not visiting a website at all?

"We are seeing the SERPs evolving and adapting results to align with how the users prefer to consume content. For example, if you type in 'gin' and 'Hendricks', you will see Google Shopping, then a knowledge graph, and a series of different visual results before you have the organic blue links. That's because what influences the decision to consume content or convert most, is a visual result, or an immediate call to action. The consumer doesn't have to go through the website and explore, the content is right there.

Google is trying to emulate how the shopping journey starts. Now, when a consumer is thinking of purchasing something, they start a shopping journey in Amazon rather than in Google. They want to type a brand, or a product, and get a list of products straightaway, without having to read or explore other content. SERPs are evolving to align with the preferences of consumers - low attention spans and wanting immediate results. Reviews and social media posts, etc., influence consumers much more than a brand's content. Now, instead of obsessing about being number one, you need to think about what number one means for your brand, and your consumers. That may be a result in the local pack, in the knowledge graph, or as featured snippet."

What is one thing that SEOs should stop doing to focus more time on serving user intent with SERP features?

"Stop obsessing over one element of the ranking factors: Core Web Vitals, PageSpeed, technical content, internal and external links. It all matters, but if your aim is to gain relevant traffic, and sales, then you always need to keep your consumer in mind. Think about how they behave online, how they consume content, how they shop, etc.

The different aspects of SEO need to come together. If you invest a lot of time on a beautiful Google Business Profile strategy, and featured snippets, but when they come to your site it's slow and it breaks, then all your efforts are for nothing. All the elements matter, however you need to focus on what is relevant for your brand and your consumers. For small businesses, it can be more effective to have a Google Business Profile strategy in place - creating Google posts regularly and updating the products and categories seasonally, etc. That can bring far more relevant traffic, and far more leads, than obsessing over chasing an influencer, which will be more expensive and may only bring temporary traffic that doesn't convert. Explore your other alternatives."

You can find Maria White over at kurtgeiger.com.

Image Search for eCommerce websites is becoming increasingly important - with Roxana Stingu, Head of Search & SEO at Alamy

Roxana shares some tips on image optimization, and the traffic opportunities available from image search.

Roxana Stingu says: "Images are now playing a bigger role in product search. If you go on Google and search for one of your best-selling non-branded product terms, you might see some of the bigger brands competing against you. If you go and do the same search on Image Search, you might be surprised to see that some of the names appearing are not the big brands you were expecting. Some of the big brands are not optimising their images as well as they could."

Is it important to have unique images on your website? I would imagine that a lot of eCommerce brands are taking images from feeds, so there could be hundreds of other websites using similar images.

"The search engines are ranking the page, not the image itself - even though it's the image showing up. You could use the same image as somebody else, if your page is better optimised for that image. It doesn't matter if your image is not unique. Just make sure you're optimising for that image better than somebody else.

The more websites that use the same image, the harder it gets to rank for it because competition is bigger, but it also depends on how the image is used. If everybody's using the exact same product descriptions and everything then, in this case, it will be hard to outrank an original website with the same image, and the same text, regarding that product. However, if you're using an image in one context, and somebody else might be using the same image in a different context, then there isn't any competition because you're going to rank for different things in the first place."

Is Image Search traffic increasing, and by how much?

"Both Google's and Bing (which has an extraordinary image search platform as well), have been investing a lot in bringing all these different features to Image Search. It's hard to say exactly what percentage of total search it accounts for because there isn't as much data around image search as I would hope for. There's an older survey, done by Google in 2019, which showed that 50% of eCommerce users used Image Search to help them choose what they want to buy. That was three years ago - imagine what it is now, with more people using mobile phones. It's so much easier to look at images than actually read text on a page on your phone."

It's obviously part of the buyer journey. Is it used at a research phase, when people know what product they're looking for but they're not necessarily sure what it's called?

"It is. People have so many different intents and reasons why they would use Image Search. They might just be looking for ideas, so they can upload a picture of a specific pattern to find a bag that uses that pattern. They might be looking for a specific style. If you're looking in a magazine, you like a combination of a pair of jeans with a blouse and you think, 'I have jeans like that, now I just want to find a similar blouse I can buy.' you're going to do more of an image search than a text search.

There is also the situation where you know exactly how the product looks, and you just want to find who's selling it, and maybe for what price. Then there are people who are just ready to make a purchase. They know exactly what they want - they just want to find the place to buy it from. There are many different scenarios where you would use Image Search."

Is Pinterest part of this image searching matrix, or is that an entirely different proposition?

"Pinterest shows up a lot in Image Search. I don't know if this is a good thing, because eCommerce websites are now competing with Pinterest. I think search engines, especially Google, are smart enough to know about the intent of the user. They can tell whether somebody is just browsing images for ideas, so they're still researching, or when people are ready to buy. The intent in their queries changes - and this is where Pinterest doesn't show up as much."

What are your general tips on file type, size and positioning, additional text, and where that text goes, when optimising for image search?

"Firstly, if you want your image to rank well, you have to give the image the importance it deserves. That means you should place it above the fold, or as high on the page as possible. If the image is not the main focus of the page, chances are you won't rank well for that particular image. It's all common sense - that's all there is to it. It's not one of those SEO techniques like putting your keyword first.

Next, your images have to be large. For example, Google recommends people use images that are 1200 pixels or more if they want to do well in Google Discover. The same recommendation works on Image Search - the larger your image, the greater the chance you have to do well.

I know large images can take up hundreds of kilobytes, which is a problem for PageSpeed, and everybody will feel the urge to compress the images into oblivion. Please don't, because sharp images tend to do better in Image Search. I always go with the lossless compression, although unfortunately, this is not always satisfying, and the image file can still come out too big.

If you're worried about PageSpeed, I'd suggest considering using responsive images instead, which is just a different way of adding images in HTML using the picture element. It allows you to give users different image sizes based on their device, and you can even have different degrees of compression. For example, you can have a smaller image for mobile. There, you don't need it to be very sharp because it will be very small and you're not going to see a lot of detail - so you can compress more, but you still give search engines access to a large and high-quality image file.

This picture element has about 96% global adoption by browsers, which means it should work for most traffic. Internet Explorer and Opera don't tend to do well with this, but every other browser works perfectly fine.

You can also look into using different image formats. For instance, you can use WebP, or a newer format called AVIF, and both can reduce the file size even further - without affecting the quality of the image. Just check browser compatibility. WebP has a 95% global adoption, but AVIF is still quite new and only covers about 70% of the browsers and browser versions that are currently in use."

What are the benefits of using WebP and AVIF instead of JPEG?

"The main benefit of WebP is you can get about a 25% compression just from the file format, without losing the quality you would normally lose if you did normal lossless compression. I haven't tried AVIF yet, but you're supposed to be able to compress it even further without losing the quality. Once more people use it, we might get better numbers on how good it is."

What about dimensions - ideally, would you be aiming for a square image?

"That is a very good question because I haven't tested it, and I don't like to talk about things I haven't tried and only heard about. Apparently, Google will prefer certain dimensions of images, such as square, or rectangular in the 16:9 ratio. This feels logical because it's easier for Google to show as much of the image as possible in the pre-set image sizes shown on image search results. If an image is really important, would Google not show it just because it doesn't have the right ratio? I'll let you know after testing."

Joy Hawkins shared a tip to include a square photo near the top of a page. So that's for the conventional SERP because Google is starting to use images as part of mobile search results next to the actual blue text listing.

"In web search, in the conventional SERPs, you can even have smaller images because they're mostly used for mobile anyway. Google doesn't care to have these big, quality images. If they are square, it's easier for Google to show them because you will know all the information in the image will be visible, and they don't need to cut it off. It definitely makes sense to use square images - if that's what you're targeting."

What about the quality of traffic from Image Search? Does it tend to convert just as well or is it a different stage in the buyer journey?

"It depends what you use Image Search for. In stock photography, for instance, we convert way better in Image Search than we do in Web Search. That's normal, because people who want to buy a specific photo will use Image Search to find it. They also use Web Search just to find websites that might have that specific photo.

For eCommerce in a classical way, I assume it's going to be the other way around. When people go to Web Search, they want to find the websites where they can buy things. That's going to have a good conversion. When they go to Image Search, they might just be in the research phase, trying to find a product in the way they were imagining it and seeing which website sells it. They might end up actually clicking from Image Search to that website and end up converting. It should still be a pretty good conversion rate from Image Search, and if it isn't - then something's not working. Maybe you've got the wrong images in there or you're showing up with your blog and not actually with your product."

If an SEO is struggling for time, what could they stop doing to focus more on Image Search?

"There are many SEO things we spend time on that don't necessarily have that much return on investment. One of the most recent examples is that we spent so much time as an industry optimising our titles for our pages. Then Google just went and rewrote those however they wanted - proving there's no point wasting a lot of time doing that. I'm not saying never do it again. Maybe just take a break from this activity and optimise some alt texts, or some image file names to make them more descriptive and help those images do better."

You can find Roxana Stingu over at Alamy.com.

SECTION 4:

CANI

10 ANALYTICS & TESTING

Learn to love Google Analytics - with Andrew Cock-Starkey from Optimisey

Google Analytics has a lot to offer, says Andrew – if you haven't spent much time in it recently, you're missing out.

Andrew Cock-Starkey says: "Everybody has Google Analytics installed, but I have come across a number of people that still have it installed the way it comes - out of the box. They haven't used any of the advanced stuff it can do, and they haven't realised what a powerful tool it is. If you just do a few things to change the out-of-the-box settings, it can give you so many great insights, and useful bits of information."

What have been the major changes to Google Analytics over the last couple of years that an SEO really needs to be aware of?

"I think one of the things that's changed is Google Tag Manager coming in. People are doing much more exciting and interesting things with that. Because it's all built by Google, Google Analytics plays really nicely with Tag Manager, and you can do all sorts of cool things off the back of that. That's what I'm spending a lot of my time doing now, with clients.

There are really powerful tools in there, like using segments in Analytics to look at particular slices of your data. A lot of things haven't particularly changed at all. They've always been there - but a lot of SEOs don't know

259

about it, or don't use it."

When setting up Google Analytics a lot of people just take the code added to the website - and that's it. What are the steps needed to ensure all the most useful data is appearing in Google Analytics?

"One of the first things I suggest is getting at least three separate views set up. You have the one that comes out of the box, with all website data, which is great. Just leave that one alone, as it's your catch-all view. You'll also need a reporting view, where you have all these lovely filters and things that you've worked out.

Before you build this view, you need to have a sandbox - a test view set up where you can experiment with things. This is essential because, if you're like me, you'll mess things up occasionally. If you don't quite follow a blog post exactly, you can break your data. Once you've broken it, it could be too late to fix, and that day's data is already gone. Mess with things in your sandbox. When it works the way you think it's going to, and everything is clean and lovely, then you can move it over into your reporting view.

The other fun task I always do with clients is setting up filters. They often don't have a filter to screen themselves out. Create an IP-based filter to screen out all the editors, and people working on your website, because they're not your customers and they're not going to buy anything.

It's always interesting when I put in a filter to screen out a client's office, and their traffic goes down massively. They always ask me what I've done. Yes, traffic has decreased by 15%, but conversions have gone through the roof comparatively."

Where are the best places to view that data? Is it more efficient to view it outside of Google Analytics?

"It can be quite overwhelming. It depends on who is looking at the data. I use Google Data Studio quite a lot, it's a visualisation tool built by Google and it plays really nicely with other Google things. Another option is Power BI, that also helps people visualise their data and make it look pretty.

For somebody in the C-suite, who isn't familiar with Google Analytics - the menus, naming conventions, and the difference between users, hits, and sessions can be very confusing. You can export data into Data Studio, or Power BI, make it look pretty and give it understandable naming conventions."

Can this be automated? Is it easy to automatically funnel all the data from Google Analytics into Data Studio?

"Yes. Because Data Studio is built by Google, it plays really nicely with Analytics. Once you've hooked that data up and told it where the data source is, it updates automatically. Automating those dashboards saves marketers loads of time rebuilding the same reports over and over again. Just point your data into something like Data Studio or Power BI and it will pull in anything.

It works really well with Analytics, Search Console, YouTube and all the other Google things. It also connects to Salesforce, MailChimp, dotdigital (formerly dotmailer), and loads of other tools where you can pull in all your information and have it nicely visualised in your dashboard. Connect it once, and it works. You have automated data that updates every 24 hours, or 48 hours, and you don't have to build those same reports. You can actually spend your time analysing, rather than just gathering data."

Can we get to a stage where it's only necessary to go into Data Studio (or wherever you're viewing the data), or do we still need to go into Google Analytics every so often?

"You probably still need Analytics in the background. You'll certainly want somebody who understands the sources of data, particularly when you're making changes. That person needs to understand the differences in the underlying data, for example, knowing that a user is not necessarily a person - because they're using multiple devices. Analytics still doesn't quite cut down to that kind of level yet. Although, there is stuff you can set up if you want to unify those sessions."

What are the key user experience Google Analytics metrics an SEO needs to be monitoring? What kind of data can they extract and utilise to improve the user performance on the website?

"That's one of the cool things you can do. Google Tag Manager is now built to start picking up things like scroll depth and putting that into Analytics. This tells you how far down the page a user scrolls when they visit your page. You can couple this data with other bits of information, and measure micro-conversions. The user might not have actually paid for anything, but they were closer to buying something. Did they subscribe to a newsletter? Did they download your PDF? Did they watch your video? How much of your video did they watch? These kinds of events suggest a deeper level of engagement than just a page visit.

Tag Manager can report all those things, push all this data into analytics and give you that kind of information. This is where you need that person who understands what the data is telling you. 100% scroll depth does not mean they read your entire content. We've all gone to a page and just read the conclusion – scrolled all the way to the bottom. You need to cut these things with additional data. Did they spend a lot of time on the page? Did they download something? Did they engage with it in the way you're hoping they would?"

Do you always recommend that Google Analytics is installed using Tag Manager?

"I can't think of a reason why you wouldn't do it that way. If you install analytics through Tag Manager, then it opens up opportunities for you to do other stuff later. You don't necessarily have to - you can just use Tag Manager to install the Analytics code. It tends to make developers quite anxious because you can do all sorts of terrible things in the Tag Manager container that you probably shouldn't. However, once it's in there, you can start to do some pretty interesting things with it, too."

From a traditional SEO perspective, what can an SEO still do nowadays, in terms of taking data from Analytics, to create strategy for their content and their keywords?

"The SEO part is a user searching for the keyword, you rank number one, and they click through to your site. The next key question is, did you convert them? Did they buy the DVD? Did they download that PDF? To paraphrase a golfer, it's rankings for show and conversions for dough. If you're ranking number one, getting boatloads of traffic, but none of it's converting, then what's the point? (Unless you're selling eyeballs and ad

---

clicks.)

You want to get conversions, and you need to see from the data how your content is actually performing. That's where Analytics plays a key role for SEOs. It's when you get people through to a page, and you learn how that page is performing once they're there. Which is your best-performing content? Blog posts about a certain topic may bring most of your revenue, but they don't bring much traffic. Maybe that's a content area you need to expand upon.

The 'not provided' thing in keywords is frustrating, but you should be able to tie some of that stuff up. That's where Data Studio can be another boon for this kind of analysis, because you can show Search Console data and Analytics data in the same dashboard. You can see when a page starts to perform better, the traffic goes up, the conversions go up, and you can start to make cognitive leaps."

Do you tend to favour an attribution model when you're talking about attributing value from traffic to a particular page to a client?

"It depends on the client's model. If you're selling things like cakes and DVDs, where it's a fairly impulse purchase, then you can start to do last-click attribution.

However, there are other parts to this, and you need to consider what your clients are actually selling. I've worked with some really big manufacturers of enormous industrial machines. This is not an impulse purchase, so people do a lot of research before they buy. If you can't buy it on the website, there's no way you could have put your credit card details in for a purchase of this magnitude.

That kind of attribution model gets a little bit blurry. It tends to be a lot more of a long-tail query, and they might have started searching 12 months ago. Eventually, they build up to making this enormous, very expensive purchase after talking to your support team and your sales team, and a rep visit to their warehouse. That kind of attribution model needs to be flexible depending on what the business is selling. I wouldn't say there is one attribution model that everybody should use."

Perhaps generic organic traffic will be higher in the funnel, so it's worth treating that differently to paid traffic, from a conversion perspective. Do you ever have client conversations that articulate the different mindset users have, depending on their stage of the buyer journey?

"I've had that conversation with clients before, and sometimes it depends on the maturity of the client. If they're a new player and nobody's heard of them, you're not going to get a high number of conversions straightaway. You need to have an awareness-raising stage. If you're pivoting a business and moving into a section you've never operated in before, that's great - people have heard of you. They just don't know that you are selling your new product.

That kind of client conversation, where you're talking to them about what function they want search to play, is key. Do they just want to show up in the search results? Often, they're quite happy to just appear quite high in the rankings and not get many clicks and traffic, because they're just planting the seed of another brand to consider. That tends to have a 'half-life' effect, where they start to pick up those purchases later down the line."

What's one thing that SEOs can stop doing to spend more time in Google Analytics?

"It's a cliché, and of course I'm going say this as a White Hat SEO, but stop buying links. Buying links is junk! I think that Google is turning the dial down on this, and they're getting much better at understanding the context and relevance of links. Yes, everybody wants a link from CNN and the BBC, but they are few and far between.

A link from a topical, relevant, and related interest area to your industry does make a difference - but stop buying those 6,000 links from various comments, spams, and blogs. It's a waste of time. It's a waste of money. If you can put a portion of that time into learning to love Analytics more, then it will be time well spent."

You can find Andrew Cock-Starkey over at Optimisey.com.

Add Google Search Console to your essential everyday SEO toolkit - with Olga Zarzeczna from SEOSLY

Another Google data platform that you need to be using on a regular basis, according to Olga, is Google Search Console.

Olga Zarzeczna says: "Always start any SEO analysis from Google Search Console (GSC). Whenever you land a new client, or undertake an audit of a new site, the first thing you should ask for is access to Google Search Console and go through all of the reports.

For instance, the coverage report will instantly tell you exactly what pages are indexed by Google, so you can take a look at all of them and make sure the right pages are indexed. Maybe there are some pages, like those with single testimonials, for instance, which are part of something bigger, and so shouldn't be indexed. This report is simple to use and will immediately provide you with useful information for your client.

The same is true for excluded pages. You can look at this report to see if there are pages within the 'Discovered - Currently Not Indexed' buckets. If there is a lot of content that your client considers as high quality, this site potentially has an equality issue. These are the best starting points, but we can move on to other reports in GSC, such as the performance reports to analyse the content side of things."

What are some examples of pages that tend to be indexed, that shouldn't be indexed?

"I recently had a client who had almost 1,000 URLs indexed, but in fact, the real pages with useful content only numbered in the hundreds. When I investigated these pages, I noticed that comments and testimonials added by clients are in the form of a separate web page. They were all indexed - even though they shouldn't be. It was due to the way the CMS was set up. It was generating separate pages, even though everything should've been on a single page."

What are some typical issues picked up by performance reports?

"The performance report lets you quickly see how the site is doing in terms of keywords visibility. If you use the tool Keywords Everywhere, and have it installed in Chrome, you can see the volume estimates for a given keyword in GSC. You can instantly see the keywords the site is ranking for, and their traffic potential. You can use the filters in the performance report to see which pages rank on the second page of Google – and this will usually provide some quick wins for you. Enriching the content on these pages will give you a good chance of going to the first page of Google."

That's a lovely tip because many SEOs think that keyword data isn't available to them in Google tools anymore, certainly with their experience with Google Analytics. You're saying that a lot of it exists in Search Console?

"Yes, everything is there for you - it will just take you half an hour to dive deep and see what's available. There's really a tonne of useful data right there, direct from Google, delivered straight to you."

Is this something that SEOs should be doing every single day?

"Definitely, they should log into Google Search Console every day. If you do this, the overview will instantly tell you if anything bad is going on. For instance, the overview will show you if your site gets penalised or if there are any dramatic spikes or drops. This is one thing everyone should check on a daily basis."

Can you map those spikes against historical trends to get a feel for whether the spikes or troughs are normal?

"You can open the performance reports and set the date range to be a specific period, such as the last 12 months. You can then compare what happened over this period with today's performance. This will give you the whole picture and allow you to see if it's a real spike or drop. Is the trough just because it is a weekend or a spike that's never happened before in the last year?

You can go back 16 months into the past, and there are lots of ways to compare data in GSC. For instance, you can compare mobile traffic to desktop traffic, image traffic to web traffic, or traffic from different countries. You can definitely take a very deep and detailed look at people coming through Google to your site and how they found it. They could have come through Images, or from Google Discover, because there are also the Google Discover and Google News reports which will appear once your site is getting meaningful traffic from those sources."

Is Image Search something that's increasing at the moment, and what percentage of traffic does this generally account for?

"Overall, image traffic is only generating a very small percent of what the sites I'm auditing are getting. However, image traffic may be a little higher for eCommerce sites, when people are looking for a specific product name and they go to Google Images to see what this product looks like. Image optimisation is potentially more important for eCommerce sites that have a lot of products with images."

Is it possible to set up some top-level reports that SEOs receive on a daily basis, to highlight whether or not there is an issue?

"There are a lot of tools that integrate with GSC that can send you those automated reports. For instance, one recent tool I have also started using is SEOcrawl, which gives you daily alerts about your visibility and other important metrics."

You also recommend starting any SEO analysis from the data in GSC. Why is this your starting point?

"Usually, if you are doing an SEO audit, the crawler will tell you what pages are indexable - it may render JavaScript and tell you if there are some differences - and it will tell you if there are any HTTPS or speed problems. Basically, all of the data you need can be found in GSC -that's why I always recommend checking here first. Once you start using other, more advanced tools, like Screaming Frog, you already more or less know what's going on.

For instance, in GSC you have the Page Experience report and the Core Web Vitals report, so you will immediately see the Core Vitals metrics, the field data, and you can identify the groups of pages with specific issues. Once you know what's going on there, you will be able to analyse what the crawler is telling you with more precision and draw the right conclusions after your audit. What you see in GSC is the information that Google wants to draw your attention to. In most cases, you will want to prioritise what you already see in GSC over what other tools are telling you."

Does this mean the data in GSC is generally more accurate, and when do you need to use other tools?

"The data in GSC is definitely more accurate, but it sometimes only gives you samples.

For instance, if you have a very large site, it will only show you a sample of 1,000 URLs with a specific issue, such as Core Web Vitals problems. You have the sample, and you can more or less know what's going on, but in most cases, you want to crawl the entire site and have the list of all of the URLs - not just the ones that Google showed you as a sample."

What can SEOs stop doing to spend more time in GSC?

"A lot of newer SEOs are obsessing about the notifications that other SEO tools are sending them. These crawling tools usually mark many things as critical issues, even though they're not. For instance, they may report that the HTML ratio of your site is very bad, and you need to change it. A new SEO may think there's a serious issue with their site and start worrying about what to do. The fact that this tool is sending you this alert does not mean that your site actually has that hazard issue.

Instead of panicking over these alerts from other tools, you should dive deep into GSC and see what Google is actually telling you. GSC tells you very loudly and precisely what's wrong, and what you can fix. In addition, Google has a very detailed guide on how to use and read GSC reports. If you spent an hour or two on that guide, you will see how much you can get just from GSC – it covers every aspect of SEO, even elements such as links, data, and rendering."

You can find Olga Zarzeczna over at SEOSLY.com.

If you aren't testing, you need to start - if you are testing, you need to start testing with your CRO team - with Emily Potter from SearchPilot

Emily suggests that you need to get started with SEO testing – and if you have a CRO team, you should be working closely with them.

Emily Potter says: "Testing is an essential component of your SEO strategy, and the next evolution is testing with your product or CRO teams, and focusing your changes on both on-page metrics as well as for SEO traffic. With Core Web Vitals, these two things are blending much more - and they're a good source of big organic wins."

Why aren't more SEOs testing at the moment?

"There's definitely a cost barrier to entry, and we're aware that solutions like Search Pilot are expensive and not for everyone. One limitation is that outsourcing may be difficult. The second issue is a lot of people just don't realise they can do it with some of the tools available to them. If you're a smaller website, you have things like Google Tag Manager - it's not my ideal solution, but you can do testing in different ways. You can even just do 'before and after' tests to get a bit of a better idea of what works. If you have more time, resource, and technical aptitude, there are tools like Edge SEO. Availability of time and resource, like awareness, is a major reason why SEOs don't test more."

What are some easy ways to get started with testing?

"Learning to split up your pages is important. I'm talking about SEO testing here, versus something like conversion rate optimisation testing. The main consideration is that you're just testing for one user - Googlebot. You want to split up your pages, and the first thing to get used to is finding ways to split up pages that are similar on your website, to test small changes. Coming up with hypotheses and getting used to the SEO testing process is one way to start.

You need to identify pages that are similar and on the same template. Maybe change the title tag on half of them and leave that running and monitoring for a while. The starting point is developing SEO hypotheses and getting used to the idea that some of these things that we think are natural, best practice, or obvious, may not be the best solution. How can we find more ways to get data, to make sure the things we're recommending are actually useful?"

What would be worth testing in your title? Would you recommend starting with an offer, such as 'free shipping', or more permanent changes?

"Yes, we've done lots of tests on different shipping offers. If you're going to roll out a promo, such as Black Friday, it's good to test offers. That way, if you see a big uplift one year, you know you can roll it out next year to get the gains.

More permanent changes, like testing your prices or titles, are something that a lot of eCommerce companies are doing. Also, changing the phrasing of how you're testing the head terms, cutting out the secondary keyword and just testing the primary keyword, and different ways of shortening your titles. It's important to focus on how you are going to change click-through rate as well, not just rankings."

Is it generally detrimental to have an offer that isn't keyword-rich near the beginning of a title? Is it more important to have something that's hyper-relevant to the offer for the reader to click through?

"The tests I've seen when we've tested offers have been negative - but I wouldn't want to say that's a blanket rule. It's important to keep what's most useful for the user towards the front of your title tag, especially if something's truncating. We've seen mixed results from shortening title tags, so truncation is not necessarily a problem unless it's truncating out the part that your users are going to find useful and informative."

Can you also split-test the content on the page, and the impact it has on SEO?

"Yes – the content still matters. We've done a lot of SEO text tests because Google is always saying that SEO text doesn't really matter, and we're finding that content is always useful. Still, Google definitely isn't at the level yet where it can just understand a page without some help allowing it to understand what that page is about. Definitely split-test on-page content. Once you start getting used to that mentality, there are all kinds of different things you can test, such as changing your images, or the compression of images, for site speed."

Are you able to give a specific number of minimum words required for pages you're trying to rank for?

"I'm not close to being able to provide a specific cut-off limit. We've had an eCommerce customer where they had no content at all, and we added a single line of copy and saw a 20% uplift to organic traffic. We've had others where they already had tonnes of content, and we added a little bit, and it did nothing we could detect. It's all relative to the page. If there's not really any existing content, it's probably going to help. Whereas, if you already have a lot of well-developed content, then it might not impact as much."

Is it important to have content quite high up within the page?

"Yes. We are seeing that the higher above the fold, the more importance you give to that content. It seems to have a bigger impact. For another customer, an aggregator of service providers website, we tested adding unique content and putting it above the fold. We saw over a 20% uplift for SEO - but a 13% decline for conversions. The net impact was still positive on conversions. Now we're trying to test it lower down the page, to see if we can keep the SEO benefit without lowering the conversion hit. It has helped, but not nearly as much as higher on the page. It appears that you get more from that content when it's further up the fold."

Is it always possible for SEOs and CROs to work together to increase the relevance of testing, or is it sometimes more appropriate to just have one of those departments developing a test?

"I find the companies doing it best have two different departments that work well together, but that doesn't always happen. Every SEO knows that you don't always see eye to eye when working with product teams. It is definitely a challenge.

There are still SEO tests that probably aren't going to have much impact on CRO - so it's more efficient for the SEO team to run their tests. When there's a test that impacts both teams, you can coordinate together to run it. There's a lot of project management required, because you can't run two tests on the same page at the same time. You always need to make sure there's not a product test going on simultaneously. Getting good ideas from each other is a good reason to work together, but there's also a business operation argument because otherwise, you're going to be clashing with each other."

Can you provide examples of tests that can positively impact both SEO and CRO?

"Adding new components to the pages. For example, on travel websites, we've seen product teams develop maps that do cool things for users and end up achieving a really big uplift for SEO as well. It's only the product team that really has the skillset to develop these types of features. Also, because the SEO team was collaborating on the test, it helps with optimising all the SEO elements, such as the headings."

How long should tests run for, and how much data is required to derive a meaningful result?

"For Search Pilot specifically, we say at least 1,000 sessions a day. Having said this, I've run tests that have worked 200 sessions a day. What happens when you lower that sample size is, you're only going to detect big wins. If you have a huge website with a big sample size, and you're getting thousands of sessions a day, you might get a result within two weeks. When you lower that down, it might be three or four weeks, because Google takes longer to crawl those pages. Usually, there's some correlation between how much traffic a website gets and how often Google's crawling and indexing it."

If you've got many different ideas you want to test, how do you determine which is likely to have the biggest meaningful impact?

"To prioritise experiments, we consider two factors. Firstly, what we think the impact of this will be – and this is informed by our previous testing. For example, we know that internal linking tends to have a really big impact, while a meta description test doesn't usually move the needle.

Secondly, we always consider the level of effort. So internal linking can provide a high impact, but there are a lot of complications around measurement, because you're changing two different sets of pages. Therefore, there's a lot more build that goes into this test. We're always playing between impact and effort."

What should an SEO stop doing to focus more time on testing?

"Optimising and re-optimising content, particularly things like meta descriptions and alt tags. Even title tags are now getting overwritten. You see more and more that these metadata changes are mattering less. They're still important to test - but the hours you spend on keyword research are not as valuable as they used to be.

Also, you have things like GPT-3 that are starting to generate content with AI. It's not at an advanced enough level to replace copywriters but can be a really useful tool - for example, generating title tags for your category pages - to save you time to do more testing.

Hopefully, AI will never be good enough to get rid of copywriters because humans have the context, knowledge, and emotions that are essential to creating superior content."

Emily Potter is Head of Customer Success at SearchPilot.com.

Take your SEO to the next level with SEO testing - with Aleyda Solis from Orainti

Aleyda shares that SEO testing has the potential to take your SEO efforts to a completely different level.

Aleyda Solis says: "I believe we have reached a point in SEO maturity, where we can stop focusing so much on avoiding SEO issues and errors or lifting credibility and executability of our websites. Instead, we can increase our focus on how and where we can build up to grow our results. Let's take our results to the next level and become much more competitive through developing and building new initiatives. There are lots of opportunities to connect to our search audience much better and using the many new SEO testing platforms will become much more of a norm. They are easier to use and cheaper so, if you haven't started using these testing platforms yet, I highly recommend you start doing so right away."

What SEO testing are you running most often? Are we talking about split-testing or something else?

"A/B testing, doing an experiment or developing events. Sometimes we are asked to prove potential returns from certain efforts to the decision-makers. This could require non-trivial efforts involving technical, content, and even product changes. I believe that we now have tools to help us that can be easily implemented through JavaScript. For example, Semrush and SEOTesting.com, which is another tool that can easily connect with Google Search Console. Then we have all the tools like Ranksense that allow CDNs to leverage CloudFlare Workers to run these tests.

Our testing can become pilot projects for bigger efforts and helps us show their impact without having to wait for ages. Furthermore, they ensure that we have good testing frameworks and establish control groups to develop these experiments in a way that actually makes sense. This means we can check and validate that something makes sense in our own specific context without implementing millions of URLs. We can remove a lot of uncertainty and move beyond generic best practice recommendations that may or may not work for us."

There are so many different things that can be tested. How would you know which thing to test first?

"There is a lot of low-hanging fruit, such as the metadata. In fact, a recent Google update has lowered our control there. A timely example is tweaking the titles and meta descriptions that we show in search results, to make sure Google picks up the actual content of title tags.

Next, there's a lot of conversations about whether more content is always better. We need to understand that it depends. What is the nature of the page? Is it a blog post or an article that only has an informational intent, or is it a category or product page? You also need to consider the role of that page in the customer journey.

Then, there are other questions such as, 'How many products should I be showing to drive traffic to product pages? How many internal links?' or, 'How can I optimise navigation to refer more traffic to the most important pages?' Testing allows us to validate a lot of best practices that we know, generally, should be good for SEO - but are often not trivial to implement. We can confirm that initiatives will actually be good for us and won't waste significant effort."

Should an SEO be concerned about the version of the test that Google is seeing? Several years ago, Google struggled with JavaScript and now it can see within JavaScript and the content that comes from there. What version of the test is Google likely to see, and is this likely to impact the SEO and the conducting of the test?

"Yes, it is a positive development that it is now able to render and process JavaScript. It's the same with CloudFlare Workers, which we can leverage to show the right version, or the tweaked the version, of the pages that we want to test directly through the CDN. This allows us to see the variations we want and learn which ones are performing better. Then, if our hypotheses don't play out as expected and we decrease in rankings or traffic – it should be ok. The idea is that we confirm if we are right or not before we release all the changes across all of the millions of URLs on our sites."

How do you select a winner? How much data is required and what kind of percentage confidence does the software need to declare a winner?

"Of course, this is not trivial, and it will vary. But you need certainty from any testing, and this framework will allow you to establish this. You need to be informed about the level of traffic, and length of time required, to run this test and declare a clear winner. Many of the tools and platforms I've mentioned allow you to establish and configure the whole testing environment, so your experiments make sense and provide you with enough confidence before selecting a winner."

Typically, are you looking at a certain number of visitors or a certain amount of time to actually make a test valid?

"Yes. If you have a website with only a few hundred visits, it will be very hard to test. You should be looking to have minimum levels of traffic. I think Semrush's SplitSignal recommends dozens, or hundreds, of thousands of visitors."

You've mentioned a couple of bits of software, such as SplitSignal by Semrush and also SEOTesting. Which tool is best to get started with? And what are the pros and cons of each tool?

"SEOTesting.com integrates directly with your Google Search Console and allows you to run time-based SEO tests as well as A/B tests. This is a good starting place if you don't have the technical capacity to implement something like JavaScript to display the changes and variations across different groups of pages. It allows you to run different sorts of tests and integrates Google Search Console.

Then you have tools, such as Semrush's SplitSignal, that use and leverage JavaScript and Google Tag Manager. Chris Green recently presented at BrightonSEO, demonstrating how you can develop your own testing framework using Google Tag Manager - so you can run this completely yourself if you want. The main benefit of tools like SplitSignals is that they provide you with a very nice interface to analyse, visualise, and easily establish how your tests are performing. However, implementing the test yourself is completely doable.

Finally, there are platforms like Ranksense. They allow you to implement testing and will run directly through the CDN using CloudFlare Workers, so you won't depend on JavaScript."

For running split-tests, I use Google Website Optimizer. Are you familiar with this tool, and is it an option for SEO as well?

"No, because these are UX-oriented. When UX people run this test, there are certain best practices we need to take so they don't get confused with the different variations - they don't end up indexing twice, or cause inconsistencies with the way we want to see our website configured. We usually canonicalize one version to the other or redirect from one version to the other. In general, these tools are designed to run this test at the user level. These are tests that are designed to test and validate how it will affect our actual rankings traffic - from an SEO standpoint."

What should an SEO stop doing to spend more time on SEO testing?

"There are a lot of rules of thumb that we have taken as a given. For example, that you need to optimise your title and meta description to include terms, and you can use certain characteristics and variations. But how much is too much? We've now seen from a recent Google update that sometimes the right title is not shown because we were over-optimising the title and it was too long.

Therefore, the title might be one of those elements that has a higher impact because it affects relevance, click-through rate, and engagement in SERPs. We can test how we are wording, or showing, information regarding the number of products that we feature, or information regarding the characteristics of certain types of pages. It's very straightforward to do a little bit more testing of our titles.

Also, effort that is non-trivial. Sometimes we recommend activities that we know are beneficial, but they are harder to implement because of their resource requirements. For example, adding certain types of descriptions on our category pages. We have millions of them - so how can we write unique descriptions for them? On the one hand, we now have tools to try to automatise this process. On the other hand, even automating a lot of this process takes lots of human effort and copywriting resources.

How do you make sure the impact will be positive from an SEO, and traffic standpoint? You can run a test with a group of category pages. This will allow you to see if the impact is positive and tell you if it makes sense to add content, and help you understand the type of content to add to those particular pages."

Aleyda Solis is an SEO Consultant and Founder at Orainti.com.

Use Agile for SEO testing - with Luis Rodríguez from Uber

Luis advises that you should be using Agile for SEO testing, in order to work more quickly and collaboratively.

Luis Rodríguez says: "You can start implementing an Agile mentality for SEO into different areas, but my first focus would be around testing. It's now very important to define your own best practices. The length of your titles, amount of content on your page, and number of links are all very specific for your domain. The key to determining the best way to do things is quick testing. We've been developing what we call testing velocity, where we are rapidly testing different concepts and innovative approaches. This has given us the path to start creating our own set of best practices. Every domain is distinct, with different strengths, approaches, and structures. Consider what makes your domain unique, test fast, and continuously learn."

How often should you involve other people in the thought process of what you're doing?

"Agile is a process for managing a project involving constant collaboration and working in iterations. You need to collaborate all the time - from the inception of any SEO project. Since you're starting to create a strategy and implementation path, it's important you involve your engineering, science, and data teams from the beginning. This is something that needs to be integrated within the project itself – if and when you need to touch base shouldn't be a consideration. It's a constant learning process that needs to be fed by different teams with different expertise."

Are there other ways you are using Agile?

"Yes. More than just how to use it, technology is a key focus area for Agile. One of the biggest frustrations for CEOs is not having tools to play with, such as for your CMS, data, and dashboards. One of the best ways to integrate Agile mentality into the technology element is using every single data point and technology you have at hand - to implement your projects in the fastest way.

The second part would be to evolve as you need. Sometimes we want to have fancy tools with a specific UI that gives us everything in a dashboard quickly and easily. In reality, it would be better to use your resources as you actually need them. If you're facing a block, or trying to launch a test that involves new technology, that's when these steps need to be taken. Having a collaborative approach to building technology will be a key part of 2022. Developing your own tools internally would be a tremendous enabler - it has been for us."

Is what you're saying appropriate for small teams, or is there a certain team size required to take advantage of Agile working?

"No, this applies to any size of teams. In fact, the smaller the team, the more Agile mentality you should have. The fewer resources you have, the more balls you need to kick off at the same time. It's a matter of making sure your resources are being used constantly, regardless of the size of your team."

What are a few areas that SEOs can focus on initially to test the value of working in an Agile manner?

"Firstly, focus on your process: how are you taking care of all of your projects? How do you launch them? How do you bring this information to the table and start creating the plan to get there? Rigidness is not a value that I would implement a lot in SEO. The constant changes in the algorithm and people's behaviour are significantly altering how we use search. Quick iterations of your plan, having a very defined vision but with a restating path towards that vision, would be a good way to implement Agile into SEO."

Is it challenging to announce at a board level that your plans have changed? Do top-level executives look for more consistency in approach?

"They are looking for consistency towards the goal, and where you are actually going. They recognise that things change quickly, so there's a need to redefine the path that takes us there in the fastest, most efficient way. It's not been a challenge with leadership. It has worked well because we've properly defined our vision, have a strong foundation, and backed everything up with data. Change is always constant - particularly in SEO."

What are some quick wins an SEO could make by iterating quickly?

"Take a look at your titles. We all know they're important, and one of the top-ranking factors, but are you getting the true 100% value from your title? For example, sometimes length is not necessarily something that is very fixed, and you can have a longer length and actually have a higher performance. Play a lot with the format of your titles. Is it all caps? Is it with dashes? We've been finding that little format changes can make a significant difference. Agile and fast testing has allowed us to quickly see the results of changes and understand what is scalable. This is great because it doesn't require heavy SEO research, just observation of what is happening in the SERP."

What technology are you using to conduct these tests?

"On the process side, we are working heavily on Smartsheets, particularly in one area called Workspace. This tool allows you to connect different spreadsheets, systems, and web pages into a single UI - enabling you to change tabs within the same tab and use different tools.

On the implementation side, we use a lot of different spreadsheets that connect to the backend of our system. This is an example of evolving your technology as you need it. So far, using spreadsheets that we hand over to engineering, or upload to a CMS, has worked well without the necessity of having a specific UI. They help us to test more intuitively. We do all of this in-house and have been working closely with all of our technology partners. We are basically acquiring a lot of data from different services, allowing us to create our own dashboards and measurement for these tests."

How significant is this within your role, as a percentage? How often should an SEO be thinking about testing in an Agile way?

"At Uber, my focus is 100% on growth and testing, so this is every day and involves two parts. One is the inception and innovation part, such as creating ideas, making sure we're constantly feeding a pipeline of different experiments. The second part is how to evolve all the processing technology. Our tests are going to be as complex as our technology allows us to make them.

My advice to everyone would be to make this a significant amount of your time. Creating ideas, and exploring how you can maximise what you already have, should be a core part of everyone's week. Maximising what you already have, is going to be a profitable use of your time."

How do you measure success? Is it on click-through rate, time spent on that page, purchases, or some other metric?

"It's always a combination of metrics. Different experiments have different goals. For example, when you're already ranking in position number two or three, you're probably aiming for click-through rate improvements. We try to create a balance between the SEO metrics we have, such as sessions, rankings, and click rates, but also how these stats are contributing to the business. There's always a money component here, and leadership will understand revenue."

How do you persuade non-technical content teams that doing a test is the right thing to do?

"Definitely one of the biggest blockers is controlling how the brand is presenting itself, and the actual words used to do this. Firstly, you have to present this to them as a one-off, cautious test - it's not a full-blown rollout that you're doing for your entire site. This is always a very convincing factor.

The second part is that you are actually basing your research on data and benchmarks. If your competitors are able to drive further performance by using certain words, then you need to play on a level playing field. If you're not able to compete by using different types of words or different writing styles, you will never be successful with SEO.

I know the content teams are always very cautious about the tone they're using. And sometimes, the tone is not necessarily the best when you're adding in search phrases or long-tail keywords. Once you have showcased the value in that through testing, you're able to present the economic benefits your idea has. There's very little argument to advocate not bringing more money to the company - regardless of what the brand guidelines are."

What should an SEO stop doing to focus more time on Agile SEO testing?

"Sticking to your plan. I would really suggest that you don't stick to your plan. A lot of plans generally change according to the algorithm or the trends of the business. Don't marry your ideas. Always make sure you're listening more to the data and the results than what you have put onto paper. What is most important is that you achieve your goals - and the goal should never be executing a plan, or executing a specific project."

Luis Rodríguez is Global Growth SEO Lead at Uber.

How to get more clicks without ranking higher - with Dan Petrovic from DEJAN Marketing

Dan believes that not enough SEOs focus on improving CTR, and that organic CTR optimization is a very worthwhile activity for SEOs in 2022.

Dan Petrovic says: "CTR optimisation is something that is a norm in paid search, but people hardly do it in SEO. It's one of the single most underutilised tactics you could do. People need to dive into their search console, check out what's happening in their click-through rates, and start asking questions. Why is this click-through rate really high? Why is this one really low? And what can you do with that information? The key is in finding anomalies. Once you find one, you can do wonderful things with it."

Why have SEOs not taken advantage of this before? Is it because the data hasn't been available, or because it's been easier to just rank new keywords higher?

"It's the mindset - because it's free. If you were paying for that click, you would scrutinise the title, the description, and the competition. You would really try to squeeze every click you can get out of that ad by improving the click-through rate. Whereas, if you have an organic result, people think, 'Let's rank higher' - that's the mentality: 'If we're ranking number three, what can happen if we push it to number two or one?' However, I've seen situations where something increased in rank and lost click-through rates.

We've seen studies done by numerous bloggers and SEOs that propose what an average click-through rate is for rank one to ten. And people think this is the model they should be using to find out what an average CTR is - but the truth is a lot more complicated. There are two main reasons for this: Google's results are not just ten results anymore and the user behaviour on the search results page is not linear. We're not going from top-down slowly scanning and moving our way down. It's more like a pinball machine. Our eyes are darting around, going here, and going there. Google's not helping SEOs - they're helping the user by providing more direct answers. There are now zero-click queries, where people ask for the weather, sports results, or lyrics, and they show up on the results page.

All these special search features tend to distract users and take away from your clicks. So as part of understanding the whole process, you also need to consider whether something has a low click-through rate because of something you did, or something Google did. For example, did you write a bad meta description? Do you not have an interesting title, or is it just that Google has something shiny next to you and there's nothing you can do to improve your situation in that particular search configuration?"

What does a great title and meta description look like that will encourage a high CTR?

"So far, we've discovered a number of things. The primary thing is that people don't read online. I've done this research several times, and we found that people scan and skim pages. Just as they don't read whole articles most of the time, they do the same thing with the search results. To create an interesting snippet, you need to be brief, concise and to the point - and have some of the power words that tend to resonate with your audience. Some of those things could be titles, phrases, or questions. Some of them are a little bit 'clickbaity' and are like a trend that will fizzle out. For example, in the movie industry, you have the current trend of calls to action such as, 'watch this now' working well. This is an instructional title that tells people what to do: 'Go check this out. Stop what you're doing now and click on 'Go watch this movie'.'

You also have your whole meta description, which gives a little bit of extra information. Then you have Rich Snippets schema available, for you to add all the wonderful, extra frills to your regular snippets. Another thing that people don't always consider is SERP geometry. Let's say everyone's packing their search results and snippets with lots of content and text. If you suddenly have a very brief two-word title and a one-sentence meta description, you'll now have a lot of negative space around you - so you're standing out.

The true key to finding out the right thing to do with your snippets is to look at your data. There's no other way to see it, because one website is different to the other. There are different industries, purposes, numbers of pages, and types of pages. You could be on information pages, evergreen content, blog content, product pages, or category pages - they all behave very differently. People may have different behaviours because they'll have different intents."

Is it still necessary to have a target keyword phrase within the page title at the moment?

"This is something you need to be careful of. When optimising your snippet for better click-through rates, you have to ensure the keywords you want to rank for are in the title. That's one of the most obvious signals to Google. You still want to follow those traditional SEO rules when writing - but copywriting is super important. Also, micro copywriting, including your titles and descriptions, is super important.

I obsess over my titles and descriptions. I sometimes spend half an hour on a single snippet, writing the title and rewriting it. And then when I'm finally happy with it, I don't just trust it - I test it over a 30-day period to compare the before and after. I'm then measuring the impact of my idea to improve the click-through rate, to see if it actually makes any difference. Sometimes it's a negative, so you could inadvertently ruin your click-through rate by attempting to improve it.

There is an important thing to remember when you're testing your click-through rates. Don't compare your data on position one and position two. It has to be position one to position one and position two to position two during that period of time. Obviously, positions one and two will have different click-through rates by default because of selection bias."

What software do you use to do this, and how do you identify the time periods that have the correct positions when you can take the data to use?

"The main software I use is Google Search Console because that's really the only thing that gives you the real query data. I start with that, and I used to use Excel. I would import all the queries from Search Console into a spreadsheet, and I would use formulas to plot a CTR curve. The CTR curve gave me an average click-through rate for each position, which I could then run against the actual position and see if it deviates above or below the expectation. Because I did this all the time for all my clients, I developed my own software - which now sits on algoroo.com. You can literally do this for free - assuming you're fairly competent at spreadsheets."

If you're ranking number three with a 10% click-through rate, and position two is getting a 5% click-through rate, will Google rank you higher because of your click-through rate (if everything else is the same)?

"Google uses click-through-rate to learn and train its systems, but they have a layer of protection against real-time CTR manipulation. For example, if I just pay 100,000 people to click on something instead of something else, Google's going to find that a bit suspicious. I would say that they are using that more as a training mechanism, but they definitely use click-through rate as an algorithmic signal. Every search engine does. If you started up a brand-new search engine, CTR would be one of your primary metrics to inform you of user behaviour on the server. Now Google has Android, Chrome, and Analytics - they know what's going on. They have their finger on the pulse when it comes to web traffic, and it's a very robust set of signals that are useful for ranking.

I wouldn't worry about using CTR to change the rankings. You should be quite interested in looking at averages, to detect anomalies and attach your ROI to different rankings scenarios. The wonderful thing about working out potential traffic you can squeeze out of extra click-through-rate, is that you can also model your ranking projections based on increases in the rank itself. You can project the traffic gains on the rank-based scenario, which is separate from the CTR increase scenario.

You can do a clever little thing by importing all your Google keywords from the Ads campaigns, and all the non-ranking keywords. You can project for the things you don't rank for using your CTR model. Then finally, you can attach your average order value. For example, if you're an eCommerce website, you can attach an average order value and average conversion rate to create a rudimentary ROI study. This allows you to make projections and inform your decisions, based on how much money you will make if you achieve certain CTR or ranking scenarios."

What should an SEO stop doing to spend more time focusing on click-through rates in 2022?

"People tend to obsess over link acquisition. I've seen too many people earn links, make links, or buy links towards blog pages when in fact, the link should be going towards the product pages you want to rank for.

I'm going to circle back to branding. If you want to improve your click-through rate, you could rewrite all your titles and do clever things. However, if a web user is on the search results page and goes through the list, they will pay attention if they see a familiar brand. That is the single most overriding factor that will make them decide. If there's a whole lot of unknowns, and suddenly there's an 'Airbnb' - they're going to click on 'Airbnb' because they're familiar with it. There's a whole range of benefits when it comes to CTR.

If you weren't busy with CTR, you should definitely invest in branding, because it will improve your CTR. If you improve your brand, you'll get more traction from link building. If you reach out to somebody and they recognise your brand, they'll be more willing to interact with you."

You can find Dan Petrovic over at DEJANmarketing.com.

Look beyond the value of the click - with Antonella Villani from Assembly

Antonella highlights that measuring clicks isn't enough, and that there are other KPIs that SEOs should be tracking.

Antonella Villani says: "We need to look beyond the value of the clicks for our keywords in position one for organic - because we all know our job goes well beyond this."

Why is measuring clicks not enough?

"In the past few years, we've seen Google give more and more space to paid features, and all sorts of other features in the SERPs. Even if you're position one, it probably means your click-through rate will be much lower than it used to be. This means it's very important that you talk about the other work that you do that might not be visible."

Is just seeing your brand on SERP providing SEO value in itself? Is it more important to focus on user experience on-site than measuring clicks?

"No. Clicks are still the number one metric we should always be looking at. However, beyond that, there are many other sorts of KPIs and factors that we can consider when we're asked about SEO performance."

What are the top KPIs to look at?

"It depends on the work you do. For instance, site speed and page speed are something that we've been talking about for a very long time. This is especially the case in the past couple of years because of the Core Web Vitals update, and we've finally got the development budget to make things happen and see the improvements we've been wanting for years.

If we said the improvements that we're measuring are only clicks from ranking improvements, it would be a disservice to ourselves. We know that by improving speed, we increase conversion rates, and maybe decrease bounce rates - not only in SEO, but across all the other channels as well."

Is it negative if someone visits a web page, and then goes back to the

SERP without clicking through to another page on the site?

"It depends. If they take the action you want to take, then it's not negative. If they don't, and are not satisfied with the results they're getting, you're just losing somebody that's landed on your page - they're not converted."

How do you differentiate between different clicks and different audiences? Some clicks will be fairly early in the funnel, and some are going to be later. Someone visiting for the first time and seeing your site for 20 seconds could be very valuable for the future, how do you measure the value of that?

"You might be looking at different sorts of attribution models. There is definitely value in somebody being exposed to your website, even if they do not take action straight away. Using a different attribution model that is not based on last-click might help you measure this."

Do you have a preferred attribution model, or do you try and understand your client's business and agree on a model based on their metrics?

"The best approach is understanding what the client is trying to achieve, and how are you going to report on that. If you've got a data science team, you might be able to develop an attribution model catered specifically for that client. There are many different ways you can do this."

What if you have a client who is only interested in last-click? How do you talk about the value of early-stage traffic that may not be ready to convert yet?

"Again, you can introduce other metrics. If last-click is all they want to hear about, that's what you're going to report on. You can try to target longer-tail keywords, for instance, that might bring you further down the funnel - so you're looking at that last click."

Are you seeing a trend towards focusing on longer-tail, bottom-of-funnel keyword phrases rather than more competitive high-volume keywords that are hard to rank for?

"Yes, and potentially they're very valuable. I think businesses are starting to do this more. Again, because of the changes in the SERPs, ranking in position three or four might end up giving you very few clicks anyway. Targeting keywords with more conversion-lead intent can definitely help you."

How do you help someone who isn't a technical marketer to understand things like click-through-rate?

"When you are doing trainings with clients, you need to make sure you talk their language. For instance, if you're talking to developers, and you tell them that increasing speed will improve conversion rates, they'll be very keen to listen if they know it will create X more revenue for the business. This goes down very well, and they also feel part of this larger project.

It all depends on who you're talking to, and what kinds of metrics and measurements they're looking at on a daily basis. You need to work out how SEO is going to help them."

What does success look like when you take a client's focus away from clicks to other metrics? What metrics should be the focus of a modern, progressive SEO agency report?

"In Data Studio, for instance, you can build dashboards specifically for the projects you're working on for a quarter. If we focus on speed again, you can overlay your improvements on base speed with conversion rates, and bounce rates. You could even look CPCs for your PPC campaigns.

Think about the value you're bringing to their business beyond rankings. Being in position one is obviously important - and you still need to monitor keyword rankings and the number of keywords you rank for - but we need to understand that the role of SEO is much wider than just looking at the keywords. We are agents for change in the businesses we work for - whether we are in-house or external consultants."

How can SEOs get better at becoming 'agents for change', and have more understanding and interaction with other areas of the business, including strategy?

"Speak the language of the person you're speaking to. Understand what they're trying to achieve and how you can support them. Make it clear to them that you can help them with their goals. We need to move away from an 'us versus the rest of the business' mentality. Instead, we're here to support an improvement to the overall website experience. We're not just here to target keywords and create technical documents - that aren't very useful if they just sit on someone's desktop."

What's one thing that SEOs can stop doing to spend more time educating clients to understand different metrics?

"Stop robotically doing SEO reports and audits. Really try to understand the business' needs and how you can best help them achieve their goals."

You can find Antonella Villani over at assemblyglobal.com.

11 NEXT GEN TECH

Find opportunities for embedding machine learning into your processes - with Lazarina Stoy

Lazarina believes that too many SEOs are manually doing tasks that could be automated, and that machine learning could be the answer.

Lazarina Stoy says: "There are three main components of embedding machine learning into your processes. Firstly, the 'What' - which is to increase your efficiency exponentially. Secondly, the 'Why' - which is to focus on building systems that skyrocket performance. And thirdly, the 'How' - which is finding opportunities to utilise machine learning.

Increasing your efficiency is something that every SEO needs to do, especially as the industry becomes more competitive and search engines continuously improve their offering and algorithms. There's a lot of hunger for good SEOs because businesses and individuals are becoming a lot more aware of the importance of developing their online brands and digital presence. They need allies to help them do this efficiently, and it makes sense to think about how to increase your efficiency as an SEO because it can save you a lot of time - which is a very valuable commodity. You need to build systems internally that can free up your time to focus on strategy, and develop scalable systems for your clients.

The most exciting way to become more efficient is to seek opportunities for embedding machine learning into your processes, and there are a couple of different steps you can take to do this. First of all, you need to become familiar with the different types of models, scripts, and tools available out there. Most of them don't even require any coding experience, you just have to get started and get your hands dirty. Then, when you're encountering a new task or project, you just have to think about how you can break this down into things that are more manageable. Finally, you just have to assess the characteristics of the task, and identify which machine learning models, libraries, or scripts can become your allies when completing these tasks. This will give you more time to focus on more scalable initiatives."

What specific SEO tasks are currently not particularly efficient, and can be aided with machine learning?

"Every task that requires you to pull exports from different systems and tools. Most of the time, we get these large chunks of data that need to be audited. The process of data science and analysis is the number one area where you can get a machine learning model or script to become your ally in identifying opportunities. Furthermore, you can easily measure the time you save after implementing a particular script model.

For things like internal linking or technical audits, you can create scripts that actually identify the top opportunities based on machine learning libraries, or even clustering content based on the similarity of this content. Obviously, it will be a lot easier for a Natural Language Processing (NLP) library, or model, to go through the content of your website and cluster it as opposed to you reading the articles and trying to make sense of them. These are great opportunities to rapidly scale your auditing processes."

Is this something that existing SEO auditing tools can offer or does this have to be set up manually without a pre-existing platform?

"It's a mixture of both, and it depends on the access to the tools you have. For instance, if you are working in-house, you might have access to very advanced, expensive tooling, which allows you to get more insights than you'd normally get from doing simple analysis yourself with basic tooling. There are some great tools out there that provide very insightful comments. If you want to do a very in-depth analysis - especially on larger websites - it's always good for you to know how the tools created the insights, so you can replicate it in your processes as well."

Can you recommend any processes and machine learning tools?

"It's quite easy to find all of the Python stuff from the SEO community on Twitter - so I'd definitely recommend following them to get a lot of amazing resources.

In terms of the processes, you can very quickly look into automating things like keywords clustering, extraction of the main keywords for a particular topic, labelling search intent based on the content of the article or based on the title, and looking into how to cluster different content using topic modelling and algorithms. If you get a massive website audit and have a huge export from a tool like Screaming Frog, exploring this data in Python is a great starting point, before incorporating different models based on what the analysis shows you.

A couple of very quick libraries to get started doing this are pandas and NumPy. For visualisation, you can incorporate things like Matplotlib and for natural language processing, things like NLTK's fuzzy matching techniques. Also, there are different clustering algorithms, but k-nearest neighbors (KNN) is the one that works well for clustering different texts.

When you have a particular task, the main thing is to break down what data you are trying to analyse. Is it numerical or is it text? Then, label the task you're trying to do. For instance, if you're analysing text data, are you trying to generate new text, cluster it, or maybe label or classify it? Once you have these two things, you can start searching for algorithms, libraries, or scripts that can help you achieve this task."

Does this mean you could use machine learning to assist you with identifying content opportunities, and determining what you should be writing about next?

"Yes – but this is the second step of topic clustering. The first step is analysing your website and content using machine learning libraries to provide embeddings for all the words in the text. They work by considering the inter-exchangeability of words and topics. For instance, if you have a lot of keywords in your content, you might imagine this is a topic that you are trying to target as well. This is the same assumption most of the tools like Semrush make when they provide you with the list of parent, seed, and 'broad match' keywords.

This analysis during the first step will show you the definitive clusters of content, and where the similarities between these clusters lie. This can give you a lot of opportunities to find out which clusters you can link together, and which are the main keywords for each cluster - so you can guide your users to discover new content.

After this, you can seek out where your topical authority is - based on the content you have. For instance, which topic is the most represented on your website? Does this align with your business proposition? If it doesn't, then you know where to expand, and invest in more content development."

Should SEOs be concerned that quality may deteriorate when so many different tasks are automated?

"This is definitely something I consider when trying to implement any sort of machine learning algorithm. People should consider these scripts, tools, and libraries as allies rather than replacements to a particular process. Imagine this is like someone on their first day in SEO, because these algorithms are not typically designed for our work. There would definitely be a quality checking step after any implementation.

Normally, you will be implementing pre-trained models. It will take additional time to fine-tune it based on the data you have if you're doing that. If you're just looking for a simple output, such as automating meta descriptions and generating them in bulk, then you'd need to quality check the output after using a machine learning tool. Similarly, you'd need to sense check things like automated image alt text generation and captions."

Can you think of anything that shouldn't be automated?

"At this point, I really don't think we should be automating content generation. The creators of GPT-3 and other models have trained them on historical data that is not updated in real-time. Of course, this will probably change in the future. The other issue is that it has a lot of biases and makes a lot of assumptions. Furthermore, when you are generating text, there is no authoritativeness. There is no trust in the text, because it's not fact-checked or providing references.

As SEOs, we know that search engines and users want authoritativeness, trust, and expertise, and we cannot safely say that our automated models can provide this yet. Until they do, I'm not sure how they can be used as the main driver of a content strategy. Things like content and user experience really need the human touch."

How far away are we from a significant percentage of the content on a website being generated automatically?

"I've seen a lot of SEOs currently running experiments with their sites, and they never put the name of the site there. You never know, it might already be the case! I really don't know - but it's an interesting future to think about. I'm sure that Google still states in their guidelines that automatically generated content is not something that is aligned with best practice. Automated content requires editing, fact-checking, and sense-checking. Hopefully, we are far away from this - but you never know."

What's one thing SEOs should stop doing to spend more time investigating the potential opportunities of machine learning?

"If you imagine an on-page optimisation project, you'll have many different mini-workstreams - such as optimising the meta descriptions, optimising the titles, and writing image captions. Break it down into chunks and try to test out all of the different scripts and models that already exist for things like generating titles, meta descriptions, H1 headings, and alt text. See how much easier it is to work with this output. Then, just edit and sense check it, as opposed to trying to generate it yourself. You can now use the time you saved from doing this to create better strategies for scaling sites."

You can find Lazarina Stoy over at Lazarina Stoy.com.

Start getting comfortable with JavaScript rendering - with Nik Ranger from StudioHawk

Nik shares that if you aren't comfortable with JavaScript rendering, now's the time to find out more about it.

Nik Ranger says: "Everyone is very aware, all around the world, that we are coming out of a pandemic. The foot traffic from the streets is moving online and everyone's looking at their websites and thinking about how they're going to make the most of that. A lot of site owners and web developers have been busier than ever creating new sites, and as a technical SEO a lot of my job has been around site migrations.

This is only going to continue, and I'm seeing a massive influx of developers wanting to develop sites using JavaScript libraries. This is absolutely fine, but there are some important caveats that we, as SEOs, need to be able to understand, and communicate to different parties for project management."

Is JavaScript likely to be better or worse for SEO, or does it depend on how you use it?

"It's a library that you can use, like anything else. The mission is often to get a site to load super-fast. You hear from everybody at the moment that site speed is really important, and it's considered a 'ranking factor'. To oversimplify things, people create a really fast site, hoping that everything else will fall into place. That seems to be the general understanding of most site owners. They go to a web developer and give a brief that just says to make the site as fast as possible. In the web development world, JavaScript is seen as the hero that is leveraged to be able to do that. JavaScript will take parts of HTML and parts of CSS and be able to combine that into simpler forms of JavaScript which is far fewer lines. Therefore, it's far less to crawl and perceive.

However, when it comes to rendering (the process whereby Googlebot retrieves the pages, runs the code, and assesses your content), Google understands the layout and structure on the site differently compared to what is seen by you. The information that Google collects during the rendering process is used to rank the quality of the page - against the content and against other pages trying to rank for those keywords. That needs to be part of the conversation in the planning process, and it's often completely excluded.

I have seen a massive influx of sites being launched that are purely client-side rendered. All JavaScript is client-side rendered by default. As Martin Splitt said, 'If you use a JavaScript framework, the default is client-side rendering. This means you send the bare-bones HTML over and then a piece of JavaScript, and the JavaScript fetches and assembles the content in the browser.' When JavaScript sites are being produced, that's part of the message that gets lost.

Client-side rendering has two main downsides. First, it can increase the likelihood of a poor user experience, because JavaScript can add seconds of load time to a page. That's counterintuitive and puts a burden on the website visitor. Secondly, it affects search engine bots. For example, Googlebot has two waves of indexing. In the first wave, they crawl and index the HTML of the page. In the second wave, they come back and render the JavaScript when those resources start to become available. That two-phase approach means that sometimes JavaScript content can be missed, and not included in Googlebot's index. That's a big thing that SEOs need to understand, and look for, going into 2022."

What common aspects can't be completely rendered, and are often missed by search engines?

"It depends on how much is actually being written in JavaScript. For example, if you're using native server-side rendering in Shopify, and use a language like React on top of that, it's like having jQuery added to a website instead of having it on the server. It means you can't server-side render because everything's been client-side – you're not going to be able to communicate with the server at all. It's not interacting in a way that can produce all the resources that were intended for that page.

A quick way to test this is to go to your site - literally copy out a bit of the text on the page, right-click, go to View Source, open the DOM (the HTML that user agents use to crawl and parse), and try to find some of the text on there. Google relies on the text and the HTML a lot of the time, to be able to parse and understand the context of a page. If it's not able to see that, it's not going to have any context for the other elements on the page. That's your canary in the mineshaft to figure out what's going on with your site, and whether it is client-side or server-side rendered. You need to know if the basic elements on the page are reflected in the HTML that user agents are able to crawl and see.

If you're using a pre-rendered solution, which can be really awesome, you're probably not going to be able to see it. You might have to reverse-engineer it through Cloudflare Workers, but that's a whole other topic."

How does an SEO communicate with the developer to make sure that everything's done the right way?

"It's all about relationships. If you want to work with developers, from a project management standpoint, you have to consider that they have a very set idea of how they want to build a site. You're there to help guide them down the pathway. To use a bowling analogy: you want to guide them down the lane to hit the pins, and not go into the gutters on either side. It's important to have a set list of questions. I've made a template structure for site migrations for my entire team because we need to have specific things.

You obviously need to understand their business workflow, but also ask whether they're changing the CMS, or the URLs of any of the pages. You want to know if they're keeping the same titles and meta descriptions or if they're planning to get rid of any pages or content as part of the migration. Also, you need to start asking if there are any technical considerations that you need to note. Be aware of who you're asking, it might be the owner - who may not know exactly what they've been told to do, or why.

Ask those exploratory questions about the technology stack – how it's going to be done, if it's going to be a custom site, if it's going to be written in Angular or React, etc. After asking those sorts of important questions you need to let them know that if you are going down this pathway, you need to be aware of how it renders. Often, they've got a directive, and the rendering part of the conversation is not even thought about. You need to introduce that as part of the planning process, and make sure that people are mindful. Then throughout the process, you can keep testing and re-evaluating those areas. There are so many different ways to server-side render JavaScript.

It's really important that you ask these questions, then you can change the methodology of how you deliver those recommendations. Developers will appreciate that you're aware of their workflow alongside your directive with the project. The whole goal is to have a successful site, and you can agree on that core principle."

What percentage of websites nowadays are using JavaScript like this, and is it increasing?

"I don't know the exact percentage. I think the growth of this will be exponential because a lot of this stuff is very new. It's new for a lot of SEOs and it's even new for Google. Martin Splitt has been a wonderful resource to the SEO community and is doing a great job of helping people to understand these new changes as it's been rolling out.

It is changing. From listening to Google, and having conversations with people on Twitter, their aim is for their user agents, tools, processes, and browsers to help you understand all different types of languages. At the same time, like everything, it is a constantly evolving process. It is using another language that needs to be compatible across systems rather than just understood. It is definitely an area that you need to be very aware of."

Is it something that only needs to be of concern during a new site design, or should JavaScript rendering be done on a regular basis?

"As soon as it's done, it's good. However, if you are using third party tools, it's always important to see what resources are loaded into that. When you're looking at how many resources it takes to load a page there might a third-party plugin, for example, that doesn't render at all. That can be detrimental. A tool might insert an iframe, and then nothing after that iframe will render properly. It's always important to be aware of what you're looking at.

Remember, when it comes to JavaScript, it does obey HTML5 protocol. There are lots of great things that you can do outside of that. You can provide caching that gives Google a little snapshot to save on your crawl budget, or, if there are render-blocking resources, you can defer it with something asynchronous, which is great. There are tonnes of opportunities. Google's PageSpeed Insights, and Lighthouse as well, are a great way to, again, be the canary in the mineshaft with that stuff."

How can SEOs save time, to free them up for finding out more about JavaScript rendering?

"There are so many amazing tools out there - Google gives you a whole suite of different tools to test how pages are being perceived by their user agents. Search Console is great and, if you don't have it, the Mobile-Friendly test is also useful. You can see the rendered HTML, and you can see the screenshot of what Google is able to see. PageSpeed Insights is awesome as well, and so is Lighthouse.

Search Console is your one-to-one way of seeing what's being discovered, but not indexed, and why. You can see the referring pages and how Google is able to find those pages. If you're not using Search Console regularly, why not? Google has made an awesome free resource for any site owner to unpack and reverse-engineer how these things are happening, and why it's happening as well."

You can find Nik Ranger over at studiohawk.com.au.

Serverless applications that run on the edge are going to be the future of enterprise SEO deployments - with Nick Wilsdon from Torque

Nick shares that SEO 'on the edge' is a game changer for enterprise SEO deployments.

Nick Wilsdon says: "I've been obsessed with edge SEO for nearly two years now. SEO teams need to understand how they can start utilising the edge, and the opportunities it provides. It's quite a complex subject with various levels of understanding around it, but I'll give a simple rundown of what you can do. The edge is CDNs, or Content Delivery Networks, such as Fastly, Akamai and Cloudflare. These were previously used for content distribution, but they've gone far beyond that. Now, we can hold data on the edge with KV-Store, we have increased processing power, and we have increased memory. We're moving into a situation where we can have a serverless environment, and we can run more complex computation on the edge. That gives huge opportunities for SEO.

As a practical example, we can start to move all our redirects onto the edge. Previously, managing and improving redirects in an ongoing process would be quite a challenge for an SEO team. Issues like flattening redirect chains, dealing with link rot and finding better contextual targets for links can be complex. If you can move these into the edge, and start developing logic around that, you can be fixing and improving redirects as ongoing workflow.

The edge can provide opportunities in everything - from dealing with redirects, rewrites, or schema, to stitching data from databases on the origin server into the page at the edge, for the end user. There are so many possibilities that you have with this technology. The edge is part of the architecture, and it has certain pros and cons against the origin server that you're currently using."

What are the pros and cons of using the edge?

"To get around problems on the origin server, there are things that should be done on the edge, and there are things that should be done on the origin server. You should always ask yourself where your problem should be fixed. When you're approaching it from that angle, your perspective changes.

To use our previous example, redirects is something that works particularly well on the edge. There's no point getting a user in via the CDN, taking them to the origin server and then redirecting them back and forth. It's a huge waste of time. By putting redirects on the edge, you provide a much faster experience for bots and users. You can save up to 800-900 milliseconds per journey. When it makes sense to serve content to the user at the point of interaction with your network, it's something you should be doing on the edge."

What size of business or website should be using the edge?

"It is primarily in enterprise. Platforms like Akamai and Fastly have quite significant costs associated with them, so they suit larger enterprises. However, Cloudflare is used by a huge number of companies, and it's very accessible. The capability is there, but it is work — it's politics to get these things deployed, and get these processes built. If you are redirecting dozens or hundreds of links, you might not go to the edge. However, for redirecting links in the tens of thousands, edge is a solution.

Like any project in SEO, it's about getting things done at the client level you're at. The edge is a toolset that you can utilise and access. It may well make sense in terms of the reward that you can get for the client, for the effort that needs to be put in. Having knowledge about what you can do on the edge allows you to bring it into your calculations, and bring it to the client as a possible solution."

What are some of the initial steps that an SEO should be taking to get started?

"First, like anything in SEO, do the background learning. You have to have a good knowledge before you start engaging. Edge involves developers, so you're going to have to have the knowledge to enter those conversations. Take time to learn edge from tools like Cloudflare - they have published a huge amount of material for people learning how this works. Set up your own test environments, do some simple 'search and replace' scripts, to take bits out of pages and present them back. You can start to teach yourself. There is a lot of politics involved with these front-end teams, and you need a certain level of knowledge to start interacting with them successfully."

Are there tools that SEOs can access for having specific services, like schema, delivered on the edge?

"There are lots of tools that are looking at how to do this on the edge. It's going to be the way forward for this kind of content delivery. Specifically, in the schema space, tools like Schema App are looking at edge delivery. At the moment, they use tags via Tealium or Google Tag Manager to insert into the page, but they're trying to move this towards edge. There are definitely SaaS platforms out there looking at how to incorporate this as well.

Edge compute is how edge has changed this year. Standard edge had standard key/value pairs and very limited storage, but computed edge is a leap to 500,000 Key-Value Stores and massively increased computational power. It's happening this year, so it's still very new for a lot of SaaS platforms, but it's absolutely the way I see them going. There will be an increased number of products and offerings, and you're going to find specialists who will help you to get these projects deployed."

Is it a set-and-forget situation, or is this something that SEOs need to be doing on a regular basis?

"It depends on what you're trying to do. For link management, the project would be set up and then used as an ongoing process. It would give you easy interfaces to manage links, upload links, and deal with REGEX - in terms of redirections. You would have a system to easily deal with issues, such as chain redirects and link rot. Often, it's about setting up this capability for an SEO to then run with.

However, edge is always evolving, it is a developing platform. You may, down the road, want to do something more complex. You might want to do different things for different users, or for different people in different locales - you might even want to integrate it into different business processes within your company. There's always room for developing on the edge, but for bringing that capacity to SEO teams, it's very much project-based work."

What are the main benefits of using the edge?

"It definitely gives you the ability to do things at scale, because you're taking the load off the origin server. It will also help with the time it takes content to load on a web page. Performance-wise, when you're delivering on the edge it's closer to the user. You will have significant page speed improvements.

There are environmental and cost benefits as well, to reducing some of the waste crawls that we have across big enterprise sites. That will become more important over the next few years. So much of the capability of the web is used up by bots. Finding ways to make this more efficient is something that's at the top of the list for Google, and for every large enterprise site. They want to decrease the costs associated with crawl efficiency, provide a faster service, and make happier sites for Google. As an added benefit, they will also become more environmentally-friendly."

How does an SEO articulate the value of the edge to a general

marketer?

"You would look at the specific use case that you're addressing. To go back to the redirects example, you may have realised that you are getting conflicts because you have redirects in many different locations around the origin server. You can explain that bringing them to the edge would simplify this, by having them in one place so that you can start to make improvements. You can talk about link recovery, because links coming in to 404 pages have very little value. It will give you a better process for dealing with that problem and bringing links into better-mapped places around your site. This will increase the SEO value, and the experience for users who are coming through from third party sites. It's the same arguments that you have for tactics on the origin server. It's just a different way of solving your issues - and it may be a better way. Use the same business logic.

Another case for using the edge is how agile and efficient it can be. There may be reasons why it's difficult for you to fix these things on the origin server, and edge may be a more elegant solution. Something that was low-priority, and was going to take several months to resolve on the origin, could be done in months, or even weeks, on the edge."

Can the edge help reduce work for the dev team, and avoid the limitations of a CMS?

"There are always going to be some things that should be done on the edge, and some things that should be done on the origin server. In certain situations, you will need to fix things in your underlying structure. You shouldn't use the edge as a way of bypassing difficult decisions about your CMS and your origin. You might find that the benefits you can see to doing something on the edge actually provides a business case for fixing the CMS, and the inherent issues that you have.

It's all about process. If the process and the solution is better on the edge, then do it. If you're hiding tech debt that you have with the CMS, then you may find that it's better to make those fixes."

What's something that SEOs should stop doing to spend more time understanding the benefits of the edge?

"SEOs need to understand scaling in order to be effective. Some SEOs are still focusing on individual fixes for large enterprises - perhaps they're still doing their meta or titles manually. That's not scalable, especially recently. Google is developing their understanding of how title tags work, and the data that they're going to pull in to form the title tag. You need to find ways to scale up. If you want to be effective, work out where to spend your time effectively. The tactics that work best are the ones that scale quickly and deliver results for the business."

You can find Nick Wilson over at TorquePartnership.com.

Are you prepared for Platform-less, server-less SEO on the edge? - with Bastian Grimm from Peak Ace.

Bastian's tip follows on from Nick's, highlighting that Platform-less, server-less SEO has the potential to make several SEO operations much more efficient.

Bastian Grimm says: "SEO on the edge, or platform-less SEO, is a really exciting topic because historically when we try to optimise different systems, such as CMSs and eCommerce platforms, it requires resource availability. You have to make business cases, and you have to fight with different stakeholders. Often, one of the key challenges in SEO is to actually overcome these obstacles and get things implemented. However, with sever-less SEO, you can take away some of this pain because you're essentially already implementing certain changes and optimisations. Not on the platform itself, but rather on what we call 'the edge'.

An example of the edge is a CDN like CloudFlare, where they have a technology called Workers. The idea is that you don't necessarily have to make changes on the respective platform. Instead, you rely on this technology, or the CDN provider you're already using, to get things done. This can be a fantastic solution for getting things done quickly, because you don't have to wait in the queue for the next iteration of development.

This means you can get things done relatively quickly, so it is definitely one of the big topics for 2022. You can essentially use it as a testing ground. You can use the edge to get stuff done right away, and then prove the impact to stakeholders. With this information, you can build your business case, and get a proper implementation done afterwards. It's a very exciting concept to help SEOs move significantly faster."

Is there any real need to consider SEO on the edge for SEOs who are happy with their current platform, have full access to everything and are in control of new platform development?

"In the rare case of a platform that's extremely flexible, and you're fully controlling, there's probably less of a need. However, server-less SEO is very easy to implement. I referred to CloudFlare Workers, and it's essentially just a piece of JavaScript. The complexity of creating something is very small. Even with very limited development skills, you can get quick fixes done in literally 10 minutes. All you do is create your couple of lines of code, hit the Workers 'deploy' button, and it's done. Therefore, in most cases, you are significantly slower, even if you're under full control of the release planning.

The other benefit is it's extremely powerful for testing, as well as classic SEO fixes. One of the things we're doing is split-testing for SEO purposes. You can do this using Workers, with very small implementation effort. This is a very nice way to benefit from this technology without having to do much else."

Is this something that all SEOs need to be aware of, or is it only relevant for SEOs in enterprises?

"There is a huge benefit for larger organisations, because they often move slower due to higher levels of complexity, stakeholders, and politics. However, even if you have smaller sites you could use it. We've been utilising Workers a lot on smaller platforms with Shopify, because until recently it didn't really allow you to change the 'robots.txt' file. It's not necessarily only for large or small, it really depends on what situation and setup you're dealing with, and then how you could incorporate it to help you be more efficient."

What specific elements will this technology be used for, and what are the aspects of SEO where you definitely wouldn't use platform-less SEO?

"The beauty - and also the danger - of SEO on the edge is that you have full access to everything, so you can test whatever you can think of. I could test anything from different title tag variations to more complex things such as changing content or moving HTML elements around. You are fairly limitless, because it gives you access to all the elements but again - this can be dangerous. If you are modifying things on the edge that are implemented differently on your platform, such as a shop or the CMS, you could introduce conflicting code or produce unforeseen behaviour. It's very important that you have proper communication when using this powerful weapon. Make stakeholders aware that certain things are being done that are suddenly happening at a different place."

What are a few initial first steps that SEOs need be aware of when they first discover this technology? What are the first few things they should probably test to get the biggest quick wins?

"You need a bit of technical experience, but not too much, which is what I really like about it. The CloudFlare technology is essentially JavaScript, and they have a very well-documented section on their homepage that gives you all the info on API's, functionality, and pre-made code samples. Entry into the topic is relatively straightforward.

You need a CloudFlare account, which is free for everyone until a certain size limit, and then you need to be somewhat familiar with JavaScript, so you can modify at least the ready-made examples. Then, to understand the complexity, you can try to access some basic elements like page titles, meta descriptions, or paragraphs with content. Modify them to see what comes out of it. There is a Workers Playground element, which is just a simple sandbox. It gives an instant way to preview and test a Workers script directly in the browser, against any site. It makes everything super-easy because you can essentially deploy anything, just in this testing stage, and see the real-world output.

There's been a lot of discussions and posts about it recently. One of the platforms I suggest for this implementation is called Sloth. It's a meta-CMS, so essentially, it's a code creator for Workers. If you don't want to write code, you could also have them support you in creating the functionality based on Workers that you actually want. There are various approaches but

I think, barrier-wise, it's fairly easy to get into it."

What are your general thoughts on best practice for page title and meta description at the moment?

"There's been a lot of recent update chatter around Google dealing with page titles differently and using values from headlines, and even anchor texts. However, on page titles, the biggest thing we still see with a lot of platforms is they're just creating internal duplication in various ways, forms and formats. I would certainly make sure my page titles are still unique, and you have certain keyword inclusion. It's not a list of keywords, or keyword-stuffing them for the sake of it. Just make them relevant and click-friendly - and take care of readability. This hasn't really changed that much. If Google decides to, for whatever reason, rewrite your titles, then maybe they weren't that great in the first place - so that's something you probably should revisit.

It's great because you can easily test these things. You can test different types. Do you want them to be a bit longer, or a bit shorter? Do you want to move the brand to the end or not? These are the things you can really test relatively quickly. One issue with testing is that people need to understand that you can't test on a one-on-one basis. You need to build groups. This is very important - otherwise, the results won't tell you much."

What are your general thoughts on the amount of time or eyeballs needed on a page title, for example, before we get statistical relevance and can be certain that something has performed better?

"Reaching the respective relevancy you need is probably one of the biggest topics in split-testing. It's not really possible to test something with 100 visitors. Yes, you might see a result - but is it actually relevant? I'd rather test chunks of pages that are somewhat the same. 20 in one bucket, then 20 in another and 20 in another. Make sure that they are somewhat comparable in terms of traffic. Also, you need to consider seasonality - when do you test, and what do you test?

As for duration, you also need to consider that Google needs to recrawl and reprocess things. Don't make the mistake of ending tests too early."

What's one thing SEOs can stop doing to spend more effort

developing SEO on the edge?

"What fascinates me is how many people still 'chase the algorithm(s)'. I'd rather not do that and focus on the stuff I can somewhat control. I would move away from this reactive SEO - running after every trend you see out there is probably not the best use of time.

I'd rather be proactive and start using this. The best reason to use edge SEO right now is to test out things very quickly. Build a rough implementation and see what it does. If it works, fantastic. Make your case and roll it out into the platform. Be more proactive and not so reactive."

You can find Bastian Grimm over at www.pa.ag.

12 PASS THE BATON

Focus on the next generation of SEOs - with Si Shangase from WorldRemit

Si closes off our expert contributions by highlighting the importance of training the next generation of SEOs.

Si Shangase says: "Focus on the next generation of SEOs that are coming into the space. This is important now more than ever, due to what has happened over the last two years. The lockdown has really shaped how we do business, how we work, and how we come together as groups. If you look at the juniors that have come straight out of university, they haven't had the opportunity to work in groups in an office environment, where you can learn through osmosis. It's been a challenge for them. There is a lot that we can do with Teams, but we all get Teams fatigue. More can be done in the SEO community to bring the next generation into SEO. We know that, with the rise of social media, SEO is not the 'cool kid' anymore."

Has the pandemic affected recruitment in terms of the types of people that are being brought into the profession?

"I think so. SEO is a broad spectrum, but the biggest stress for people who are recruiting is that they don't hire people outside of the traditional norms. Most businesses always recruit from the same university, and the same channels, so the diversity of people working in that space is shrinking. During the pandemic we also saw a decline in the number of women working within SEO. That could be for several reasons, such as childcare responsibilities, but the pandemic has caused a shift in the demographic that's been coming into SEO. The younger generation need access to the things that we've always known to do in SEO. We need things like Meets after work, including those sponsored by companies or organisations, to bring new people into the space. That's been a lot more challenging."

What can more senior SEOs and recruiters do to make SEO more appealing to the younger generation?

"It isn't one-size-fits-all. You should become more aligned with universities, and have workshops that can involve junior members coming into the SEO space. Also, offer more work experience with team members, which could be structured as well. We have platforms that allow structured training, such as EdX and Coursera, where we can upload and record our knowledge. That can help bring more people in. We also need to show the potential of what can be done with SEO, especially with a lot of business going digital and having a digital transformation. Show the career trajectory, and the successes of people that have actually come into the space. We can do a lot more to highlight that.

Also, look at where society is going, and things like ESG, so that we can highlight how SEO benefits the wider community. Bring people up to speed on the fundamentals there, because that could be a huge selling point for us as an industry - and as a community. Young people coming from university are going to be big on climate change and social equity. We, as a community, need to highlight how we are a lot more forward-thinking than most industries."

Because of the current SEO climate, is there an issue with retention or is it more about training?

"It's a bit of both. It's an issue with a sense of feeling connected. When you're a junior starting off in your career, working from home, your space hasn't really changed. You've been doing that throughout university. When you have an opportunity to go into the office, the space does change, and you have an ability to learn from people who have been there for a long time. You don't get that kind of contact when you work from home, especially starting off.

A lot of businesses weren't ready for this new transformation - working from home almost full time for the past 18 months or so. There weren't processes in place for training, particularly for the younger generation who haven't been in SEO for a long time. That meant that new people coming in have become dissociative learners. They don't get any positive reinforcement, or an arm around the shoulder. There haven't been senior members of the team giving mentorship on a regular basis. Some things can be done online, but you miss out on daily opportunities - those 'water cooler moments' that can't happen on Zoom or Teams."

What's your sales pitch for encouraging someone to choose a career in SEO?

"SEO is life changing because the skills are transferable. You learn a lot about how digital works. There are also so many pathways. If you're creative - become someone who creates amazing content marketing campaigns. If you're really into data - become an analyst, deep diving into analytics and looking at user behaviour through numbers. If you like to build things - create code and build new tools and applications within SEO. All those skills are transferable to any part of your life. Even if search engines cease to exist, the skills that you learn in SEO are ones that you can use for the rest of your life.

SEO is a great place to start your career because it gives an insight into all areas of digital. Starting out elsewhere, like social media, you wouldn't get the same big-picture view of what is happening in digital, and in marketing as a whole. At Moz they call it a 'T-Shaped Marketer', and SEO sits centrally at the top of that shape. Underneath, you've got all the other different channels, and they form a support for what you can do. SEO is a foundation, from which you can branch into other channels. The learning curve will be much longer for someone entering SEO from another channel than it is for someone transitioning elsewhere from SEO. SEO is the gateway."

How do you encourage other people in an organisation to have a better understanding of SEO, and to keep it at the forefront of their minds?

"Consider the different stakeholders. If you're thinking about business executives, from an agency side, the key is demonstrating how effective SEO can be as a performance channel. Show how much business can be incrementally generated for your clients or customers, and how much they could drive their business as well. Also, communicate how SEO can support other channels. You might have a paid social budget running on Facebook or Instagram, but once users have landed on a website, how are they navigated to the information that they need? Once you have users engaged with content on a web page, how can they convert? SEO needs to be working with other channels, such as CRO, to support business growth.

It's business metrics that matter. Once you can show the benefits and impact of your SEO work, at the business and revenue level, you will get buy-in. SEO is effective, and it's not a medium that is 'paid for', which is quite attractive. Well-executed websites, information, architecture, and design can hold the business for years to come."

Should we focus less on rankings, and more on the revenue that a business is getting as a result of SEO?

"In this environment, yes. The last couple of years in particular have been about cold, hard cash. It's about metrics that matter. Some businesses don't just want to drive incremental sales and revenue. They want to have a voice and be at the forefront of consumers' minds when they search for a particular subject matter. Digital can allow them to have their voice shared. SEO is a much more long-term approach to that, both from a training and a buy-in point of view. A lot of the work that you do with junior members of the team should be looking at least five-years ahead, instead of at short-term horizons. Fast-acquisition channels, that are paid, are driving almost quarter by quarter metrics that are easy to measure. With SEO, you're looking at a much longer period - three years plus."

What's one thing that senior SEOs should be doing less of to spend more time developing their team, and supporting the next generation of SEO?

"Reduce your manual tasks. For a head of SEO, or an SEO director, you need to find out what you can outsource that you are spending a lot of time doing. If recruitment has become a challenge for you, as a senior member of the team, focus on recruitment - outsource everything else. You need to have the right processes in place so that you can delegate, to the point of abdication, to your team members. If you are a head of SEO, the way you do a technical audit should be recorded, or trained to your team members, so that it can be outsourced to them.

A lot of SEOs are just focusing on optimising their websites for Core Web Vitals at the moment. Pay attention to your competitors, plug it into an automated dashboard, like Google Data Studio, and just measure how you're doing against the competition. Spending a lot of time trying to optimise for the best benchmark, using live data, is not the most efficient use of your time. Try and automate that through an API, and a good dashboard - but also train the team about the metrics that are being displayed. Then, when you do see a competitor is making changes and optimising for something, you can prioritise that. The key thing at the moment is to focus on the growth of the team. Google's given us so much time this year to plan for Core Web Vitals. It's time to start training your team."

Si Shangase is Global Head of SEO at WorldRemit.com.

12 Pass the Baton

CLOSING THOUGHTS

Si encouraged you in the last chapter to pass the baton, but you haven't passed the baton yet – you are holding the baton, and you need to decide how to use it.

If you've managed to read every single piece of advice in 'SEO in 2022' thus far, congratulations. You've absorbed many SEO tips that will hold you in good stead throughout 2022 and beyond.

Which tips are right for you?

But what's next? You need to decide on which tips are right for you, right now – which tips you should run with, and which tips aren't the best use of your time at the moment.

How do you decide? It's a combination between your personal passions and abilities, where you see your career going, what industry you're working in at the moment, the current strengths and weaknesses of you company's SEO, and where your current knowledge gaps are.

Take a few of the tips in the book and run with them – don't attempt to try to do everything by yourself, or you won't do a great job at anything.

Why not get started by selecting a single tip from each section of the book and run with that? After you select the tips, learn more about them, and then implement what's suggested in your ongoing SEO strategy, before reviewing their effectiveness.

Of course, the tips that are right for you are unlikely to be the same tips chosen by another SEO – and that's the way that it should be. Nobody's circumstance is exactly the same.

Enterprise SEO example

For example, if you work in an enterprise SEO environment, you may decide to focus on the following four tips:

1) Kerstin Reichert - Convince your stakeholders to make SEO a priority

Seek to bring decision-makers on board with your SEO strategy. Make sure that all your wonderful ideas actually have a chance of coming to life.

2) Helen Pollitt - Employ intent mapping for every core page on your site

Intent mapping should dictate everything about the content, and the user journey, from your landing page through your site.

3) Aleyda Solis - Take your SEO to the next level with SEO testing

SEO testing has the potential to take your SEO efforts to a completely different level.

4) Nick Wilsdon - Serverless applications that run on the edge are going to be the future of enterprise SEO deployments

The edge is CDNs, or Content Delivery Networks, such as Fastly, Akamai and Cloudflare. SEO teams need to understand how they can start utilising the edge, and the opportunities it provides.

Choose a selection of tips that are right for you

I'm not suggesting that you necessarily run with the above tips – they are just an example of what you may choose to focus on if you happen to work in an enterprise SEO environment, and you've identified that those particular tips are the most valuable ones to be focusing on in your individual situation.

Thank you

However you decide to use the knowledge contained in their book, thank you so much for being part of 'SEO in 2022'.

Remember, if you haven't done so already, we'd love for you to join in the discussion. Why not share what resonated with you most using the hashtag #SEOin2022 @ Majestic on Twitter?

Of course, 'SEO in 2022' was produced as a free video and podcast series as well as a book, so check out the links to the video and audio episodes at SEOin2022.com if you haven't done so already.

Maybe we can even include you as a contributor in a similar, future series? Here's hoping. Don't be a stranger… let's keep the conversation going!

David Bain
Author, *'SEO in 2022'*
Founder, *CastingCred.com*

Made in the USA
Middletown, DE
01 May 2022

64888661R00186